HE SHOOTS, HE SAVES

★ ★ ★

THE STORY OF HOCKEY'S COLLECTIBLE TREASURES

JON WALDMAN

ecw press

Published by ECW Press
2120 Queen Street East, Suite 200
Toronto, Ontario, Canada M4E 1E2
416-694-3348 / info@ecwpress.com

LIBRARY AND ARCHIVES CANADA
CATALOGUING IN PUBLICATION

Waldman, Jon, author
He shoots, he saves : the story of hockey's
collectible treasures / Jon Waldman.

Issued in print and electronic formats.
ISBN 978-1-77041-002-2 (pbk)
Also issued as: 978-1-77090-653-2 (PDF)
978-1-77090-654-9 (ePub)

1. Hockey—Collectibles. I. Title.

GV847.W34 2015   796.356075
C2014-902574-2   C2014-902575-0

Editor for the press: Michael Holmes
Cover design: Tania Craan
Cover image: © Francisblack/iStockphoto
Back cover image: Jon Waldman
Printing: Friesens 5 4 3 2 1

We acknowledge the financial support of the Government of Canada through the Canada Book
Fund for our publishing activities, and the contribution of the Government of Ontario through
the Ontario Book Publishing Tax Credit and the Ontario Media Development Corporation.

PRINTED AND BOUND IN CANADA

This book is dedicated, first, to my wife, Elana Waldman, who has fallen in love with the sport unlike anyone else I know. Her ability to absorb my hockey ramblings is amazing.

I also dedicate this book to my late uncle, Brian Fleishman, who introduced me to the world of hockey, taking me to countless Winnipeg Jets games as a kid; and to Elana's late grandfather, Sam Meyrowitz, who knew more about how the game is played than anyone I've ever met. Without them and their inspiration, this book would not have been possible.

ACKNOWLEDGEMENTS

Thank you to my wife, Elana, who has continued to show an insane amount of interest in my rambling about hockey and graciously given up most of our basement for my collection/museum; the fine folks at ECW Press, who continue to have faith in my book ideas; my always supportive family, my best word-of-mouth marketers; my friends who either collected with me or talked puck endlessly; my editors and co-writers from the last decade-plus writing about shinny, who at least humoured me when it came to my suggestion of hockey memorabilia articles; all of the industry officials who were open (and frank) with me over the years; and the NHL stars, past, present, and future, who graciously shared memories of their childhoods and their love of collecting.

COLLECTING HOCKEY!

BY PHILIP PRITCHARD,
VICE-PRESIDENT, CURATOR,
HOCKEY HALL OF FAME

Arguably, there is no better collection of hockey souvenirs, memorabilia, artifacts, and research material in the world than at the Hockey Hall of Fame in Toronto. With more than 70,000 square feet of display area, the Hall of Fame has it all. Built with the mission to collect, preserve, and honour the greats of the game and to promote the 3 E's — Education, Excellence, and Entertainment — the Hall of Fame appeals to all hockey fans, from the most serious devotee to the newcomer. Visitors to the Hall of Fame are thrilled and in awe of the sights and sounds of this great game.

However, like a lot of places, expansion is almost inevitable. In September 2009, the Hockey Hall of Fame opened the D.K. (Doc) Seaman Resource Centre in Toronto to house its archives. Located in the heart of a four-plex arena facility at the bottom of Kipling Avenue, the MasterCard Centre for Hockey Excellence is a dream for hockey fans everywhere. The Toronto Maple Leafs practise there, the Toronto Marlies operate the facilities, Hockey Canada has office space, and there is also as an international-sized rink. The Ontario Junior Hockey League, the Canadian Women's Hockey League, and

the Toronto High School Hockey league all play regular season games there. It is such a hockey institution that the National Hockey League (NHL) Alumni Association moved its offices there too. But tucked behind all of that active hockey, in the back corner of the building, is all that history of the game too.

All of the collections and libraries, negatives, photos, film reels, and so on that were not on display at the Hall of Fame were moved to the resource centre, along with the curatorial staff. The space is perfect and the conditions are perfect, helping to ensure that this vast collection — comprising millions of pieces of hockey history ranging from photos and scrapbooks to pennants and jerseys and everything in between — will not only be preserved for generations to come but will also grow. Today, hockey is played in more than 70 countries around the world, and hockey history is happening every day. From a first goal for a minor player to a gold medal at a World Championships, the Hockey Hall of Fame tries to be there.

It is always amazing to me to see how the game is preserved: an almost limitless array of hockey cards, jerseys, magazines, and souvenirs are being collected by diehard fans of this great game.

Hockey cards have been a staple in the collecting world since the early days of the game. Sure, the style, size, and look of hockey cards have changed a bit over the years, but the original cigarette cards circa 1910 are a great example of how hockey has influenced its surroundings. Today, the colour of the cards and the limited-edition game word cards have kept up with the interest and demand of the market.

While tickets, programs, and magazines are still very similar in design from the early days, they supply what is needed for the fans, the players' family and friends, and scouts: the lineups, the back stories, statistics, and some great creative advertisements. However, in today's economy, some teams provide only a yearly program, while others rely heavily on ads and sponsors to fund them. Each way is unique but provides fans with what is needed.

The game-worn jersey market has grown significantly over the last couple of decades, with many of today's jerseys documented by the team or a third-party company as certification for serious collectors. And there are plenty of great-looking jerseys out there for fans who just love the colours, logos, and

designs of all those teams around the world.

Equipment has evolved considerably over the years too, providing more protection while becoming more lightweight and durable. For collectors, each tweak to a piece of equipment is a dream come true, as the modification can be as unusual as some of the styles themselves. The goalie mask, however, seems to be the most popular item within this market. The style and of course the artwork of each goalie's mask is as unique as the goaltender himself.

Coins, stamps, pennants, magnets, and all the rest are becoming more and more popular forms of memorabilia around the hockey globe and all have a deserving place in the world of hockey collectibles, presenting unique tributes to the sport's teams, players, and leagues.

Most of all, collecting is fun! It connects the fan with the player, team, and league. Visit the Hockey Hall of Fame to see how it's done. We are here for the game, yesterday, today, and tomorrow.

WHAT IS MEMORABILIA?

"It's part of our game; it's a way of life for people around the game." Martin Brodeur understands the memorabilia world. As one of the pre-eminent stars of his generation, the New Jersey Devils goaltender has been in demand for autographs, endorsements, and memorabilia contracts. He's far from alone. Whether on a local, regional, national, or international level, hockey players recognize that their time isn't always their own. They're expected to pose for a photo or sign a trading card at a moment's notice; and while this might seem intrusive, the hockey hero knows how much meaning it carries.

"People come up to me and tell me that they have a program [from a] particular game," says Hockey Hall of Famer Frank Mahovlich. "It's nice that [they] kept that program all these years and that it meant something."

The goal of preserving a memory is what drives collectors to buy, trade, or otherwise acquire mementos. They will spend hours carefully sorting their new treasures, buy protective casings reminiscent of what you'd see in a museum, and, without batting an eye, spend up to the equivalent of a month's worth of groceries on used hockey gear.

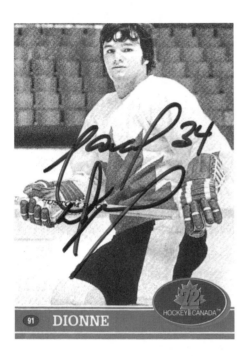

91 DIONNE

Memorabilia can be any souvenir that's preserved because of the moment associated with it: a ticket stub from a game that father and son attended together, a hero's autographed photo, or, for the lucky, a puck that went up and over the boards. At least that's how it was in a much simpler era — when memorabilia was less about dollar value and more about sentiment.

Years ago, owning a Bobby Orr rookie card or a game-used Patrick Roy stick meant something different: a feeling of connection to a hero or a moment in time. Now that sentiment can be easily lost, as trade shows and auction houses make the memorabilia industry a kind of stock market.

Still, an endearing nostalgic element to collecting endures. While some see the jersey of a recently retired player or the signature of an up-and-coming star as a speculative investment, others acquiring these items do it out of fandom, something even players themselves did as children.

For example, Tampa Bay superstar Martin St. Louis grew up like many Canadians, collecting hockey cards. "As a kid, you remember collecting those," he says. "When I was a kid, I had an uncle who would send or buy me cards whenever he'd see me. I remember having some of Gretzky's cards and Mario Lemieux's cards. Those were the ones I enjoyed. I used to put the cards on my bike and make the funny noise with the wheel like every other kid." St. Louis shows that same penchant for collecting cardboard to track his own career. "I remember a few years ago I was so excited seeing my first cards. Now, it's been a few years and there's quite a few more, but it's still exciting being on something you used to collect."

Other players, unfortunately, weren't as keen about their career mementos but in later years have put together collections that commemorate their time on the ice.

"It's funny. I was never a collector, and if my mother had never kept scrapbooks, I wouldn't have anything from my career," Hall of Famer Ted Lindsay remarks. "Since I've retired, I've become interested. I wish I would've known this 40 to 50 years ago because I would've saved certain things. I've done pretty well; I've got a nice basement in my house with a lot of stuff on the walls. It brings back good memories."

Lindsay's ability to recapture his career is thanks to the dedication that fans have shown both to him and to the sport over the years, especially those creating and preserving hockey's history.

JON WALDMAN ▼

Cy Wentworth   Jimmy Ward

Tommy Gorman
Russ Blinco
Bob Gracie
Earl of Robinson

Harvey Teno
Des Smith
M. Croghan
Baz O'Brien
Baldy Northcott
Tommy Cook
Glenn Shields
"Charlie" Smith

Bill Beveridge
Bun Cook
Harv Trottier
Gus Marker
Chuck Johnson

"Pep" Kelly
Drew Diller
"Ink" Burton
Babe Davidson
Tom O'Neely
Syl Apps
"Buster" Jackson
Chas Conacher
Buzz Boll
Nick Metz
Reg Hamilton

Dave Schriner
James Carr
Art Chapman
Eddie Wiseman
Joe Lamb
Tommy Anderson
Jack Shill
Johnny Gallagher
"Happy" Day
Al Murray
Tommy Bell
Nelson Stewart
Joe Jerwa
Earl Robinson

"Red" Horner
"Jimmie" Fowler
Bingo Kampman
Murph Chamberlain
Bill Thoms

1

★ ★ ★

THE
COLLECTIBLES

★ ★ ★

Memorabilia comes in a multitude of forms. From two-dimensional photos to three-dimensional figurines, from game-worn jerseys to replica goalie masks, almost everything imaginable is available for the collector. Some of these items are standard — autographs, for example — while others are more hardcore, as you'll see later on.

In the pursuit of these items, millions of dollars are exchanged each year through hobby shops, auction houses, and online outlets. Novice collectors may be intimidated by the enormous variety of pieces available, so for the fresh face to the hobby, and for the grizzled veteran, here are some stories about your collectibles.

THE SIGNATURE

Simply put, there is no better experience than meeting your hero; and there is no better reminder of this moment than an autograph. A scribble on a piece of paper may not seem important to an outsider, but ask anyone who's ever had a signature of a hero and he or she will understand its importance. "Everyone has an idol or someone they look up to. For some people it's a parent or grandparent, but for most people it's a celebrity. The majority of people are never going to meet that celebrity, so the next best thing is an autograph," explains Hersh Borenstein, president of Frozen Pond, a Toronto-based memorabilia company that specializes in autographs, selling signed items through their store and arranging autograph sessions for past, present, and future heroes. He remembers his first signature. "When I was a kid of nine in '79, I wrote a letter to Wayne Gretzky. I wrote it to the Edmonton Oilers at the Edmonton Arena. I said, 'You're my favourite player . . .'" Borenstein recalls. "[Finally] in

1983, I was sent an autographed 8x10 in the mail. I still have it."

Borenstein's memory is hardly unique — most collectors will remember the signatures they acquired decades ago. "I remember Ted Lindsay coming into my hometown. We got his autograph on a stick," Frank Mahovlich, a hockey superstar from the 1960s and 1970s, remembers. And even when he himself was a star, Mahovlich would pick up a signature from players he admired. "I've got a signed bat and a signed program of Eddie Mathews," he says. "He was with me when I was traded to Detroit. He was staying at the same hotel that I was. I got to meet him and know him. That was the year the Tigers were in the World Series. He gave me one of his bats and signed it to me."

Acquiring autographs today is easier than ever before, between special player appearances at collector shows, sending requests through the Internet to players or their representatives, and the growth of hobby shops that carry signed items. But the core of the hobby still remains at hockey arenas. Fans of all ages will glowingly share stories from their days of waiting for their heroes outside locker rooms and arenas. It inspires them to stay connected to the game. "For me to get something autographed from a professional hockey player was just off-the-charts amazing for a kid growing up in a town of 700 people," says Delaney Collins, a three-time national champion with Hockey Canada's women's program. "I remember going to my first Winnipeg Jets game, and my dad took me down to get Brett Hull's autograph. I was so scared. He signed something for me and I said, 'I'm going to be the first girl in the NHL, you know.'"

For many fans and collectors,

getting that single autograph from their favourite hockey hero is sufficient; but for others, getting a photo or puck signed by one player just isn't enough. Dating back to pre-World War II, autograph seekers embarked on multi-signature projects with themes such as members of a Cup-winning team or 500-goal scorers. The reason for these ambitious projects that can take years to complete is simple. "More than anything it's the pursuit," Borenstein says. "People like projects. A '72 Team Canada piece that you've been painstakingly working on for 10 years for everyone to sign . . . a '67 Leafs piece that you've taken around yourself or mailed around to get signed . . . it's not about the value."

WHAT TO GET SIGNED . . .

In the purest form, it doesn't matter what an autograph is affixed to — virtually anything will do. There's no better proof of that than today's collectors, who still ask for autographs on plain pieces of paper or index cards. It was these early forms that dominated the pre-collectibles autograph market, primarily, as Borenstein describes, because of what was actually signable in an era before a gold Sharpie was around for pucks or silver paint pens for jersey crests.

"Back in the day, it was an index card or recipe card. There weren't souvenir pucks . . . sometimes there was a team-issued photo, but not very often — as recently as the 1950s there are very few signed photos." As such, he continues, if you did want a piece of equipment signed in the pre-Sharpie era, you pretty much had one option. "There are more team-signed hockey sticks going back 50 years ago because there was nothing else that could get signed."

Today, there are more pieces for signing than one can even imagine. Just about any memorabilia can and has been signed. Jerseys, pucks, cards, photos, tickets, programs, helmets, skates, posters, pennants . . . yeah, there's an endless array of options; and when a "standard" item doesn't suffice, fans get creative in their pursuits. Borenstein recalls one item in particular: "A fire hydrant painted blue and white — the guy was getting it signed by all the Leafs. He would bring it in on a wagon."

AUTOGRAPH TABOOS

Part of the autograph game is recognizing that players are human and have certain preferences. An experienced collector will freely share advice with you on what a particular player will and will not sign, and often from these tips come urban legends. Borenstein remembers one of the more famous stories in the hobby. "I've been told several times that Paul Coffey won't sign Detroit stuff. I haven't asked him personally, but there is Detroit stuff out there. Apparently, his reason is that he hated Scotty Bowman; he was so pissed when he got traded for Brendan Shanahan. I asked Scotty about it, and he said, 'No, I'm friends with Coffey, and there's no ill will.' I hear that one more than anything."

Similar stories are told of other players but have less to do with emotional ties and more to do with incentives. "Gary Leeman won't sign Montreal cards and that's for financial reasons. He thinks eventually he'll sign and there will be huge demand," Borenstein comments. "Mike Bossy — whenever he signs a McFarlane [a figure produced by McFarlane Toys] — will only personalize it and put the personalization right into the signature so you can't rub it off. I asked him about it once, and once again it's for financial reasons."

Other players simply don't sign often. During his playing career, Mark Messier was an infamously hard signer, rarely putting pen to paper. Since his retirement, he's softened his stance and is now a major

signer for companies such as Steiner Sports. Other legends, including a famed Habs goaltender, have stood firm and are extremely hard to get an autograph from. "Ken Dryden is always difficult," Borenstein notes. "I heard rumours that he turned down $100,000 for appearances. About five years ago, I sent an email to his campaign office offering him $60,000 for an appearance. Within five minutes I got an email back from his campaign office saying, 'Thanks, but we're not interested.'" But even Dryden isn't full-out impossible. During his time in politics he would occasionally sign along the campaign trail, and while he was with the Toronto Maple Leafs he made a rare fan-friendly appearance at the closing of Maple Leaf Gardens.

A step beyond Dryden lies the truly impossible autograph subjects.

There are several tales of how some players are practically reclusive and do everything possible to separate themselves from the sport that made them household names. George Armstrong, a Toronto Maple Leafs legend and Hall of Famer who stayed with the franchise as a scout, for example, is infamous for staying clear of any autograph opportunities.

THE AUTOGRAPH BIZ

Generally speaking, hockey players have grown to understand the nature of autographs, especially as the sport has evolved into a multimillion-dollar industry. At the same time that sports memorabilia grew from a child-hood hobby into a business, so, too, did autographs. The fans who once would wait outside arenas or in line at department stores for a player purely to meet their hero would soon line up not with a single item but with as many as a dozen. This soured some players on autograph requests, while others grew to accept it as being part of their job. "When I started in the league, there weren't really autograph seekers," Mark Messier explained in a 2003 interview. "You signed an autograph because a person wanted it for themselves and it was on a piece of paper or in a note-book. As we all know, it's completely different now. It's a business — I think everyone knows and accepts this."

Brian Propp sees this business side through his website and in his everyday interactions. It's a reality — with the fame of being a hockey celebrity, there's bound to be auto-graph seekers. It's something that he doesn't shy away from — rather, he embraces it. "I don't look at it as being hounded — I look at it as they're chil-dren or adults who are trying to col-lect for their family or themselves," he says. "I know that through my website, brianpropp.com, we get a lot of requests. As people join my web-site, I'll send out a picture. I've always been very forward with having tons of pictures and I carry them with me wherever I go. In my work world, I've always got people that I meet, and I give pictures to kids down the street."

Propp doesn't see an autograph as just an autograph — he sees it as an opportunity not only for the col-lector but also for himself. "I might be a bit different than most people who might look at it as a bother, but I look at it more as a branding of yourself," he says. "On my pic-tures, I've got the logo of the com-pany that I work with that can help people in Canada and the U.S."

But as Messier describes, the value of a signature became less about how much it meant to the recipient and more about its potential resale value, heightened by the arrival of eBay in the mid- to late 1990s. As a result of resellers, a new industry emerged — the autograph business. Now, players routinely charge a fee for their signatures at organized events such as collectibles shows. And it isn't uncommon to see a special guest player sitting at a table at events large or small, willing to sign any item for a price. Naturally, this has led to some controversy, with many believing it unfair for a fan to have to pay at a public signing. Yet here's the stark reality: the lead-up to the fan arriving at an event. "Someone has to pay for the athlete's time, photos, advertising, etc., and then figure a way to recoup most of that," Ryan Rajmoolie, a former promoter with the Toronto Card Show, said in 2011. "For the most part, the people who come to the signings, who are actual collectors, know why [there is a fee]. Collectors are educated in the behind-the-scenes events that lead to a public appearance by an athlete at something like a sports card show."

For those unable to attend an event, there are always other oppor-tunities to acquire the signature of your favourite hockey superstar. Companies will hold private auto-graph signings, where fans can order an item to be signed, often with the sort of personal inscription (e.g., to Michael, my best friend) one would get at an in-person event. Otherwise, these companies will stock items in their own stores and distribute to other retail outlets.

The offshoot of this dynamic has been a new level of security for the secondary market. Almost as soon as autographs became commodities, forgeries increased dramatically. Scammers would — and still do — routinely post autographed items with claims of their authenticity.

But with a recognized dealer — one who has proven to be trustworthy and has a solid relationship or full licence agreements with leagues, teams, and/or players — a collector now has a resource that confirms the legitimacy of the autograph, more often than not augmented with a certificate of authenticity. In addition, any autograph that has not been previously certified can be taken to third-party companies for verification.

RETURN TO INNOCENCE

With forgeries a still-present concern, an increasing number of collectors are wary of purchasing a signature that has not been certified authentic. In that respect, the autograph market has, to an extent,

come full circle. Now, even in cases where an athlete will charge into the three figures for a signature, a more genuine collector has emerged, one whose relationship with the player has returned to the fan state that existed prior to the memorabilia boom. For the players, this is a very welcome opportunity. "I remember being a kid and wanting to get autographs of guys I looked up to," says 500-goal scorer Keith Tkachuk. "I don't mind signing at all for anybody. These are people that come watch us play, these are people who, hopefully, you can make a difference in their life and the most important thing is to try to help them out, especially kids."

It is that pay-it-forward mindset that makes hockey unique — that you're doing the same thing for a kid that your heroes did for you. When you come into fortune, you share your goodness with others around you. "Johnny Bower never had two nickels to rub together and used mattresses as goalie pads. Gordie Howe grew up with no money," Borenstein says. "When you come from humble beginnings, you're more willing to go above and beyond to make the fans happy. Hockey players are just down to earth."

GAME GEAR
★ ★ ★

When a ticket, program, or photo just won't cut it anymore, collectors will take their collections to the next level with a piece of the action — game gear. Gear comes in many different forms but shows a higher level of dedication to the hobby. Items generally carry high price tags, acting as a dividing line between the casual collector and the serious hobbyist.

More often than not, purchasing these collectibles focuses on personal heroes. Take, for example, Barry Meisel. As president and COO of the MeiGray Group, a leading distributor of game-used jerseys, pucks, and sticks that partners with hockey leagues and national bodies, he sees hundreds of game-used pieces go out to rabid collectors. Naturally, Meisel has his own assortment of memorabilia. It doesn't even take him a second to identify his favourite item. "The major theme for my collection, as it is for most people, is my favourite team — the New York Rangers. So the number-one jersey in my collection is the white jersey Craig McTavish was wearing during the Stanley Cup Finals."

JERSEYS

At the baseline, a jersey will usually start as low as $100 for lesser-known NHLers and some minor and junior squads; but the price tag for those worn in special events or by top-rank players can go well into six figures.

Today's jerseys are fairly easy to navigate. Teams, along with partners like MeiGray, will include tags inside the sweaters that act as a certificate of authenticity, indicating what year the jersey was worn and potentially what "set" it came from (helping discern whether it was a pre-season, regular season, or playoff tog, for example) along with a registration number. These tags are invaluable to collectors who want to know as much as they can about their new prized possession. Where collectors may run into trouble, however, is in the vintage market, where a jersey from other eras cannot easily be authenticated. As a result, collectors will look to the experts to ensure they are getting the authentic piece they desire, and reputable companies will do extensive research and put

their name and reputation on the line each and every time they put a jersey up for sale.

"Obviously, you can't go back in time and put a tag in a vintage jersey," Meisel explains. "Our knowledge and willingness to do the research and stand behind the products that already existed takes knowhow and a discerning eye to say when you're not sure. We would register jerseys when we would say we were sure. There were many ways to do due diligence, but we also took a very conservative approach that we'll only stand behind items that we know came from the correct sources — that we're correct."

This knowledge drives the value of gamers; but after that, a number of other facets come into play. "I think the most important factor [in a jersey's value] by far is the absolute authenticity. Two jerseys being equal and authentic, the collector will go for the one that's been worn more," Meisel says, "but that has to be counter-balanced by the importance or popularity of the player who wore the jersey, or the year or the moment behind the jersey." These moments become a factor that push the ordinary player's equipment to extraordinary values and the superstar's numbers into the stratosphere. Meisel reports that the jerseys and equipment he sold from the Boston Bruins and Los Angeles Kings' recent Stanley Cup runs were much more sought-after than regular-issue items.

One might be surprised to know that, unlike just about any other collectible realm, the "jersey fails" of the world — those that had only a brief moment on the ice because of their horrid style — have a place of honour in the game-used jersey market, including the "Burger King" jerseys the Los Angeles Kings wore in the waning days of the Gretzky era. "Those are among the most popular and valuable jerseys," Meisel says. "In our hobby, something so bizarre, different, and grotesque becomes coveted for collectors because of the scarcity and wackiness of them."

STICKS

Much like jerseys, sticks can be expensive, climbing into three, four, or in extreme cases five figures at auction. This wasn't always the case, however. As recently as the 2000s, old-fashioned wood models could be found for under $50; but just as

JON WALDMAN ◄

materials changed to more expensive composites, the aftermarket followed suit.

Unlike jerseys, sticks were easier to come by for the casual fan. From time to time, kids would walk home with a stick after a hockey game, given out by the player, a trainer, or the equipment manager. Additionally, sticks are easier to authenticate than jerseys. Routinely, a trainer would stamp the stick with the date of the game and the name, nickname, or number of the player who used it.

What makes game-used sticks even more attractive — and certainly more unique than other game gear categories — is that a signature on the blade or shaft is not only acceptable but welcome. While jersey and puck collectors shy away from these markings, considering them to lower the level of authenticity (after all, what player signs their jersey before they step on the ice?), stick collectors are more than happy to have that extra piece of certification as part of their valued collectible.

PUCKS

Collecting hearkens back to the roots of the game, where fans would scramble to nab a puck that flew over the glass and into the stands. The primarily black (or sometimes blue) vulcanized rubber disks are easy to collect, given how inexpensive they can be, at least at the introductory level.

Once you get into serious collecting, chasing older and considerably rarer pucks, you get into high-dollar items. "It's attractive to any budget," says Andy Schmidgall, owner of puckfanatic.com, whose personal collection numbers between 3,000 and 3,500 slugs. "If you really wanted to spend very little, a buck or two bucks at a time, it's pretty easy to do.

And then you've got the guys where money really is no object, and they go after the high-dollar stuff that's vintage and they'll pay whatever it takes to get it."

Generally speaking, there are two types of pucks — souvenir and game-used. Souvenir pucks, naturally, are plentiful and tend to have a much different look than gamer pucks. They will often be part of a seasonal series, issued with a similar design across all teams, or mementos for a season or event such as the Winter Classic. If the puck is built in to a commemorative event and only available once, the collectibility builds up almost instantly. "Sherwood is printing all these specialty pucks by team, say, for retirement nights. Sherwood sells them to the team, so that's the only place you can get them and it's usually just for that night," Schmidgall says. "For all the puck collectors out there, you can go to that arena that night and they're usually 15, 25 bucks apiece, then the next day sell them on eBay for 75 dollars. They're just that rare."

On the other side of the hobby is the game-used market. Here, authenticity can be an issue — when a puck comes off the ice and into the crowd it won't have any certification, and there have been stretches where certification programs from leagues and organizations didn't exist. At times, a puck sold or traded won't have the authentication one would expect for an autograph or jersey — instead, you're basing its authenticity on an anecdote and trusting the individual you're purchasing from and their reputation in the puck-collecting community. "I've bought several collections from people who were an on-ice official or their family, and I've listed many as game-used," Schmidgall remarks. "You pretty much have to go by my word because that's what I'm doing — I'm going by their word."

Today, leagues and teams will either distribute pucks themselves or work with third-party companies on certification programs. Interestingly enough, this isn't the first time in hockey's history that such a program has been in effect. For a couple seasons in the early 1970s, "any time a goal was scored they would take that puck out of the net, write down what game it was from, who scored it, and sell it for $10 apiece through magazines," Schmidgall recounts.

But the only sure way to guarantee the authenticity of a game puck is to be one of the fortunate few who actually catches the puck yourself. Like in baseball, the situations where a puck has been "forcibly" retrieved by officials have been few and far between, aside from the urban legends of the FoxTrax puck, which purport that attendants would rush to the spot where the puck went over the boards.

You remember those pucks, right? Engineered by the geniuses at the American television broadcaster best known for cartoons like *The Simpsons* and *Family Guy,* FoxTrax was created because network execs felt that the American audience had trouble seeing a black puck on a white hockey surface. The device, which debuted at the 1996 NHL All-Star Game, had built-in sensors that unleashed a colourful trail during broadcasts. The pucks only lasted for two years but have since become some of the most in-demand collectibles in hockey.

GOALIE MASKS

Like pucks, goalie masks are extremely collectible, both as actual game-used pieces and as souvenirs.

Masks have been produced for NHL goalies since the 1960s, but it wasn't until the early 1990s that they were heavily pursued by collectors. It began simply with trading cards and prints that depicted masks both current and through the ages, making instant names of otherwise forgettable goalies such as Gilles Gratton and Gary Bromley. But the goalie who created the market more than anyone was Patrick Roy. The Montreal Canadiens star already had a Stanley Cup ring and individual trophies to his credit when the goalie mask explosion hit. Roy's simple yet sophisticated mask became the spotlighted piece, making waves when Pro Set created the first card dedicated to the mask in 1991–92. (Following this, companies made mask cards an annual tradition.)

Soon after the card market sprung up, replica mask companies popped up, selling full-size or miniature versions. The old-school style of mask — the full face shield without the wire cages — was hotly in demand. Among these was Gerry Cheevers's famed stitches mask. As the story goes, Cheevers would add a mark every time he was hit in his mask with a puck, representing where on his face he'd have to be stitched up had he gone without the mask. It became a living testament

mask. Card company Upper Deck pulled off the same precision in the early 2000s with the Mask Collection series that included both current and past models. But the key to a mask's success was that it had to correspond to a player. Riddell, who at that time was doing monster sales on miniature football helmets, made generic team masks that didn't quite catch on with collectors.

Game-used masks, however, are a true rarity in the secondary market. Players will hold on tightly to their signature masks, wearing them multiple years (a stark contrast to pads, which may be replaced multiple times in a season). Those masks that do reach the populous often do because they are tied to special events, at times with a charity involved. Montreal Canadien Carey Price, for example, wore a Remembrance Day–themed mask for a couple games in November 2011, which would later be auctioned off for an impressive $15,000, benefitting four local charities.

to those who would otherwise feel that the mask was intrusive to a goalie's sightlines.

While the mass market was either priced out or disinterested in these masks, they did swarm to more affordable models. McDonald's had major success with a two-year promotion at its restaurants in the mid 1990s, while EA Sports created beautiful replicas that mimicked the real deal perfectly, right down to the foam protectant behind the

THE TRADING CARD
★ ★ ★

Like its American cousin, the baseball card, the hockey card had its beginnings in tobacco products. The first full-out sets appeared in 1910–11, produced by Imperial Tobacco. Unlike baseball cards, however, hockey cards were hard to come by before 1910. Baseball stars were often part of multi-sport series like Allen & Ginter's cards; hockey players, meanwhile, weren't often subjects in these products. Those early Imperials, three sets in total, were classified as "C" by *American Card Catalog* author Jefferson Burdick. Modern manufacturers Topps and In The Game would pay tribute to these first series by using their design to showcase modern players. The floodgates opened soon after World War I ended, as more cigarette series were produced. The turn to kid-friendly products followed as companies like Paulin's Candy entered the growing fray.

The first products that teased hockey's soon-to-come "modern era" in hockey cards was a short run by O-Pee-Chee in the 1930s, including oversized and undersized (by today's standards) cards, as well as a unique pop-up product. Companies like Sweet Caporal and World Wide Gum also produced series, while European issues began to pop out of cigarette and confectionary packs the same way they did in North America. With the onset of World War II, however, cards were again shelved, as O-Pee-Chee ceased production.

In 1951, the hockey card market changed forever when confectioner Parkhurst issued its first set. Amid this era, the focus turned from the cards helping to sell gum to gum helping to sell cards. Boys and girls hunted for the series that, at first, still featured art renditions. The company would later be joined by American card king Topps, soon after it had disposed of baseball rival Bowman (ironically, the cards were actually manufactured by O-Pee-Chee). After Topps's arrival, a split occurred, whereby Parkhurst produced cards of the Canadian teams and Topps took on the U.S. squads. There would be a slight shift a couple years into the structure as Parkhurst would also begin producing cards of the Detroit Red Wings. The split between the two companies lasted through the 1963–64 season, when Parkhurst folded after issuing its perhaps most iconic design, with the pre-maple leaf Canadian flag or American flag in the background of primarily posed shots. With the closure, Topps had the hockey market cornered until the 1968–69 season, when O-Pee-Chee produced its first series under its own brand name. O-Pee-Chee mirrored the Topps sets, except for two differences: O-Pee-Chee had more cards and included French text on the reverse.

The O-Pee-Chee–Topps split continued through the 1970s and 1980s, with the only major difference being that O-Pee-Chee had the market cornered on World Hockey Association (WHA) products. Occasionally, the two companies would experiment — O-Pee-Chee did a "big" series in 1980–81 and produced "mini" series in 1987–88 and 1988–89. Topps, for its part, broke its 1981–82 series into regional series, and later brought its "Tiffany" premium boxed sets into the market. The only true interruption during this time was a two-year layoff for Topps (1982–83 and 1983–84) when they didn't produce any cards for American fans. But the

monopolistic bubble for the O-Pee-Chee–Topps tandem burst for the 1990–91 season when three new manufacturers entered the market and hockey cards went from being bicycle and flip game fodder to stock market desirables.

The rest of hockey card history breaks down as follows:

1990-91

- Pro Set, Score, and Upper Deck, three companies who had entries in other sports, join the hockey market. Each comes loaded with its own specialty — Upper Deck has, arguably, the most premium feel (and inarguably premium pricing), along with a French parallel series and exclusive rights to the Canadian World Junior team; Score hits the ground with an exclusive for Eric Lindros cards and split editions for Canadian and American audiences; and Pro Set . . . well, it had lots of errors.

- While Topps rests on its laurels for the most part, O-Pee-Chee introduces Russian stars like Sergei Fedorov and Arturs Irbe in its main set and later issues its own premium series, O-Pee-Chee Premier. The set did so well that demand pushed pack prices to the $10 mark.

1991-92

- All five companies return with guns blazing. Pro Set, Score, and Upper Deck introduce the hockey market to in-pack certified autographs with Patrick Roy, Bobby Orr, and Brett Hull signatures respectively.

- Pro Set also reintroduces Parkhurst to the hockey market in conjunction with brand rights holder Dr. Brian Price.

- Upper Deck expands on the World Junior success, first by getting the rights to Canada Cup cards and later expanding its World Junior line to include all participating teams (while also producing an exclusive series for issue in Czechoslovakia).

- Upper Deck partners with McDonald's for the first of many series issued through the fast-food chain.

- Topps and Score push the premium brand further with the introduction of Stadium Club and Pinnacle, respectively. O-Pee-Chee tries to keep up with Premier, but the lustre is already gone.

- Draft pick sets become all the rage as overnight companies Ultimate and Arena join card veterans Star

Pics and Classic. Ultimate also issues the first mainstream retro series with Original Six (which also included autographs).

- The first true Summit Series retro product is issued by Future Trends. The company would release one more series the following year, commemorating the 1976 Canada Cup.

1992-93

- The hockey card market reaches its true boom. Baseball magnate Fleer joins the hockey market, while most of the other brands soldier on.

- O-Pee-Chee issues its sole base brand series that is completely different from Topps.

- Topps and Pro Set (via the Parkhurst brand) introduce the hockey market to parallel cards – pieces that are similar to a 'base' card save for a different feature, usually added foil.

- Pro Set, one year after filing for Chapter 11 bankruptcy in the U.S., issues its final series.

- Classic, the last draft set standing, signs Manon Rheaume to an exclusive contract, making her the first woman to appear in a mainstream hockey series.

1993-94

- With Pro Set gone, baseball veteran Leaf/Donruss gains a hockey licence.

- The NHL and NHLPA limit the number of hockey card series that can be issued, effectively ending the boom era in the process.

- An O-Pee-Chee series is not released for the first time in decades, as both Topps and its Canadian cousin issue Premier series in its place. Topps continues Stadium Club and teases the arrival of Finest one year later.

- Score signs Alexandre Daigle to an exclusive and in doing so creates the first redemption card (a card that offers a replacement upon notification by mail or online registration) in modern hockey card history.

- The World Junior licence is burst

open and available to all card manufacturers; only Score cashes in on the opportunity, while others like Fleer and O-Pee-Chee and Topps concentrate on the 1994 Olympic squads.

- Upper Deck gains the rights to produce Parkhurst cards, including a "Missing Link" set that fills in the gap year of 1956–57 when no hockey card sets were produced (the reason for this is unknown to this day).

1994-95

- The autographed card market is blown wide open as Upper Deck teams with the NHL Players' Association (NHLPA) to issue the first Be A Player series, which includes one autograph per pack. The set is an immediate hit, and packs can be seen hitting the $20 mark.

- O-Pee-Chee issues its final series as a company.

- The NHL lockout plays havoc with intended redemption programs, including the You Crash the Game set in Parkhurst. The program "officially" launches successfully one year later.

- Upper Deck releases the first "SP" pack series, a brand that would splinter into several sets in subsequent years.

1995-96

- Topps issues its supposed last sets in hockey (in actuality, they teamed with Fleer for a set called Picks one year later and a sticker set the year following). The Topps series includes an O-Pee-Chee parallel (as it would for the Picks series), keeping the brand name alive in hockey.

- All licencees combine for a set titled NHL Cool Trade. Each company also has redemption programs for parallel versions of their respective entries.

- After splitting with Upper Deck, Dr. Price opens Parkhurst Products Inc., with a European-only distribution chain. Naturally, some product makes its way to North American shores.

1996-97

- One year after acquiring the McDonald's licence, Score (now known as Pinnacle Brands) gains the Be A Player licence from the NHLPA and produces the series for the first time with NHL licensing in tow.

- Pinnacle also purchases Donruss/Leaf, expanding its stronghold in the hobby.

- Upper Deck issues hockey's first memorabilia cards — cards with swatches from game-worn jerseys.

- Fleer produces its final sets (at least for the short-term).

1997-98

- Pacific Trading Cards joins the hockey card market in a flurry of series.

- The Upper Deck's experiment with jersey cards continues, and Pinnacle joins in the growing craze.

- Topps gains a licence with the Canadian Hockey League (CHL). It's the first time a dedicated set for the league has been issued since 7th Inning Sketch (yes, they were a hockey card company) folded after the 1991–92 season.

- Pinnacle issues printing plates in its series, a first for hockey.

1998-99

- Mere weeks after issuing promotional cards for an intended Donruss series, Pinnacle closes up shop suddenly.

- Be A Player is launched as its own trading card company and carries on the one-autographed-card-per-pack tradition.

- Topps returns to the NHL market officially. O-Pee-Chee cards continue to be part of its programs as the company issues O-Pee-Chee Chrome. The CHL licence is imported to the NHL series for the first time since the early 1990s.

- Upper Deck regains the

McDonald's licence in the wake of Pinnacle's downfall.

- Upper Deck issues the first retro jersey cards, cutting up a Winnipeg Jets jersey of Bobby Hull.

2000-01

- Pacific blows up the memorabilia card concept, issuing three products that promise one jersey card per pack. Upper Deck and Be A Player follow suit in subsequent years.

- Be A Player gives hockey its first ultra-premium series, Ultimate Memorabilia. Packs for this set hit the three-figure mark.

- Be A Player causes a major stir in the hobby as it announces it is cutting the only known set of goalie pads worn by Georges Vezina. As a result, the cards themselves hit four–figure values.

- After a couple years layoff, Be A Player reintroduces the Parkhurst line via an insert series. One year later, the set is once again a stand-alone.

- Upper Deck gains the CHL licence.

2001-02

- The NHL and NHLPA announce that players must appear in an NHL game before one of their cards can be featured in a licensed product.

- Topps officially reintroduces O-Pee-Chee as a base brand series.

- Fleer gains a limited NHL licence, allowing it to only produce cards of retired players.

- Pacific and Upper Deck cross into the bobblehead world with Heads Up and Playmakers, respectively, as box toppers on products.

- Upper Deck brings mini masks to NHL products with Mask Collection.

2002-03

- As quickly as they re-enter, Fleer re-exits the NHL market, having produced only three series in its short tenure.

2003-04

- Topps issues its final full-out series in hockey. One year later, their last true hockey card is issued, in the Chronicles set, commemorating the lost season of the NHL lockout.

- Be A Player changes its name to In The Game. Among the premiums offered for box buyers is a series of miniature Stanley Cups with its Memorabilia series.

- Pacific issues its first (and only) American Hockey League (AHL) series.

2004-05

- Upper Deck gains an exclusive agreement with the NHLPA, ending the tenures of most of its competitors.

- Pacific issues its final NHL series. In anticipation of the resurrection of the WHA, it signs a licensing deal for the new league.

Only two promotional cards are issued before Pacific shuts down and is sold to Donruss/Playoff Inc. (then primarily a football card company).

- In The Game retains an NHL licence and also signs on with the Professional Hockey Players' Association (PHPA), CHL, and AHL (along with limited licensing with international licensors). As a result, it produces the first mainstream cards of Sidney Crosby and Alexander Ovechkin.

2005-06

- Upper Deck signs a five-year contract with the NHL and NHLPA for full exclusivity, effectively pushing In The Game out of the major hockey card market. It also gains the coveted licences for McDonald's and the Be A Player brand (both of which were shut down during the lockout) and Parkhurst.

- Sidney Crosby, Alexander Ovechkin, and their rookie brethren push hockey card collecting into an echo era.

- Upper Deck buys out Fleer and brings its brands back to the NHL.

- Upper Deck releases The Cup, an ultra-premium series that only the most affluent (and risk-taking) of collectors can indulge in.

- In The Game continues its CHL and AHL contracts, as well as signing current and former NHL players on an individual basis.

2006-07

- Upper Deck gains the O-Pee-Chee licence, reviving the popular brand while also issuing the last Parkhurst set that will be seen until the 2011–12 NHL season.

- In The Game produces its first cards with Hockey Canada licensing. The contract lasts for two years.

2009-10

- Topps issues the Puck Attax game card set, fuelling rumours it will return to the NHL market in full when the exclusivity contract with Upper Deck expires at season's end. It doesn't.

- The final full-out McDonald's series is released.

- The final Be A Player series is released.

2010-11

- Sticker magnate Panini, who the year prior purchased Donruss/Playoff Inc., gains an NHL licence and immediately makes an impact, bringing in favourites from the Score/Pinnacle, Donruss/Leaf, and Pacific eras.

2012-13

- With the NHL lockout slicing the season, the NHLPA makes the unique decision to hold any debuting players over for the 2013–14 trading card year.

2013-14

- Upper Deck regains exclusive license for NHLPA trading cards at season's end.

Needless to say, it's been an interesting few years since the boom era, and those days aren't going to end soon.

THE STANLEY CUP
★ ★ ★

Hockey's ultimate prize has been called the most famous trophy in all of sport. It has travelled the globe in player celebrations and has been the symbol of excellence that every shinny-loving boy and girl covets, and thanks to keen memorabilia companies, it has been reproduced countless times over. Here are just a few samples of products that pay homage to the Dominion Hockey Challenge Cup, better known as the Stanley Cup.

37

JON WALDMAN

JON WALDMAN

DETROIT
RED WINGS

2007-08
STANLEY
CUP
CHAMPIONS

CANADIEN
79

RTOIS PRES.
AN V.P.M.D.
U V.P.C.A.
AL COLLINSON
LOYD CURRY
LAUDE RUEL D.P.D.
WARD GRUNDMAN
AN McCAMMON D.
CK D.

HES   GILLES LUPIEN
RVIS   PIERRE MONDOU
ERT   MARK NAPIER
AY   DOUG RISEBROUGH
NTE   LARRY ROBINSON
CQUE   SERGE SAVARD
UCHE   STEPHEN SHUTT
AIRE   MARIO TREMBLAY
HAK H.T.
UR A.T.

ARENA REMNANTS
★ ★ ★

The experience of seeing a hockey game live beats out any other. You can sit at home with all the creature comforts of your couch with beer cozies, a large bowl of chips, surround-sound speakers, and high-definition TV with the commentary from your favourite broadcaster, and still it doesn't compare to the experience of sitting with 14,000 of your closest friends, generally all cheering at the same time and wearing the same jersey or coloured T-shirt.

There's something so ritualistic about it — you cheer for the same players, boo the same opposition, sing along to "Stompin' Tom" Connors, and belt out the same chants. It happens 41 times a season, more if you make it into the playoffs. And when I use the word *you*, I do so with no sense of exaggeration whatsoever. Sure, you may not be the one actually on the ice, but as any hockey player will tell you, and as cliché as it sounds, the crowd really does influence their play — it can drive them to succeed or just plain drive them crazy.

Unfortunately, capturing memories from these games can be overlooked amid all that excitement. In the hype of souvenir shops and post-game meals, the simplest memorabilia can be missed by the untrained eye; but collectors know that every piece they encounter can carry that sentimental value (heck, that's why items like hot dog rotisseries sell at auction when an arena closes). At times, the items one can get from an arena can be quite majestic. When an arena closes to be replaced by a more modern facility, it's not unusual for its seats and bricks to be sold off. The most successful of these sales, of course, was conducted by the Montreal Canadiens, who sold off countless seats from the old Montreal Forum. Those seats, especially those signed by legends like Jean Beliveau, are still among the most in-demand items in auctions and private sales. It seems that you're not considered a true Habs fan unless you have a Forum seat in your home (whether you use it or not).

Other pieces that go at auction range from game clocks to out-of-town scoreboard signs. All can be had if you're willing to pay enough and have the balls to dare enter a public auction.

The reason for wanting these pieces of buildings that once stood proud and tall is simple — the memories of how majestic they once were and, to borrow from the cliché, how they just don't build them like they used to. "I don't think you'll ever be able to catch the old buildings. I don't think you could ever build anything like the Boston Gardens, Chicago Stadium, Maple Leaf Gardens," notes former player and now coach Scott Arniel. "I don't think the building inspectors would let you put them up that way anymore."

Those types of memorabilia are still few and far between, however. For every collector who bought items at the closing points of Chicago Stadium or Maple Leaf Gardens, there are hundreds of collectors who are shut out of such opportunities simply because there just isn't enough to go around. But every collector or fan worth their salt would have at least a few of the next collectibles.

SEC ROW SEAT
GOLD21 B 3
EAST GATES
$92.50
INCL. G.S.T. #R103491981
game no.
TORONTO MAPLE LEAFS
1997-98
SATURDAY, JANUARY 24, 1998
TAMPA BAY
lightning
MAPLE LEAF GARDENS
jan. 24
7:30PM
INCL. G.S.T. #R103491981
9-19955 $92.50
EAST GATES
GOLD21 B 3
SEC ROW SEAT
JON WALDMAN ▸

TICKETS

Over the last few years, ticket collecting has evolved in two ways — it's now easier to get intact pieces, and overall tickets look a heck of a lot better than they did even 25 years ago.

Let's talk first about intact tickets. One of the more difficult factors to getting a good piece — one that is worthy of framing or display — is that tickets are hard to find from older times since they would routinely be ripped (and rather carelessly at that) by check-in staffers at arenas. Even once the proper tear-away piece was perforated for easier separation, you'd still often get chunks taken out of your ticket. Indeed, the only way you're going to get a truly good ticket would be to miss a game and keep the memento. Today, ticket takers use barcode scanners, leaving the memento intact. And as long as fans are careful with their ticket and don't stuff it into their wallets, they're left with a reasonably good-looking souvenir of the game.

That brings in the second factor — aesthetics. Usually, hockey teams will produce two tickets — one general or "game day" ticket that has the look of a standard Ticketmaster issue and one well-designed ticket reserved for season ticket holders, either reflecting the team or spotlighting one of the marquee players. Some of these designs have been quite spectacular, with beautiful art or fantastic photography used on the face.

Tickets from games generally carry a value with little to no variance; but some hold higher prestige, such as those commemorating milestone games like the first or last for a franchise, a record-breaking performance, or the debut for a new star. Even more valuable are those from special tournaments, especially the 1972 Summit Series, the 1980 Miracle on Ice, or the yet-to-be-nicknamed 2010 Winter Games. Adding to the effect of a ticket is an accompanying program, which naturally must be in strong condition to be a good sale; but collectors will be more forgiving if it has been marked up a bit, say, with statistics written on the back, crossmarks through a player's name who didn't end up stepping on the ice due to injury, or devil horns coloured in on the heads of opposing players. Hey, they add character.

The interesting part of the ticket-collecting market is that very few tickets make it to the open market. While 15,000 to 18,000 may be printed and used (or much fewer if you're in a city like Phoenix), very few make it to the collecting community. That's what makes collecting tickets such a challenge and so enticing to a hungry market.

Unfortunately, ticket collecting may soon be a completely retrospective hobby. In 2012–13, several NHL teams did away with season ticket production, issuing reusable seat cards instead to subscribers. One-game issues are also dying off with electronic tickets or home printouts via Ticketmaster.

POCKET SCHEDULES

If you thought tickets would be an obvious collectible to find in quantity, then you surely thought that pocket schedules would be even easier to find; but that's not always the case. Dating back to the early days of the game (some have been found from senior leagues as early as in the 1900s), pocket schedules have been the single best marketing tool a team can employ. Want to know the next time your team is playing? Simply stop into a gas station and pick up one of the hundreds of thousands of paper schedules printed up. Yes, even in these Internet-heavy days, the pocket schedule is still widely available in any hockey-mad city for every level of play.

04-05
SCHEDULE

WHL

Scott
Niedermayer

Kamloops Blazers,
1990-92
New Jersey Devils
1992 to Present
• 2003-04 NHL's Top Defenceman
• 2004 World Hockey
Championship Gold Medalist,
Team Canada
• 2003, 2000 & 1995
Stanley Cup Champion
• 2002 Olympic Gold Medalist,
Team Canada
• 1992 Memorial Cup
Champion and MVP
• 1991 NHL Entry Draft,
3rd Overall, N.J. Devils
• 1991 World Junior
Gold Medalist, Team Canada
• 1990-91 WHL & CHL Scholastic
Player of the Year

Western Hockey League
...Full Scholarships & World Class Hockey

Here as well, designs become intricate and will more often feature a superstar or cult hero on a team, which as a result draws player collectors into the frenzy. A Mario Lemieux collector, for example, will hunt for the 1985–86 Pittsburgh Penguins schedule that features a sketch of the Hall of Famer on the cover along with the Calder Memorial Trophy. But as mentioned, the number of schedules that make it to the secondary market is minimal. Most will be marked up by fans throughout the year, while others have so much damage from transport (they are called pocket schedules for a reason) that they would be worthless on the secondary market. That's why a collector chases schedules so hard. A true collector, like Brian Cantrell, will also tell you that it's not the NHL schedules that are difficult to find — most fans will attempt to grab those and keep them. Instead, it's other leagues that are troublesome. "The toughest schedules always seem to be the Canadian Junior Leagues, OHL, WHL, and QMJHL [Quebec Major Junior Hockey League]. It seems that way for me anyways," he says. "Sudbury and Moose Jaw always are tough to get every year. There's a few minor hockey here in the States that are just as tough, but with more collectors here, they are more easily found one way or the other."

GAMEDAY GIVEAWAYS

When on-ice success or a superstar isn't a drawing ticket, the next trick for teams to get butts in the seats is to give away products that are either exclusive to a particular contest or free on a specific day when they'd cost fans money under normal circumstances. In the early days, these giveaway promotions would primarily come in the form of posters and calendars — the sorts of memorabilia that had little to no collector value but would instead drive kids who received them crazy. Now they tend to focus more toward the collector, who will pursue a bobblehead doll or miniature replica of the arena they are sitting in.

The promotions have varied over the years. Perhaps the most unique item given in an arena promo was done by the AHL's Philadelphia Phantoms in 2005, when the team cut up one of their Calder Cup banners and embedded the swatches in an oversized team trading card. But the pure display items that look the best in a man cave may be replica retirement banners, which mirror those that hang in the rafters of the hometown arena. These banners are definite must-haves for any team collector, and given that quantities usually range from 5,000 to 10,000, they are fairly easy to retrieve in aftermarket areas like eBay.

CROSSOVER APPEAL

At various junctures, the hockey memorabilia world has intersected with other popular collecting markets.

Primarily, this has occurred in three areas — coins, stamps, and action figures (we refuse to call them dolls, of course). These hobbies have been around for decades, with hockey being part of several commemorative series. Despite the glut of product seen in recent years, coins and stamps are wildly popular in both the sport collecting world and in the niche hobby markets.

COINS

The use of metal currency dates back millenia, but coins that celebrated our beloved sport are more recent creations.

Before going too far, it's important to establish the difference between "true coins" and other circular metal pieces. Coins refer to pieces that are actual (or at least have the markings of) currency denominations, such as pennies, nickels, dollars, and so on. Others are more often referred to "medallions"; and while they aren't as popular with coin collectors, they have their spot in the sports world.

Medallions arguably had their biggest success in hockey in 1983, when Starter Mint Ltd. of Calgary created team-focused lines. Issued in plastic bags with a perforated "card," the Starter coins carried a suggested retail price of $1.50 and had the appearance of a silver dollar. The faces of the coins (appropriately) featured the visage of the particular player and his name, while the reverse featured the team logo and the year of issue (assuming there was intent to create additional series).

In later years, other medallions were issued, including a popular series by card maker Pinnacle for the 1996–97 and 1997–98 NHL seasons. Named Pinnacle Mint, brass coins were paired with cards that had circular cutouts for the combined display. Rare coins in the series were even created from pure silver or gold. Other companies have created medallions over the years, including a 1998 series issued by McDonald's for the Olympics and various series produced by The Sports Vault that were issued through newspaper promotions. In a different vein, for the 2005–06 season, American company Merrick Mint used U.S. quarters to create painted coins. In many cases, the teams depicted mirrored the state coin struck in that era (e.g. Tampa Bay Lightning player Martin St. Louis appeared on a Florida state quarter), either in the standard issue or in the gold-plated parallels.

By far, the most intricate and eye-catching coins have been created by the Royal Canadian Mint. Several themed coins have been created, including a silver dollar for the Stanley Cup Centennial. More recent years have seen the Mint strike coins that paralleled Canada Post player issues or focused on Canadian teams, depicting painted jerseys or masks. The most visible commemorative coins, however, are those that made it into Canadian circulation. In 2009, to commemorate the Montreal Canadiens' centennial, the Mint struck a commemorative loonie featuring the Habs' season logo. As was the case with most Mint coins, both regular circulation and commemorative, high-quality encapsulated coins were issued. The same year, leading up to the 2010 Winter Games in Vancouver, the Mint also began issuing commemorative quarters for different Olympic sports. This included hockey, sledge hockey, and a 2002 gold medal commemoration release. As was the case with the Habs coin, the Mint also had commemorative edition coins, but additionally there were 1 million coins with red colouring struck for each sport that made their way into circulation.

Over the years, other currency coins were created with a hockey theme, but these, like 50-cent pieces and silver dollars, are rarely found in change at a grocery store. Most recently, these included a 50-cent piece celebrating the return of the Winnipeg Jets to the NHL. But when it comes to hockey coins, there is nothing — absolutely nothing — that compares to the "Lucky Loonie." In 2002, Canada

put together its formidable team for the Men's Winter Olympics tournament, with the singular focus of winning the gold medal. The Games took place in the heart of the U.S. (Salt Lake City, Utah, to be exact), and a Canadian icemaking team — led by Dan Craig — was hired for the competition. Buried at the centre faceoff dot was a loonie, and, after the Men's team won their championship game (followed up by a gold medal victory by the Canadian women), Wayne Gretzky was handed the good luck coin by the crew. That coin made its way to the Hockey Hall of Fame, where, much like the Blarney Stone, it was put on display and was open to be touched by the public for luck. After a while, however, the coin had to be sealed off completely because the face was deteriorating from the number of rubs it received.

In subsequent international tournaments, including Men's and Women's World Championships and future Olympic championships, the Lucky Loonie has become a permanent part of the crew's master plan for rink setup and has been buried in the ice, taped under benches, or stuck into goal nets. The Mint got on board with the unique story and now strikes a commemorative Lucky Loonie in both circulated and uncirculated versions before each Olympics.

STAMPS

While less common and less popular in North America, stamps are huge pursuits for collectors globally. Stamps are a bit more complicated than coins, since used pieces rarely hold any value because they're usually marked with a postal imprint. Commemorative issues, like coins, are created and are primarily released in sheets with printer edging, with the other popular collectible format being "first day issues," which are usually issued on a commemorative envelope.

Hockey historian Joe Pelletier, in a 2009 entry on his blog *Greatest Hockey Legends*, talked about the history of hockey stamps. "The first hockey-themed stamps came in 1948," Pelletier wrote. "The Swiss issued 4 different stamps to commemorate the St. Moritz Olympics that year. The hockey stamp . . . featured a maskless goaltender." Pelletier further documents that the first Russian stamp came in 1949, while Canada's first was issued in 1956.

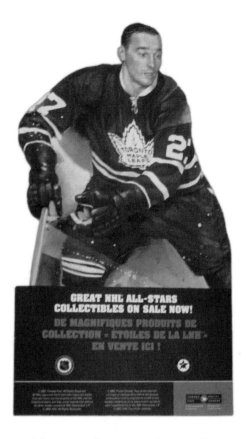

GREAT NHL ALL-STARS COLLECTIBLES ON SALE NOW!
DE MAGNIFIQUES PRODUITS DE COLLECTION - ÉTOILES DE LA LNH - EN VENTE ICI !

▲ JON WALDMAN

The NHL has teamed up with Canada Post on a couple occasions, primarily for landmark seasons such as the 75th anniversary of the league and the Stanley Cup Centennial. There was also a commemorative series issued for a four-year period that spotlighted some of hockey's all-time legends, including Wayne Gretzky, Milt Schmidt, and Larry Robinson. During this time, Canada Post also did a barnstorming tour where players would appear at collectibles shows and Canada Post outlets, signing the stamps and assorted collectibles that accompanied them, such as commemorative prints and coin holders. While the NHL stamps were popular during their period, they pale in comparison to national team releases. Across the globe, countries have produced stamps that feature their hockey heroes (or artistic depictions of generic players), primarily around Olympics time. Some, shall we say, less ice-friendly countries fete field hockey more than our beloved cold-weather game; but northern countries like Canada, the U.S., Sweden, Finland, and Russia have all produced stamps that depict ice hockey. Pelletier noted, however, that some of these warmer-climate countries did produce Olympic hockey stamps. "In fact, countries like Mongolia have more hockey-themed stamps than Canada," he points out. "Why? Revenue is the simple answer. Countries that don't even know what a hockey puck is will issue stamps, almost always to commemorate the Olympics, knowing that world collectors will be buying but never using the stamps. It is no different here in North America, and it is big business."

There's no question, though, that the elite piece in hockey stamps does not come from Canada or the U.S. or even Egypt. Instead, it's a Swedish issue from 1995. This particular stamp features hero Peter Forsberg, who, in a shootout, tallied the 1994 Olympic gold-medal-winning goal for the Tri Kroner. The stamp itself is beautiful as an artistic rendition of the famed overhead photo. No other stamp even comes close in the duality of commemoration and brilliance in visage.

FIGURINES

When photos and trading cards don't give player tributes their true dimension, collectors turn to a different medium to commemorate their heroes — figurines. Either solidly built statuettes, poseable figures, or something in between, these "toys" have been a mainstay in the hobby for two decades. While one-offs like the Wayne Gretzky Mattel doll had occasionally appeared, and there were team- (but not player-) specific bobblehead figures produced in the mid-20th century, it wasn't until the early 1990s that hockey fans had their first crack at a dedicated toy line.

In this span, from Starting Lineups to Sports Picks, we've seen everything from mass production and almost generic figures to true collector pursuits and detail we

never imagined possible. There are also some very niche products. Witness Hallmark, for example, which for years crafted a line of hockey figurine Christmas ornaments, paying seasonal tribute to the likes of Wayne Gretzky, Mario Lemieux, and Sidney Crosby, or Elby Gifts, which created ceramic figures. There have also been regional series made, such as the famed Provigo figures of the Montreal Canadiens.

STARTING LINEUP

Commonly known by the acronym SLU, Starting Lineup figures were produced by Kenner, perhaps best known as the toymakers of Star Wars and DC Comics action figures. In 1988, the company produced its first series of baseball players, later

adding the other "big four" sports, with hockey coming in 1993. The original series featured a dozen figures, including Mario Lemieux, Brett Hull, and Ray Bourque, but there were two curiosities about that first edition: the absence of a Wayne Gretzky figure (thanks to an exclusivity deal he had with the Upper Deck Company for memorabilia); and the inclusion of two goalies, Grant Fuhr and Patrick Roy. For whatever reason, the goalie figures, especially the admittedly light-skinned Fuhr figure, became extremely popular with collectors, who immediately put a premium on these pieces over their skater counterparts.

What was unique about the SLUs was that their program included both a figure and a trading card, more often than not produced by one of the full-out sports card companies (Score, Fleer, Upper Deck, and Pacific all at one point had the coveted licence). The merger of two collectibles helped spur action in the secondary market, especially for card-crazed kids who wanted to collect those pieces almost above the figurines. This led to a collector conflict. Toy collectors, of course, are notorious for wanting their figures to be kept in packages. For the card collector new to the toy market, this meant that few of the cards would escape their packaging at first and created additional demand.

The SLU craze continued in subsequent years as more players were added to series and retired greats appeared in the multi-sport Timeless Legends series (eventually, a dedicated product line was created just for shinny). These included a Mike Eruzione figure from the 1980 Miracle on Ice squad in an Olympics-themed release. Adding fuel to the SLU fire was a series of multi-figure packs that included, for example, Brett and Bobby Hull together, show- and club-exclusive figures that demanded strong premiums over their retail-issue counterparts, figures with push-button action moves, and other unique variations. But the

SLU pièce de résistance came when Kenner and Upper Deck teamed up, ushering in the opportunity for Gretzky figures to be created. Among those produced were those that depicted him holding aloft the Stanley Cup and a "Freeze Frame" boxed set that featured Gretzky in four slap shot poses, depicting him with each of his four NHL teams.

The four-inch figures, however, became victims of a changing figurine landscape in 2001. The mass production look, which did not give much detail, began to tire with collectors, especially as highly detailed pieces like McFarlane Toys figures became popular in the market. As a result of decline, Hasbro, who had taken over Kenner, made the decision to cease the product line, leaving behind a cult group of fans who to this day consider SLUs one of the best figure lines in all of sports.

BOBBLEHEADS

No one has ever successfully explained the allure of the bobblehead. They're more often comical recreations than actual portrayals and . . . well . . . their heads move. Okay, they're absurd; yet somehow the figures continue to be popular, especially when it comes to give-away nights at hockey arenas.

The first run for bobbleheads came in the Original Six era and were far cries from the figurines we see today, resembling tubby boys instead of athletic professionals. The kitsch appeal of these figures lived on for several years, and even now, in an era when realism is in demand, the chubby original bobbles can be found in high demand at auctions, while newer versions — including customized figures — have their own following.

But the bobblehead story doesn't end in this initial phase. In the early 2000s, the bobblehead enjoyed renewed interest from collectors. Quickly, two manufacturers bobbled their way to the top of the toy world — Alexander Global Promotions and Forever Collectibles — and licences were snatched up quickly. NHL, AHL, junior leagues, international . . . you name it. If you wanted a bobblehead of your favourite player, you had easy access. The peak for the figures came in 2002 and coincided with the Winter Olympics. At that point, Alexander Global created bobbles of both Team Canada and Team USA. The Canadian figures were quickly swept off of store shelves by

a nation rabidly backing their boys in their pursuit of the first Olympic gold in 50-odd years. The U.S. figures, meanwhile, were only available at the Games themselves. In the end, there were three versions of the Canadian figures released: one with a white base, one with a gold base, and one that featured the players — and team execs like Wayne Gretzky — with gold medals around their necks.

Even after the Olympics, bobbles continued to be popular; partnerships with trading card companies led to more exposure for the toys. But like so many other trends in sports collectibles, the bobblehead craze eventually died off and retail outlets were left with a huge amount of inventory. Where stores had trouble with the figures, hockey arenas found them to be a smashing draw for fans. Bobblehead giveaway nights became signature events on the schedule for teams of all competitive levels as highlight players and team mascots were highly coveted. Today, these regional pieces are exceedingly in demand on eBay as collectors attempt to barter with cohorts outside their area and add that head-shaking (in a good way) piece to their collections.

SPORTS PICKS

The appeal of the figures created by Todd McFarlane — perhaps better known as the man who brought Spawn, one of the greatest antihero comic book creations, to the world — is best explained by one of his subjects.

"It's the definition and the way they really approach it," explains Marcel Dionne, who was not only in the Legends series but was a key cog in the agreement that brought the first legendary figures to market, acting on behalf of the Hockey Hall of Fame. "Everything has to be approved, and the likeness has to be close. There's only so much you can do, but I thought it's pretty good. If you look at it, they also don't really flood the market. They make it so the collector can really enjoy this."

This attention to detail came from Todd McFarlane's own frustrations with what had been previously produced. "If you collect bubblegum cards and you look at any card, everything's there," McFarlane said in a 2002 interview, "and then all of the sudden, because I have to take that thing from 2-D to 3-D, the stick can't be in proportion, you can't have the logos right, you can't have the markings? All of a sudden you have to start taking away from the reality of what I see on TV and enjoy? A lot of other collectors didn't have a problem with it, but I did. If we're going to do sports, then, damn it, we're going to do it right. If it doesn't look like the guy, then what are we doing it for?"

The debut of McFarlane's statuettes came amid the decline and eventual cancellation of the Starting Lineup series. Standing in the neighbourhood of six inches, the first series of McFarlanes depicted NHL superstars like Steve Yzerman and Patrick Roy in sendups of their uniforms and were solely licensed by the NHLPA. It took one other series of realistic figurines before McFarlane was able to convince the NHL that they were worthy of the coveted licensing contract. Agreements were also made with equipment manufacturers and even the goalie mask artists.

In a flurry, series were produced that commemorated current and past stars from hockey. Virtually every name player (and a few not-so-name players) have been part of the Sports Picks lines. Some truly creative pieces have been issued,

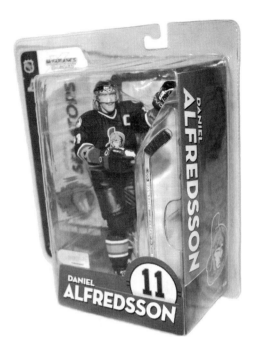

▲ JON WALDMAN

including players jumping over the boards, hat-trick celebrations that include mini ball caps on the ice, and Stanley Cup hoists.

In recent years, Sports Picks has seen a decline in popularity as other trends catch collector eyes, but the company continues to soldier on with popular lines that have included Olympic heroes and autographed figures.

HARDCORE
COLLECTIBLES
★ ★ ★

What happens when collector interest turns from enjoyment to all-out passion? Well, let's consider hardcore memorabilia. A multitude of organizations has helped feed the need for hockey souvenirs that go well beyond the local hobby shop or sports store — many of these next items are more likely found in retail outlets, bars, or restaurants, while others have their origins in arenas both standing and demolished. These collectibles are usually premium offerings, touting the credo of "Want this? Buy this first." Yes, it appeals to the kid in us who would buy the box of wretched caramel-coated Cracker Jack just for the surprise toy, and yes, it works. It *really* works.

Of course, even this extreme has its limits, and those limits are often exceeded. Witness the collector who will not be satisfied with a mini mask from McDonald's and will jump at the opportunity to also own the in-store display. Now *that's* hardcore.

RETAIL

If you've ever been through a Canadian grocery store in the winter, chances are you've come across ads for hockey collectibles. We can all remember those anxious moments as we spotted the familiar uniform of a hockey player as we were dragged up and down aisle after aisle by our shopping cart–pushing parents, and seeing the hockey prize within reach somehow made the entire trip worthwhile. At times, this has been as simple as a store teaming with traditional memorabilia companies such as card and figure producers to offer exclusive products or host an in-store autograph session. But more often there will be a premium offered for purchasers of products, either included in (or on) packaging or available by a mail-in offer. Among the favourites for collectors are the following collectibles.

BEE HIVE

The history of Bee Hive hockey products, as outlined on the archival

George (Red) Sullivan

site beehivehockey.com, started like this: "In 1934, the St. Lawrence Starch Company Ltd. hired a photographer for sessions at Maple Leaf Gardens with a few of the Toronto Maple Leafs 'star' players. These photos were to be made available for free through a promotion campaign that was about to start-up."

The series was broken into three "groups" — the first from 1934–44, the second from 1944–63, and the final from 1963–1967. As one might expect, the popular players of the day received the most requests; thus, lesser names were produced in much smaller quantities, leading

JON WALDMAN

replica hockey masks, magnets, and even spoons.

Preceding these lines, however, was arguably one of the most artistic card sets ever created — the 1986–87 Kraft Singles line. Inserted one-per-pack of the delicious cheese slices (okay, at least they were delicious when you were a kid) were renditions of black-and-white sketches featuring players on the NHL's eight Canadian hockey teams. The checklist was pretty extensive, giving recognition to both superstars, like Peter Stastny, and role-players, like Perry Turnbull. Tougher to locate these days than the cards, however, are the blown-up poster editions, which tended to be given out regionally. There was also a mail-away redemption for a Wayne Gretzky poster that required UPC codes from Kraft products and a mere $3.00.

to them being the most coveted by modern collectors. Along with the famed photography, Bee Hive also issued series of pins, rings, tie clips, team crests, and other souvenirs available in the same mail-in style promotion. Other photo series created by Bee Hive include Olympians and World War II planes.

KRAFT FOODS

Kraft's hockey-related marketing kicked off during the 1989–90 season. Through its popular Kraft Dinner products and Singles cheese slices, the company issued trading cards and stickers. It would be the start of a run that would go almost straight to the 2004–05 NHL lockout, with other products like Jell-O getting into the mix (pardon the pun). Also produced were paper

SHIRRIFF

As if the delicious pie fillings and pudding that Shirriff has created for families weren't enough over the years, the company was also involved in what was arguably the best run of memorabilia during the 1960s. First issued in the 1960–61 season, the famed Shirriff "coins" were either composed of plastic or metal, featuring a given player in a posed shot with their jersey visible. At first, the reverse of the coins had limited information, primarily urging kids to collect all the coins in the set; but later on statistics were included. The initial run for the coins was three consecutive years, with a fourth set released in 1968–69.

Alongside the coins issued in packages of its popular mixtures, Shirriff also offered, by mail-in redemption, a full series in a black presentation box (1960–61 set) and shields to display all the coins from a team (1961–62).

CONFECTIONARY

While the trading card market emerged out of the cigarette and bubblegum industries, chocolate treats were just as influential in the founding of the beloved hobby. In these early times, cards were, surprisingly for the era, photographic. The first two series were issued in 1923, one dedicated to hockey (Paulin's Candy) and the other a multi-sport release (Willard's Chocolates).

In more recent years, companies have taken a different spin, using cards to sell confections rather

than the other way around. In 1983, Neilson produced a Wayne Gretzky candy bar, and a decade later Clark issued a Mario Lemieux "bun" of chocolate and marshmallow. Trading card manufacturer Pro Set also got in on the action, creating a chocolate/nougat/caramel treat in 1991 that included three trading cards in the packaging. Needless to say, the series wasn't too popular. Since that time, there has been little in terms of candy/hockey combinations outside of a partnership between the NHL and chocolatier Zaini, who produced Kinder Surprise-esque chocolate eggs that contained various toys for kids to put together, including Stanley Cup displays and Zambonis.

CEREALS

Between Post, General Mills, Kellogg's, and other cereal companies, no child ever left for school hungry or lacking in hockey swag. These promotions date back to the 1930s, when Quaker Oats issued its first series of player photographs via a mail-in offer, similar to the Bee Hive promotions. Later, cards and other collectibles like marbles and plastic "shooters" (think

free-standing table hockey players) appeared inside packets of cereal or on the box backs; but the boxes themselves have become quite collectible when they feature a player on the face. Not surprisingly, Wheaties commands the most attention for this, having the likes of Wayne Gretzky and Olympian Karen Blye as part of their champions-themed packages.

ACTIONMATIC

When the retail store just doesn't have enough goodies for kids to indulge in, vending machines located near the exits have historically been great hits. In early days (and still occasionally seen), these machines would issue small- or regular-sized trading cards. In more recent times, the NHL has teamed with Actionmatic on a series of kid-friendly niche collectibles, ranging from "Buildables" generic hockey players to miniature mugs. But the gem of these is a series of keychains the company inherited one way or another that were originally issued during the 1983–84 season by a company called Souhaits. These back-to-back plastic cards were issued as team-focused keychains and included the likes of Bryan Trottier, Lanny McDonald, and Marcel Dionne.

JON WALDMAN ▶

ZELLERS

Retail stores themselves got into the hockey memorabilia program game. Former retail chain Zellers had the most famed promotion in the mid-1990s with its Masters of Hockey promotion. The program began with an annual hockey card series that commenced in 1992–93 and ran for four years, featuring the likes of Gordie Howe and Maurice Richard. But the true draw for the program was a series of autographed items that were available via the redemption of "Club Z" points. These started with autographed copies of the cards and continued to equipment that included multi-signed pucks, sticks, and jerseys.

ESSO

Esso has been somewhat light in the collectibles game despite its long association with the NHL and Hockey Canada. Most often, the Canadian gas company's logo has been emblazoned on pocket schedules for the full league schedule, but a few times it has ventured fully into the memorabilia realm, including a series of records released in the 1960s, featuring the Toronto Maple

▲ JON WALDMAN

Leafs, and two series of "stamps" (one issued in 1970–71 and another during the 1988–89 NHL season). Alongside these efforts, Esso has produced hockey-themed cash cards, and has also created commemorative pucks, crests, and assorted other souvenirs as part of its "Medals of Achievement" program for young hockey players.

COLA COMPANIES

When fans weren't interested in an alcoholic beverage (or weren't of age), they would turn to the next best drink — soda pop. In doing so, they would also stumble across some cool collectibles. For the most part, the two main soda providers — Coca-Cola and PepsiCo — celebrate hockey (along with other major sports) by adorning their cans with team logos or other themes. Regionally, this has included commemorative cans that celebrate a team's Stanley Cup victory, while national programs have seen team jerseys splashed across the sides of cans. Both companies also used the NHL in cap promotions in the days when their soda would come in bottles.

Between the two companies, Coca-Cola unquestionably has the advantage, primarily thanks to its longstanding relationship with the International Olympic Committee. The partnership has produced commemorative Olympic cans for years, including a special gold can for Canada's 2010 gold medal teams. The Coke tie-in with the Winter Games has also included commemorative pins over the years.

RESTAURANTS

At first glance it seems like a no-brainer: take the kids to a local eatery, where they get a hockey toy when they order off the children's menu. Go with the guys to the local sports pub and take home your NHL playoff stein. Finish our 52 oz. steak in a half-hour and have your name engraved on a personalized miniature Stanley Cup. (Okay, the last one hasn't happened, yet . . .)

But despite the logical progression, the promotions between hockey and restaurants have been sparse, at least on a nationwide basis. Regionally, promotions aren't uncommon (such as Little Caesars in Detroit producing trading cards of the Red Wings), but national programs with chains are few and far between. More often than not, these promotions are overly kid-oriented, like Wendy's or Pizza Hut toys, but some outlets — like 7-Eleven, which had a couple cool promotions in the mid-1980s, and Tim Hortons, which capitalized on its Sidney Crosby sponsorship with a unique cash card — got into the collector mindset.

The exception to this general lack of hobby love has been McDonald's, whose near two-decade run stands as the ultimate dedication to hockey collectibles (and the money it brought in for its restaurants). Through a longstanding partnership with the NHL, its Players' Association, and other organizations such as Hockey Canada, beginning in 1991 annual McDonald's promotions offered what was the major source

of hockey paraphernalia for fans and fry addicts and some of the most coveted collectibles that small amounts of money could buy.

Although McDonald's promos started before that fateful year (there was a sticker series in the 1980s and a Russian hockey stick available in 1990), the craze really began just a few weeks prior to the 1991–92 season's All-Star Game. That year, McDonald's teamed with Upper Deck to produce a series of hockey cards and hologram stickers that were sold in packages of four to anxious customers. This, of course, was at the peak of the boom, and McDonald's cashed in big-time. The cards, which were only distributed in Canadian restaurants, quickly became the hottest set on the market, and over the course of the next several years the set would evolve to include rare inserts, redemptions for blow-up cards, autographs, and jersey cards. The licence for the set would bounce around among Upper Deck, Pinnacle, and Pacific.

Likely the most memorable — and arguably most controversial — card in the entire run was Sidney Crosby's 2005–06 piece (he could not be included in subsequent years because of an agreement with Tim Hortons). Because it was issued during his inaugural NHL trading card season, many, including price guide *Beckett Hockey*, deemed it a rookie card, a designation never before even thought of for a non-mainstream card set. The debate over whether the card garnered the coveted "RC" designation still rages on to this day.

Amid the hills and valleys of hockey card popularity, however, a new tradition had been established that arguably matched the anticipation for cards — a semi-regular non-card program, which began in 1996 with miniature masks, kicked off another obsession. Rather than simply admire the beautifully designed goalie masks on the ice, collectors wanted to own replicas. While it would still be a few years before more authentic masks would be produced and become readily available for the mass market, the plastic versions that McDonald's created satisfied fans who wanted inexpensive reminders of their heroes.

Two other factors drove popularity on the secondary market for the two years McDonald's produced the masks. In the first season, the masks were produced in very limited quantities as a test run. The next year, McDonald's really struck it big as it did a full series, with some mask models, such as Kirk McLean's and Damian Rhodes's, being only available regionally. For collectors who were still of the mindset that

they could own every piece, this meant huge chases, especially in an era when eBay was not yet born and online trading was very much in its infancy. In subsequent years, McDonald's would add a variety of other miniature replica equipment pieces, including jerseys, sticks, and helmets. It would also tie in its Olympic sponsorship to produce commemorative pucks and coins.

By the time the 2009–10 season rolled around, there was a not-so-hushed feeling of anticipation over what McDonald's and its partners were cooking up for the 2010 Olympic Winter Games. The Vancouver location, of course, fuelled speculation that the company would go all out in a tribute to the nation's favourite sons. But then an odd thing happened. For years, McDonald's had not so subtly announced what would be the collectible for the year via an advertising card insert in packs of that year's card product. No such card, however, appeared in the 2009–10 Upper Deck series. Collectors naively hoped that McDonald's was lying in wait for the Olympics to end for a tribute series to be issued, rather than an anticipatory product; but the collectibles line had indeed met its end.

Roughly a half-year later, McDonald's formally put a halt to its hockey card line as well. A near 20-year relationship had ceased as McDonald's had chosen to move in a new direction, one that left collectors out in the cold. "At this point in time, premium programs (including non-card memorabilia) are not part of our strategic focus," Louis Payette, national media relations manager of McDonald's Restaurants of Canada Limited said. Payette attempted to assuage collectors that a return could happen, but the magic of McDonald's tie to the NHL had disappeared. The legacy for these collectibles, however, lives on as collectors attempt to complete the full run of McDonald's memorabilia.

JON WALDMAN

BEER

Beer and hockey are pretty much the single-most famed pair of sport and food (and, yes, I say that in full recognition of baseball's tie to peanuts and Cracker Jack), so it's not surprising that Canada's major ale producers have also been some of the most influential players in the memorabilia market. Primarily, these collectibles would be issued in cases of beer (or at times as mail-in redemptions) either right before or during the NHL playoffs, and as such the two would often be tied together in one form or another.

Not surprisingly, it is Canada's two largest breweries that have been most active.

LABATT BREWERIES is best known for its miniature Stanley Cups. Issued between 1999 and 2001, the Cups stood roughly four inches tall, perfect as trophies for table hockey games. In a somewhat unorthodox move, especially in comparison with other commemorative giveaways, the Cups bore the logo not just of teams that had raised Lord Stanley's mug in victory

these, making the logos accurate to the club that hoisted Lord Stanley's mug. Other collectibles would range from commemorative banners (primarily used by bar owners) to mini kegs that featured the Stanley Cup to bottles emblazoned with the logos of the Original Six.

MOLSON, Labatt's chief competitor, has primarily been associated with the Montreal Canadiens and the three-star-inspired Molson Cup given out by each Canadian NHL team (aside from the Quebec Nordiques, which had the O'Keefe Cup instead). But the brewery has also produced a few memorable collectibles over the years. For the 1992–93 season, for example, Molson produced cans that were emblazoned with the logo of the 100th Stanley Cup anniversary celebration.

Where Molson truly struck gold was with its adored mini keg, the Bubba. Paired with an infectiously catchy song, the popular canister's branded look was twice altered by Molson, once with jerseys from Team Canada and once, perhaps more famously, with images of Don Cherry's famed multicoloured suits and his signature "thumbs up." There were a few variations of

but also the entirety of the league's membership club roster. This, of course, led to many jokes that it would be the closest thing many teams would get to having any sort of connection to hockey's most enduring championship.

If collectors wanted something that didn't commemorate the Nashville Predators with the Cup, however, Labatt made a few other Cup-themed products that collectors could more easily identify with. Right off the hop (or is that hops?) was a 2001 series of commemorative bottle caps featuring the logo of a given season's Cup-winning squad — and by given season I mean that in the truest sense of the phrase, as every NHL Cup victory was represented. Labatt did a remarkable job with the Bubba, generally with different patterns or colour schemes. A few, ironically, also featured Cherry's dog Blue. Molson has also issued commemorative team patches, Stanley Cup champion posters, and a trading card series with Panini.

After the "big two" in Canada come some unique offerings from U.S. companies. **BUDWEISER**'s most notable contribution was a series of Stanley Cup USB keys emblazoned with team logos. Originally designed for an online contest, the keys are still popular among fans, especially since they came in a clear display case. Budweiser has also produced a number of commemorative bottles and cans over the years, dedicated to Stanley Cup champs and the Original Six squads, and used its secondary brand, Bud Light, to issue a series of beer steins as well as bar flags.

Regional companies have also been a part of the action. Around the time of Mario Lemieux's first retirement and induction into the Hockey Hall of Fame, longtime brewer **STROH**'s issued commemorative cans depicting a caricature of the legend. Other companies have taken a more "hands-off" approach.

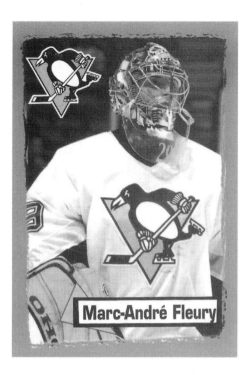

Marc-André Fleury

JON WALDMAN

HEINEKEN, for example, issued a series of "Did You Know?" coasters dedicated to the sport.

KID ESSENTIALS

Kids don't care about the value of collectibles (for the most part) — they enjoy their souvenirs. They put them up in their rooms and lockers just as children of the 80s did with these keepsakes.

STICKERS were at their peak in the 1980s when O-Pee-Chee, Topps, and Panini were producing sets. Many can still be found with their backs intact.

Still a favourite in kids' bedrooms, **PENNANTS** have been issued for ages, primarily targeted toward teams. Vintage pennants can command decent dollars in the secondary market, while modern models are favourite pieces for autograph hunters.

Unlike their movie counterparts, **HOCKEY POSTERS** have never been ascribed much value. Still, there are some collectors who frame up a piece once it has been signed.

Even in today's e-crazy world, printed **PROGRAMS** and **MAGAZINES**, primarily older issues that commemorate special games, still have a spot in the collections of young and old fans alike.

JON WALDMAN ▶

2

★ ★ ★

THE
NATIONAL
HOCKEY
LEAGUE

★ ★ ★

In 1917, the sport of hockey changed forever.

Created primarily from teams abandoning the National Hockey Association, the National Hockey League (NHL) has undergone numerous changes over its history as executives have come and gone and its member clubs have joined, moved, and/or folded. Today, the NHL is the unquestioned king of sports organizations in Canada, and depending on who you talk to south of the border it's either growing, receding, or maintaining an even-keeled cultlike status. Like most sports leagues, the NHL as an entirety has at times been the subject of collectibles, but more often the case is that the league is distantly secondary to its member clubs and highlighted stars. More often than not, an artifact that is a "league" collectible is a historic item like a rule book, a league-wide pocket schedule, or, more commonly, a commemorative program from showcase events like the All-Star Game or the NHL Entry Draft.

THE TRINITY
★ ★ ★

Debate about who has been hockey's greatest player has raged on in living rooms, cars, pubs, and rinks. It's a battle of wills between fans who will present every stat and nuance with a *Rain Man*–like ability to reel off information supporting their heroes or countering the argument for someone else. The collectibles realm has seen it too, and barter sessions can become particularly fierce.

But unlike the pub talk, the collecting universe has been more willing to anoint a triumvirate of hockey superiors, and while new superstars emerge year after year, three names can unequivocally be dubbed hockey's holy trinity — Wayne Gretzky, Gordie Howe, and Bobby Orr. These men did more to change the game of hockey than any other — they made it an art form. Howe's arms were dually purposed to punish skaters and netminders, Orr's legs pushed him to the brink as he went coast to coast, and Gretzky's eye for the way plays developed was unparalleled.

While the three never appeared on the ice together, they did appear as twosomes. Several times in their NHL careers, Orr and Howe appeared on the same NHL All-Star Team, while Gretzky and Howe famously played alongside each other in the WHA's 1979 All-Star contest. Orr and Gretzky's time together, however, is a little less well known. In 1979, Wayne and Bobby were brought together for a charity hockey game in Winnipeg. In the end, fans can make all the connections they want, but there will always be the one thing that drives them apart — that debate over who, indeed, is the greatest player in NHL history. (And for the record, what follows is organized alphabetically—it's not how I would rank the players.)

WAYNE GRETZKY

There's no question that during his career, Wayne Douglas Gretzky was the single biggest name in hockey. His popularity bordered on insanity. It seemed like you could not walk into a store without seeing some sort of promotional item featuring The Great One's visage.

Between his time in Edmonton and Los Angeles (let's be honest — the less said about St. Louis and New York, the better), Gretzky conquered the hockey world on either side of the 49th parallel and as a result created legions of fans that picked up any item that featured him, whether they were in his teams' cities or not.

And despite being retired for more than a decade, Gretzky is still the single biggest name in the hockey memorabilia world. In fact, he's created his own brand, WG Authentic. Through his online store, one can purchase everything from spectacularly framed photos to replica gloves.

But true Gretzky fanatics go miles beyond collecting autographs and trading cards. Because of his popularity, Gretzky has memorabilia of just about every sort. A Classic Collectibles auction in October 2004, for example, included a single lot that gave a small window into the breadth of collectibles devoted to The Great One. It included:

- pinback buttons;

- Gretzky's *Above and Beyond* video (VHS);

- The Wayne Gretzky "Rocket Hockey" tabletop game and video game;

- a skate box bearing his likeness;

- a Wayne Gretzky thermos (likely an accompaniment to the Wayne Gretzky lunchbox widely available in the 1980s);

- a flattened box of Honeycomb cereal depicting Gretzky with the New York Rangers

- NHL and team media guides; and

- numerous magazines with Gretzky on the cover.

That, of course, is only the tip of the iceberg. Stuffed pillows, his own candy bar, hockey equipment . . . if it could feature Gretzky's likeness, it likely has, and with good reason.

At retirement, Gretzky owned or shared more than 60 NHL records, an unfathomable number by any stretch (and this is before you get super geeky). He won four Stanley Cups, all with the Edmonton Oilers, and appeared in two additional Cup Finals, has more NHL assists than anyone else has points, has more NHL hardware than anyone else in history, and, to top it all off, has seven international medals, including three golds from the Canada Cup.

◄ JON WALDMAN

Gretzky's NHL career began after he turned pro at the tender age of 17 with the Indianapolis Racers of the WHA. While in the Rebel League, Gretz would end up being sent to the Edmonton Oilers and would make NHL history in short order. His first season in the league saw him tie Marcel Dionne for the points lead, though he would lose out to the Kings star over goal-assist

RONALD ENG ►

differential in the Art Ross Trophy race. He would also be denied the Calder Trophy for Rookie of the Year based on the technicality of having already played in the WHA.

Almost immediately, Gretzky became an icon. In just his third NHL season, he set the all-time goal record with 92 tallies and earned the first of four 200-point seasons in his career. Just two years later, he would win the Cup for the first time.

Even with all the success the Oilers had with Gretzky as their star, it was inevitable that he would leave. In 1988, Gretzky was sent to Los Angeles in the biggest trade in NHL history. That year's trading card by Topps and a miniature card produced by O-Pee-Chee featured Gretzky holding his new Kings jersey from the famous press conference in L.A. As legend has it, he

signed his corresponding O-Pee-Chee card — a posed shot in the new L.A. duds — for his daughter, Paulina, and has vowed never to sign that piece for anyone else.

Once in L.A., Gretzky became a bona fide Hollywood star too. He would become the first NHLer to host *Saturday Night Live*, and his marriage to Janet Jones gave him added cachet. It was here that he broke Gordie Howe's all-time point and goal records and continued to add to his trophy collection (albeit missing a Stanley Cup), up until a sooner-than-expected departure. During the 1995–96 season, he was traded to St. Louis, where he was united with 1980s rival Dale Hawerchuk and 1990s rival Brett Hull. The team, however, underperformed and, amid word of disagreement with head coach Mike Keenan, Gretzky rejected a contract offer from the Blues and signed instead with the New York Rangers, reuniting with one-time Oilers teammate Mark Messier (though Messier would wind up in Vancouver just one season later). Gretzky's career came to a close after the 1998–99 season. Not only was the three-year waiting period for Hockey Hall of Fame entry waived, but his No. 99 was retired NHL-wide as a testament to his greatness.

The Great One wasn't done with hockey. Prior to the 2002 Winter Games, Gretzky was tasked with assembling a Canadian squad that would avenge the poor performance of 1998. The team took the gold, and in a moment reminiscent of its 1987 Canada Cup celebration, Gretzky the team executive and Mario Lemieux the team captain embraced and posed for pictures together. Later, he would become part of an ownership group that purchased the struggling Phoenix Coyotes, and for a short time he would coach the club.

Today, more than a decade after his retirement, Gretzky remains among hockey's most in-demand players. Collectors will aggressively pursue his memorabilia, which has yet to stop being produced. Look no further than his continued relationship with the Upper Deck Company and the constant demand for his autograph as evidence of this, as well as the high-dollar values his gear and collectibles receive at auction. But of all the collectibles that have come out over the years, there's one that sticks out — a particular hockey jersey. As both Oilers and Kings fans will lament, Wayne's incredible career ended on Broadway. By this time, game-used Gretzky memorabilia was already at an insanely high level of demand, both from private collectors and collectible companies, so it wasn't uncommon for Gretzky to wear multiple sweaters in one season.

On October 30, 1997, The Great One suited up in a jersey that was, well, memorable for all the wrong reasons. Despite his being the all-time NHL scoring leader and holding more records than most teams had record books, the brain trust in the equipment room of Madison Square Garden misspelled Wayne's last name as *Gretkzy* that night. (Incidentally, the Rangers lost that game to the New York Islanders). Since that fateful night, the Gretkzy jersey has been well travelled, making appearances at conventions and at the Hockey Hall of Fame, but has not found its way into a private collection. While no company has created a jersey or other product to commemorate the error, "tributes" do exist. Witness the "jersey foul" like the one dug up by one Greg Wyshynski, a.k.a. "Puck Daddy," a popular hockey blogger on Yahoo! Sports. On February 5, 2009, Wyshynski reported that an eBay auction came up with an L.A. Kings "Gretkzy" jersey. No big deal, right? "But here's the thing," Wyshynski wrote. "Gretzky *actually signed* this Kings version of the Rangers jersey foul, and it comes with a Certificate of Authenticity. Our obvious and only question: Did he misspell his autograph in accordance with the jersey?"

No matter how you spell his name, there is no denying that Wayne Gretzky's influence is unparalleled in hockey, and he will continue to be the one of biggest names in the sport for decades to come.

GORDIE HOWE

When you speak of legends of the game, none resonates with fans of all generations more than the man dubbed "Mr. Hockey" — Gordie Howe. Born in Floral, Saskatchewan, Howe began playing organized hockey at age eight — late, considering many children today are already lacing up skates before their fifth birthday. After Howe reached six feet in his early teens, pro hockey came calling when he was 15. He was invited to try out for the New York Rangers, but he was unable to secure a developmental spot with the club. Soon after, however, the Detroit Red Wings snapped him up, and he began to play in the club's developmental system. By 1946, Howe was up with the senior club. He wore No. 17 in his rookie campaign and gained his famed No. 9 one season later. The debate rages on as to whether Howe or Maurice Richard is the greater player to wear the number (your side chosen primarily by whether you speak French or English). The argument is valid on both sides, but Howe's numbers outstrip Richard's — 801 goals, 1,850 NHL points, both NHL records at the time of Howe's retirement. Howe won the Hart Trophy and Art Ross Trophy six times apiece, numbers that are rare in professional sports. More importantly, Howe was an integral part of four Stanley Cup campaigns for the Red Wings. It was perhaps no coincidence that this time coincided with Howe's pairing with Ted Lindsay

JON WALDMAN

and Sid Abel as part of the famed Production Line. When the line was broken up by Abel's retirement and Lindsay's trade, it spelled the end for Howe's taste of Stanley Cup glory.

Gordie was more than just a brilliant shooter and playmaker — he was also as rough and tumble as they came — a power forward before that term was born in the 1990s. Unlike a Gretzky or a Crosby, Howe was in no need of an enforcer — he fought his own battles and did so with such gusto that NHL reporters coined the term "Gordie Howe Hat Trick" for a player who had a goal, an assist, and a fight in a single contest.

After retiring in 1970–71 due to a wrist injury, Howe turned down an opportunity to be the incoming New York Islanders first head coach. Instead, he took on a minor office role with the Red Wings until the WHA came calling. It was the Houston Aeros that would breathe new life into Mr. Hockey, offering him the opportunity to play with sons Mark and Marty — a first in hockey and a generational feat rarely seen in sport. Howe and his kids would become the leaders of the club, with Gordie winning the WHA's MVP award in 1974, then known as the Gary L. Davidson Trophy but renamed in his honour the following season. That year would also see Howe and Co. win the Avco World Trophy for the first of two consecutive seasons. The year 1974 also gave Howe a rare opportunity to suit up for Canada as the best WHA players born in the nation suited up against the U.S.S.R. This team, while having superstars Howe and Bobby Hull on their squad, was not nearly as powerful as the '72 Summit squad and fell to the Russians. Only recently, mainly thanks to trading card companies Upper Deck and In The Game, have the crew and their admittedly impressive jerseys been shown in memorabilia.

In 1977, the Howes moved to Hartford, Connecticut, to join the team then known as the New England Whalers. A short time later, in 1979, Howe was back in the NHL for his final season of pro hockey. Late in the year, the renamed Hartford Whalers pulled off a trade with fellow WHA alumns the Winnipeg Jets and acquired Bobby Hull, marking a rare occasion that two superstar rivals ended their careers together. Howe's final game gave him instant entry into the Hockey Hall of Fame, an honour rarely bestowed, but if there ever was anyone who deserved it, it was Gordie. Howe would go on to have a fairly quiet retirement — that is, until the memorabilia world beckoned. In the early 1990s, he became a regular on the burgeoning autograph circuit. His signature would quickly become one of the most sought-after in the hobby world as fans across North America would go well out of their way to meet the superstar.

It was also during this time that Gretzky, once one of Howe's biggest fans, would begin an all-out assault on his NHL records. The first major record to fall would be the all-time NHL points lead, followed by the all-time goal mark and combined professional hockey points mark (NHL and WHA). Howe still, however, holds longevity marks, playing more games and seasons in the NHL and in professional hockey overall. His consistency is also unparalleled, as he holds the NHL record for most consecutive 20-goal seasons (22). Howe's association with hockey doesn't end there. In 1997, Howe signed a one-day contract with the International Hockey League's (IHL) Detroit Vipers and, just short of being 70, suited up for the club for one shift, marking the first time any pro athlete competed in six different decades.

This tells the story of Howe's hockey career, but his business career is a study in and of itself. As mentioned, Howe earned the moniker "Mr. Hockey" during his career. This would end up — literally — becoming his trademark, as for several years memorabilia companies were contractually obligated to title cards and other paraphernalia depicting Howe as "Mr. Hockey." Howe also would very frequently include the moniker in his autographs during this period. Today, Howe drives more memorabilia sales than just about anyone. In particular, signed photographs of Howe and Gretzky (either of them holding the 1,850 and 1,851 pucks or the famed photo of Howe and his school-age protégé) remain on every hobbyist's want list, along with the Hartford Whaler collectibles that have recently become available.

BOBBY ORR

For whatever reason, defencemen are not hotly pursued by hockey collectors in comparison with forwards or goalies. Very few blueliners break

through a glass ceiling to become must-haves for collections. Despite this, it's a D-man, not a goalie, who is the non-forward in the hockey hobby trinity, a man who took the attention of a team of Bruins execs in one fateful game.

"I was working for Boston and assigned to be the general manager and coach of the Kingston Frontenacs in the Eastern Professional Hockey League, Boston's number-one professional development team," recalls Wren Blair. "I heard that Parry Sound was coming to Gannanock to play a Bantam C team. I told Lynn [Patrick] that there were a couple of kids in Gannanock that I was following. In the end, the owner of the Bruins went, our chief scout went, Milt Schmidt, the coach of the team, Lynn . . . about 12 of us went. About three minutes into the game, Lynn was standing behind the screen, I was on the side. I went to Lynn and said, 'Forget the kids on the Gannanock team. There's a kid on the Parry Sound team that is unbelievable. Watch that team and see if you spot the same guy I do.' Lynn said, 'Who, number two?' I said, 'Yeah.'"

That player was none other than Robert James Orr.

After the game, Blair spoke to

Bucko McDonald, the Parry Sound coach. McDonald informed Blair that Orr was headed to Detroit. The following Monday morning, Blair visited the Orr family at their home in the small Ontario town of Parry Sound. Orr was 12 at the time, two years before he would be eligible to attend a Bruins training camp. The dedication by Blair paid off, and Orr indeed donned the black and gold of Boston.

Orr would go on to become one of the game's greatest innovators,

becoming the first true offensive defenceman. He won eight Norris trophies during his career and, more impressively, also led the NHL in scoring, captured the Hart Memorial Trophy, and was *the* marquee name on a club that sported the likes of Phil Esposito and Gerry Cheevers. He was also an integral part of the NHL's continued domination in hockey when the WHA attempted to take control of North American shinny.

Not surprisingly, Orr's heroics

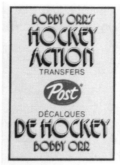

Face off / Mise au jeu

later led to hobby immortality. Amid the sports card boom in the early 1990s, Orr was the first retired player to have his autograph randomly inserted into trading card packages (1991–92 Score Hockey). He was also the subject of figurines from Starting Lineup and Todd McFarlane Productions, started his own memorabilia chain (which still runs today) and is easily one of the most requested signatures in the entire landscape of hockey. Even in his playing time, Orr was heavily desired by young fans. He was the face of several promotional NHL products and even had a doll in the days before sports action figures were mainstream.

All this before we even talk about Orr's signature moment, known simply as "The Goal."

In the 1971 Stanley Cup Finals, Orr and the Bruins battled the St. Louis Blues. Orr was at his usual peak offensive play when he accepted a pass from Derek Sanderson and potted the Cup-winning goal behind a sprawled Glenn Hall. What made the moment even more special was that Orr was simultaneously being tripped by ruffian Barclay Plager. Orr was airborne, in a victory leap unlike anything ever seen in sports history, when the puck crossed the goal line. Amazingly, the moment was captured, photographically, frame by frame, and as a result the number of collectibles that memorialize it vary. Trading cards, framed photos, artwork . . . It's all very easy to track down and often for a reasonable price (except when it's autographed). The most unique collectible depicting Orr "scoring and soaring" was issued by McFarlane Toys in the late 2000s. Just a few years prior, the toy company produced its first figures of

NHL Legends, and as soon as the announcement came, fans began to crave a statuette of the famous Orr pose. The figure was quickly snapped up and remains one of the most popular McFarlane pieces ever.

Orr's heroics weren't limited to NHL ice. In 1976, the Canada Cup tournament was staged for the first time. After being forced to miss the 1972 Summit Series due to a knee injury, Orr's condition had deteriorated even further by the time he received his 1976 invite. Orr initially refused an offer to join the Canadian squad but later relented and showed remarkable determination for a player of his condition. His play was impeccable, and it seemed like the pain completely disappeared. En route to leading Canada to the championship, Orr potted seven points to share in the tournament lead and take home MVP honours.

Like so many legends who wore the black and gold, however, Orr did not finish his career in Boston. With knees that could no longer take the rigours of a full NHL season, at least at the calibre of play he was accustomed to, Orr's final games of NHL hockey were played with the Chicago Black Hawks. The team didn't get as much out of Orr as they would have liked; he managed to play in just 26 games before he was forced permanently to the sidelines. In the aftermath of his career, Orr was granted exceptional status and immediately inducted into the Hockey Hall of Fame. His No. 4 was retired by the Bruins, and he routinely battles Wayne Gretzky for the honour of being called the greatest player in NHL history. Many of his records are still intact, and accomplishments like being the only player to win the Art Ross, Hart, Norris and Conn Smythe trophies in one year will likely never be equalled.

Today, Orr continues to be one of hockey's most pursued legends and makes occasional appearances. He has opened his own online hockey memorabilia store. Orr has also become a player agent to men like Jason Spezza, who are still awed by all he's accomplished. "I don't think I have a true feeling for how great he is. I have so much respect for him," Spezza told fyiottawa.com in 2001. "I watch him on tapes and it's just ridiculous how good he was compared to the guys he was playing against. He's a great guy and you don't even know it's Bobby Orr, the way he talks to you."

THE TEAMS
★ ★ ★

What you will see in this section are not strictly the top players in their respective teams' histories. Rather, they are a sampling of the players who made such an impact on the squads and resonated with its fanbase that they are emblematic of their teams.

Having a single player representative is a unique task. Squads like the Montreal Canadiens have multiple stars who could easily fit the bill as great representation, while newer clubs like the Winnipeg Jets aren't as easy to pick from. So early on, I set a couple parameters:

1. **A PLAYER COULD ONLY BE LISTED WITH ONE TEAM.** This meant making a choice for some of hockey's greatest heroes. Certainly, Mark Messier could have been listed with the Edmonton Oilers, but as great as he was in the City of Champions, he had a greater impact in the

hockey world when he came to the Rangers and led the team to the promised land of the Stanley Cup.

2. **THE "TRINITY" OF HOCKEY IS REMOVED FROM CONSIDERATION.** This one was a difficult decision to make at first, but when you think about it, giving Gordie Howe, Bobby Orr, and Wayne Gretzky their own space was very well justified.

3. **CURRENT TEAMS ONLY.** I'm not alone in the belief that a defunct or moved franchise has its own history. Listing Dale Hawerchuk in the Phoenix Coyotes section or Peter Stastny among Colorado Avalanche greats borders on sacrilege.

Just as the players listed are parts to the overall story of an NHL team, so, too, are the highlighted memorabilia items I've selected to talk about. By no means are they necessarily the most valuable or most desired items (especially in the case of the Anaheim Ducks entry); but in identifying the treasures I discuss here, I wanted to give a bit of air to some of the rarities and oddities the collecting world has spawned.

THE ORIGINAL SIX
★ ★ ★

The Boston Bruins, Chicago Blackhawks, Detroit Red Wings, Montreal Canadiens, New York Rangers, and Toronto Maple Leafs were the only teams to do battle in the NHL for most of the 1940s, 1950s, and 1960s. Between the folding of the New York Americans in 1942 and the expansion period in 1967, these squads fought valiantly through tough, rigorous schedules that resulted in some of the greatest rivalries in sports (although every team's focus seemed to be the Montreal Canadiens, who were, by far, the most dominant squad).

The close confines of the six-team league meant only the most elite players in the world were able to earn spots on an NHL roster. Simply put, if you weren't top rate, or if you were anything but Canadian, it was near impossible to get a break — unless you were an American recruited to play for the Blackhawks. The action of the era was, to say the least, intense.

Helmets were scarce and players were fearless — despite the notable lack of a union to protect them, players would stride across the ice with reckless abandon. Additionally, a player was more likely to play for a team for his entire career, unless you angered management like Ted Lindsay did when he began setting the wheels in motion for the emergence of the NHLPA. (Fun fact: Vic Lynn is the only player of the era to suit up for all Original Six teams.) It was a great time for the sport: families would gather around the radio or television to listen to Foster Hewitt's *Hockey Night in Canada* broadcasts, and names like Maurice Richard, Gordie Howe, and Bobby Hull were iconic in Canada, fuelling schoolboy dreams from coast to coast.

Today, the Original Six teams enjoy varying degrees of success on the ice but are still the most popular in the league. Part of this can be attributed to the natural generational condition of following the same team your father did and his father did, but the efforts of the NHL to promote the attractiveness of seeing the now lowly Habs still burns brightly. Remarkable anniversaries such as the Canadiens' recent centennial (which included the mass reproduction of yesteryear jerseys, no matter how horrid they looked) certainly helps this notion. But let's leave aside the artificial nature of the Original Six branding and instead focus on their years in the league and the (proud) traditions they carry that attract players and dollars. There's a mystique about being able to don the Broadway Blue or *bleu, blanc, et rouge.*

BOSTON BRUINS

If there is any true oddity that has surrounded the Boston Bruins over the course of their long history, it is that few of their legends retire while on the team's roster — a stark contrast to the other Original Six teams. Look throughout the history of this storied franchise — from Shore to Orr to Bourque — to see the trend of players ending their careers outside of Beantown. But there is an unmistakeable mystique to the time each one spent in Boston, whether at the original Boston Gardens or the modern arena, wearing the team's colours, be they the modern black and gold or the older brown and gold combination.

Yes, you read that right — the

team has had two colour schemes. When the Bruins franchise was founded in 1924, the colours were chosen to match those of owner Charles Adams's shop. The original sweater did not feature the now familiar spoke-wheeled B. Instead, it had the crawling bear that was recently reintroduced when the team uniform was redesigned, adding a tribute to the original logo on the shoulders of their main jersey and as the central image on the team's third jersey. The more familiar B debuted in the 1940s after a period where the team featured player numbers on the front of the sweater (they were already on the back), and almost immediately the team began a series of commemorative jerseys, the first being the new logo with the numbers 24 and 49 on two spokes, commemorating the 25th anniversary of the squad. Later on, they would wear all-gold jerseys with the word *Bruins* scrawled across the chest in a script-style font. Remember — this was in the 1940s and '50s, well before commemorative jerseys became regular fare in the NHL.

The tradition of unique jerseys continued on for years for the Bruins, and it's no surprise that they were among the first teams in the NHL to adopt third jerseys; but, man, did their choice cause a lot of controversy. In the mid-1990s, the team debuted the new yellow-gold-dominated jersey, which, instead of the spokewheel B logo, had a bear's head as the main crest. Even considering the ugliness of this jersey, a game-used Bruins tog is considered one of the best you can get. For fans who want something more artistic, however, there are some extremely affordable options. Witness, for example, a series of collectible prints and associated items produced by Maple Leaf Productions Ltd. that show a timeline of a team's jerseys. While they were produced for all NHL clubs (and even some defunct squads), none quite compares to the Bruins'. Original watercolour artworks of the timelines were later made available to the general public through Heritage Sports Art.

These artistic depictions tell a very colourful and illustrated history of the Bs, but they don't come close to telling the full tale of a team whose history has seen a mix of success, failure, and several in-between years. The Bruins won their first Stanley Cup in 1929, one of three under the watchful eye of Arthur Ross, an icon in Bruins' management history for more than 30 years. Ross certainly had a lot to work with in his favour. Early on, he was able to snipe Eddie Shore and later was able to add star names like Dit Clapper before forming one of the most dangerous trios in all of hockey, the Kraut Line. Composed of Woody Dumart, Bobby Bauer, and Milt Schmidt, the Kraut Line was a trio of players who lit up the NHL during their time together while also banding as brothers and taking leave from the NHL to fight in World War II (along with several other players of the era). The trio led the Bruins to the 1941 Stanley Cup, a victory that would be their last until the Bobby Orr era.

Over the next several years, the Bruins saw up-and-down seasons. They would at times challenge for the Stanley Cup and other seasons find themselves basement dwellers among the league's six teams. Slowly but surely the returning heroes from the pre-WWII Cup team disappeared. Players cycled through the system until a stable lineup took shape in the early 1960s. The era also saw the Bruins break hockey's colour barrier, as Willie O'Ree became the first black hockey player to crack an NHL lineup.

In 1966, the slow building process was amplified by the debuting Bobby Orr. Already considered a hockey superstar before he played his first NHL game, Orr would prove to be a strong force for the Bruins right out of the starting gate. Soon after Orr's call to the big league, the Bruins pulled off a remarkable trade, acquiring Phil Esposito, Ken Hodge Sr., and Fred Stanfield from the Chicago Black Hawks. Other players like Derek Sanderson and Gerry Cheevers were added to the team, and the team won two Stanley Cups in the 1970s — in 1970 and 1972 — in a decade that was otherwise pretty much otherwise dominated by the Montreal Canadiens.

Ah yes, Les Habitants. The teams crossed paths for decades in the Original Six era, but it was in the 1970s that a true rivalry developed between the two clubs. The feud started in the 1971 Stanley Cup Finals, where Orr and Co. ran into a hot young goaltender by the name of Ken Dryden. The Canadiens' victory was a stopping point between Cup-winning campaigns by the Bruins, and the feud only escalated

later in the decade when the Bruins lost in the finals. The back-breaker came in 1979, however, when, in Game Seven of the playoff semi-finals and up by one goal, the Bruins were called for having too many players on the ice. The Habs stormed back during the power play, scoring the game-tying goal during the power play and then putting the Bruins on the golf course during overtime.

The era of Cup contention began to slip away from Boston's control in the 1980s. New talents like Ray Bourque, Rick Middleton, and Cam Neely helped guide the club to the Stanley Cup in 1988 and 1990; unfortunately they were both times stacked against a far superior Edmonton Oilers squad. By the time the 1990s rolled around, the team were more pretenders than contenders. The only true success during the decade came in the defeat of the rival Canadiens in four playoff series. The low point for the club would come in 1997, when, for the first time in 30 years, the Bruins missed the playoffs. That off-season, the Bruins had the first overall selection in the NHL Entry Draft and selected Joe Thornton, the team's eventual captain. But

even with Thornton at the helm and a cast that included Glen Murray, Bill Guerin, and Brian Rolston, the team struggled both before and after the lockout. It wasn't until a journeyman goalie by the name of Tim Thomas emerged as a strong netminder, and prospect Patrice Bergeron took on a leadership role within the club that they again started to sniff around as a potential Cup threat.

That run came in 2011. After soldiering through the playoffs, they met the heavily favoured Vancouver Canucks for the Cup. The Bruins were a team possessed, with Thomas putting on a performance for the ages, particularly in Game Seven where he put on 60 minutes of shutout hockey as the Bruins took the Stanley Cup home for the first time in nearly 40 years.

Following that incredible year, the Bruins continued as a playoff team but were besieged by off-ice drama surrounding Thomas, whose political campaigning and disinterest in continuing with the team after the 2011–12 season set the club on a new path, something this squad was no stranger to. Thomas's understudy, Tuukka Rask, would step in quite well and help guide the

Bruins to the Stanley Cup Finals for the 2012–13 season, showing once again that the Bruins legacy would continue on strong.

★ RAY BOURQUE ★

"When I got the call today, I didn't know how I was going to react. I was on the golf course . . . I had shivers everywhere and I had a hard time playing golf after that." That was Raymond Bourque's reaction when he got the call to the Hockey Hall of Fame back in 2003, capping an incredible run in hockey that saw him stake his claim as one of the best defencemen in NHL history.

Bourque debuted in the NHL the same year as Wayne Gretzky, taking home the Calder Trophy on a technicality (Gretzky was deemed ineligible for rookie honours having already played at the pro level in the WHA). While some questioned whether Ray was the true winner that year, he would never be questioned as a superstar through the 1980s and 1990s as he put together a run in Beantown that included leading the entire NHL (you read that right) in shots on three occasions.

Bourque's career in Boston spanned 21 remarkable seasons, during which he became one of the leaders of his generation of blueliners. He sits atop the leaderboard among defencemen in career goals and points, won the Norris Trophy five times, and was named to 19 post-season First or Second All-Star Team berths while in Boston (in addition to one during his time in Colorado). Bourque also accomplished another rare feat in Boston — the former captain had memorable runs wearing two numbers for the Bruins. While most players, especially those with significance to their franchise, will wear one number their entire career, Bourque changed his jersey from his inaugural No. 7 to No. 77 midway through his run in tribute to fellow Beantown legend Phil Esposito.

The only accomplishment Bourque was unable to achieve in Boston was winning the Stanley Cup. Instead, Bourque was given his opportunity to go to another team — the Colorado Avalanche — and taste the championship during the famed Mission 16W (16 wins needed to claim the Stanley Cup) campaign in 2001. After all was said and done, and Bourque was called to the Hockey Hall of Fame, he reflected on his time spent with both teams, finding both tenures to be amazing.

"Twenty-plus seasons in Boston were incredible. I came as part of a special team, and for me it was an incredible experience," he said. "Then I made a tough decision to move to Colorado to chase the one thing that was left for me to win and it happened for me. I think it was a great experience for me not only as a hockey player, but as a person, and seeing a different organization and living out the full experience of living it out there."

For Bourque collectors, that team mentality sticks as well. While a single signed photo is coveted greatly, there's something unique about having the captain's jersey signed by an entire team who support him, and this is especially the case with a player as well-liked and respected as Ray Bourque.

CHICAGO BLACKHAWKS

Before getting into the story of the Windy City's boys, let's clear the air on something right off the hop — the original name of their beloved franchise was the Blackhawks. As Liam Maguire cites in his trivia book *What's The Score?*, the original spelling was discovered on the team's charter in 1986. For many years prior, the moniker "Black Hawks" had been used, but once the discovery was made, the one-word name stuck.

Another misconception should be cleared up right away — the team's history begins not with James Norris but with Frederic McLaughlin, the man who outbid Norris for the rights to the 1926 expansion franchise (yep, expansion has really been around that long). McLaughlin named his team after his World War I infantry division, who in turn had been named after Chief Black Hawk.

The team's foundation was built on American-born players and fielded the first all-American lineup in the history of the NHL. Within the first decade of their existence, in 1934, the Hawks, on the strength of goalie Charlie Gardiner and defenceman Cy Wentworth, were Stanley Cup champions. They repeated in 1938. But although success came quickly to the Hawks, it was fleeting. Though crowds at Chicago Stadium cheered louder than in any building in the NHL (if not all of sport), the fans were saddled with bad teams. Between the 1938 and 1961 Cup titles, the team twice went on runs of five or more years without making the playoffs and in that entire time only won one playoff series.

In the 1960–61 season, the team's fortunes finally turned around. With the tandem of Bobby Hull and Stan Mikita leading a squad that included future Hall of Fame goalie Glenn Hall, standouts Elmer "Moose" Vasko, Pierre Pilote, and others, the Blackhawks finished third behind the Maple Leafs and Canadiens. The squad counted back-to-back six-game series victories against the Habs and Detroit Red Wings en route to just the third Cup in franchise history. It would be the only time that legends Hull and

Gordie Howe would square off for the coveted Cup.

One year later, Chicago was once again in the Finals, but this time they were battling a team with destiny on their side — the Toronto Maple Leafs. The Hawks were so unwilling, as the story goes, to relinquish control of the Cup that they hid it on the team bus prior to the final game of the series.

As the Original Six era wound to a close, the Blackhawks returned to their ineffective ways, only winning one more playoff series before the 1967 expansion. After the NHL moved to 12 teams (and through later expansions), Chicago put together some decent squads. Even when Hull left for a bigger payday in the WHA in the 1970s, Mikita was able to lead the team into the

JON WALDMAN ▾

playoffs and occasionally to series victories. In the 1980s, Doug Wilson and Denis Savard became the darlings of the Windy City as the team continued to show promise. It would take the team until 1991–92 to return to the Stanley Cup Finals. Led by Chris Chelios, a recent import from the Montreal Canadiens, Chicago powered to the finals with young stars Jeremy Roenick and Ed Belfour maturing almost minute by minute. The team, however, could not overcome the Mario Lemieux–captained Pittsburgh Penguins.

It would be the closest the Blackhawks would come to a true "hurrah" for several years and was the final true glorious hockey moment for Chicago Stadium, which would host its last hockey action in 1994, as a Mike Gartner goal eliminated the Hawks from the 1993–94 Stanley Cup Playoffs. Following that season, the Hawks moved to the United Center and seemed to keep things on track; but the departures of by then team leaders Roenick and Belfour left giant holes in the team's lineup, and in 1997–98, the Blackhawks missed the playoffs for what would be a run of a decade with only one post-season berth.

The less-than-mediocre play, however, gave rise to a new tandem that seemed destined to bring the Hawks back to Cup glory — Patrick Kane and Jonathan Toews. The two high draft picks led the Hawks all the way to the Conference Finals in 2008–09 (just their second season in the NHL) and, one year later, returned the Cup to Chi-Town. The suddenness of the rise took many by surprise, but the seeds for the revival of the Hawks franchise began just after the NHL lockout, when Duncan Keith and Brent Seabrook were introduced to the NHL, and a series of players like Dustin Byfuglien, Patrick Sharp, and others brought the squad new hope. That off-season, with salary cap woes present, the Hawks were forced to trade or leave several players open for free agency, including Antti Niemi and Andrew Ladd. Still, just three short years later in 2013, the Hawks once again captured the Stanley Cup after establishing an NHL record for the longest winning streak to start a season

Throughout the Blackhawks' history, the centrality of the team has been in the aforementioned Chicago Stadium, where an old-fashioned organ famously played through game after game until its closure in 1994. The organ, which was first played by famed poet Ralph Waldo Emerson, was moved to the 19th Hole upon the closure of the stadium and later put into storage in Arizona, where much of it succumbed to a fire. The original console, however, is still intact and is the property of organ collector (yes, there is such a thing) Phil Maloof of Las Vegas, Nevada.

For all the hoopla one would expect from the closure of such a historic building, there was little done at the time to commemorate its shutdown. Newspaper articles, stadium seats, and bricks are the primary remnants fans hunt for. But one curiosity does exist: a patch commemorating the last year of Chicago Stadium was produced, yet was never worn by the Hawks during their last season of play in the old barn.

★ BOBBY HULL ★

There are two reasons Bobby Hull's name continues to be one of the most in demand on autograph circuits and in memorabilia offerings, despite a proliferation of products dedicated to the Golden Jet.

Those reasons? The Chicago Blackhawks and the Winnipeg Jets.

Of all the players listed on teams in these entries, none have quite the two-franchise cachet that Hull does. Yes, the likes of Messier, Gretzky, and Roy have virtually equal demand in two cities, but Hull's demand covers two leagues — the NHL and WHA. Between the two, Hull's bigger impact may have been in the WHA, as he gave the young league a feeling of legitimacy that it needed out of the gate. But in the grand scheme of hockey history, he is better remembered as the man who, alongside fellow list member Stan Mikita, brought Chicago a rare championship and ultimately changed the sport of hockey forever with the use of his trusted stick. Hull was not the first to ever use the slapshot, but he mastered it, creating booming shots that hurled toward opposing netminders with unheard-of speeds once clocked at more than 118 miles per hour. Hull's advantage partly came from a unique stick that he and teammate Mikita used during their careers, often referred to as the "banana stick." The duo curved their blades rather than keeping them flat. As a result, Hull's already threatening

H. M. COWAN

BOBBY HULL

slapshot became even more intimidating, and the "Golden Jet" became hockey's most feared shooter.

With his innovation in hand, Hull broke the NHL record for most goals in a season, setting a new standard of 54 in 1965–66. He broke his own record just a few years later, counting 58 in 1968–69. In total, Hull won three Art Ross trophies, the Hart Trophy twice, and the Lady Byng once. In addition to these honours, Hull was the WHA's

MVP twice during his run with the Winnipeg Jets. He would help guide the team to three Avco World trophies (the league's championship) before retiring once. When the Jets were absorbed into the NHL, Hull joined them for a short stint before being traded to the Hartford Whalers, where he would team with one-time rival Gordie Howe. The duo nearly retired together after that period, though Hull did attempt one final return with the

New York Rangers, one that ended in the following exhibition season.

Hull also suited up for Canada on two occasions, once in 1974 during the WHA Summit Series (he and other defectors were disallowed from playing in the more famed series) and in the 1976 Canada Cup. Hull has also been honoured by both the Blackhawks and Winnipeg Jets by having his number retired and together with his son Brett holds several other father-son distinctions.

The era in which Hull played for Chicago was known for unique collectibles, and perhaps none speak to this more than painted tiles issued by HM Cowan during the 1962–63 season. Interestingly, the tile depicts Hull with the number 7, before he made the switch to his more famous number 9.

DETROIT RED WINGS

Without question, today's Detroit Red Wings are the pre-eminent American hockey franchise. For a generation they have been the most feared opposition of every other team. In the decade before the NHL lockout, the team had three Stanley Cup celebrations, and even in the years following, when there

has been a reversal of fortune for so many NHL clubs, the Red Wings have had continued success, winning one Stanley Cup and reaching the finals one other time while continuing a decades-long streak of playoff appearances. Even after the retirement of Nicklas Lidstrom left a big question mark on the team's future, they still managed to reach the Conference Finals in 2012–13.

"They've been the most successful team in the league over the past 25 years. That's often caused the American networks to build their programming around the Red Wings," explains *Windsor Star* reporter Bob Duff. "So when there's been a national broadcast, be it on ESPN, Fox, or NBC, the Red Wings are always a big part of it because of the ratings."

The draw, however, goes beyond simple success in Duff's eyes. "They're a high-end, skilled team. They're just fun to watch. Even if you're not a fan of the Red Wings and just a fan of hockey, you've got to enjoy watching the way they play the game."

A similar scenario has existed throughout the Red Wings' history. Founded as the Detroit Cougars back in 1926, Detroit began as a collection of players bought from the failing Western Hockey League. The team was first renamed the Falcons before James Norris bought the team, choosing the Red Wings and the new logo, the famed winged wheel.

A decade after their founding, the Red Wings captured their first Stanley Cup and repeated the following season. This was before the Wings put together their most famed trio, the Production Line, which featured Sid Abel, Ted Lindsay, and Gordie Howe. The line first came together during Howe's second season in the NHL and propelled the club to two straight Stanley Cup Finals appearances, where they were defeated both times by the Maple Leafs. During the 1949–50 season, however, the fortunes turned in favour of Detroit, who won the Cup. Captain Ted Lindsay celebrated the victory with a lap around the Olympia Stadium rink, igniting a new tradition.

Just a couple years later, the Red Wings were again Stanley Cup champs led by the Production Line, this time with another new tradition. During the playoffs, local fish shop owner Peter Cusimano threw an octopus onto the ice as a good luck charm symbolizing the eight victories needed to win the Cup. Despite protests from the NHL that have resulted in alterations to the celebration, the octopus throw continues to this day.

Two Cups later, however, the winning ways for the Red Wings were over. Lindsay was sent to Chicago as punishment for helping start a players' union, as was Glenn Hall. Howe, now paired with Alex Delvecchio up front, was unable to secure another Cup for the Red Wings despite multiple Finals appearances.

All this happened before the "Dead Wings" era started.

For all the success the Red Wings have had for the last couple decades, they were equally unsuccessful in the years previous. Detroit was a bottom-dwelling franchise, seeming at times on the brink of all-out collapse. This, Duff attributes, to team ownership, which at the time when the team started to collapse was still in the charge of a family who had owned the team for nearly half a century.

"The Norris family certainly saved the franchise back in the 1930s and turned it into a power in the 1950s," Duff explains, "but by the time the 1970s had rolled around, Bruce Norris, the son of James, had squandered much of the family fortune and there was no money left to invest in the team. The result was what you saw on the ice. They were a laughing stock. From the late 1960s into the 1980s, they were pretty much one of the worst teams in hockey."

Enter a new owner — Little Caesars magnate Mike Ilitch. "The Ilitch family bought the team in '82, decided to invest in the team, and put money into it," Duff says. "He made it clear he was going to win, and by the start of the 1990s, they were getting to be a better team."

As Ilitch described in interviews prior to his 2003 induction into the Hockey Hall of Fame, his first taste of interest in hockey ownership came from the passion he had at the amateur level for the game. As his business, Little Caesars Pizza, grew, so, too, did the opportunity for him to be more financially invested in hockey, first as a season ticket holder, then as a suite holder. "I started to learn more about the business because I started to know the people around the rink," Ilitch told reporters during a scrum. "You start to think 'Boy, it would be a dream to

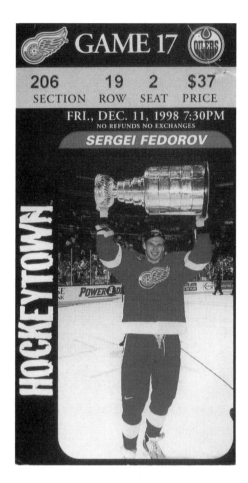

buy an NHL team.' I didn't think it was possible."

But the franchise's misfortune was just the opportunity that Ilitch needed. As he recalls, "They fell so low that the price wasn't that big, so it was timing and luck." Soon after, the turnaround began with Steve Yzerman being drafted by the Red Wings in 1983. Suddenly, there was a new attitude in the Detroit locker room — one of hope and promise. As the 1980s rolled on, new heroes were starting to emerge and incredible drafting of players like Sergei Fedorov and Nicklas Lidstrom helped solidify a franchise that was on the upswing.

What put them over the top, however, was one particular move. "I think the real key to what made them the most dominant team in the league was when Scottie Bowman came here," Duff says. Bowman was the bench boss for many Montreal Canadiens Stanley Cup winners, most notably in the 1970s when the team was in its dynasty days. He joined Detroit in 1993, soon after being inducted into the Hockey Hall of Fame, and shaped the team immeasurably. During Bowman's days and into the era of today's team, the focus of the franchise has been developing within. Sure, they'll pick up a couple missing pieces through trades like any other franchise, but the key players come up through the system. This attitude of development over acquisition comes from the squad's mentality behind the scenes. "They work themselves up the system much the same way players have," Duff reports. "Kenny Holland [for example] started out as a scout and is now the GM." In

total under Bowman's leadership, the Wings won three Stanley Cups, including a memorable two-year run when they captured their first in 1997 and repeated in 1998, dedicating that second win to fallen hero Vladimir Konstantinov, permanently injured in an auto accident days after the first Cup celebration.

Through it all, traditions continue to reign in Detroit, and there's one that's a little more unique (not that octopi aren't, but still . . .). As Duff points out, a particular piece of head gear has become a unique symbol in Motown. "From a quirky standpoint, they [the Red Wings] used to sell these hats that were basically a wing nut. That's what they looked like," he recalls. "That's one thing that has been popular in the late 1990s. People really wanted to get them."

★ STEVE YZERMAN ★

"When Yzerman came in '83," Bob Duff explains, "the Red Wings had a marquee name to build the team around — someone people were willing to pay to see."

Steven Gregory Yzerman was destined to be a special player in the NHL. Born in Cranbrook,

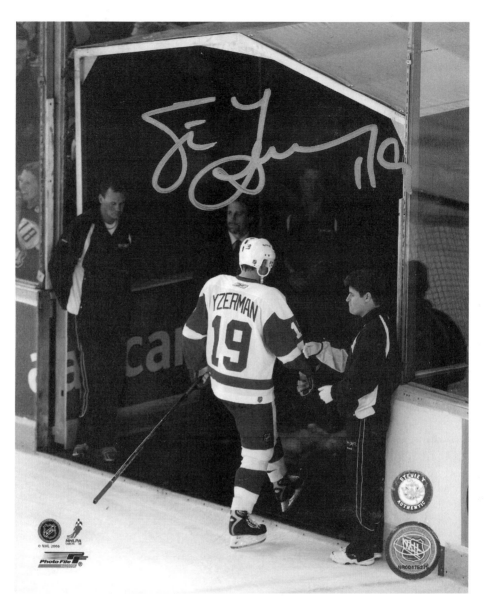

B.C., Yzerman moved to Nepean, Ontario, during his youth. He played both Junior A and CHL hockey in his development before being taken fourth overall in the 1983 NHL Entry Draft (behind, among others, fellow Hall of Famer Pat LaFontaine).

Little did new Red Wings owner Mike Ilitch know back then just how valuable that pickup would be. Yzerman became the youngest player to ever participate in an NHL All-Star Game (at 18 years of age) and tally 87 points by year's end. Yzerman's high-scoring ways would continue through the 1980s and well into the 1990s. During his first 10 years, he would score more than 100 points six times (including an astounding 155 points in 1988–89), go over the 50-goal mark five times, and become one of the biggest names in the sport, solely on this prowess.

Perhaps it was for this on-ice display that Yzerman was named captain of the Red Wings at such an early age. Just three years into his career, Yzerman was given the C after Danny Gare left the Wings and never looked back. But it wasn't until 1993 and the arrival of Scotty Bowman to the squad that Yzerman truly developed into a full leader. Bowman insisted that Yzerman develop his skills as a two-way player. The result? Two years later Yzerman led the Red Wings to their first Stanley Cup Finals appearance since 1966, and in 1997 the team ended its age-long drought. Yzerman was the first to raise Lord Stanley's mug over his head. Yzerman would again lead the Wings to the Cup one year later, in the process earning the Conn Smythe Trophy as playoff MVP, and also bring a Cup home to Detroit in

2002. Along the way he would take home the Frank J. Selke Trophy (best defensive forward) in 2000 and the Masterton Trophy in 2003. The only other major individual trophy Yzerman won was the 1989 Lester B. Pearson Award.

When he retired following the NHL lockout, Yzerman did so as the longest-serving captain in Detroit and NHL history, 19 seasons in all. He ranked sixth among the NHL's all-time point leaders at retirement and continues to be one of the most highly sought-after personalities in the memorabilia market, his autograph a coveted mark for collectors young and old.

But for all the collectors that have swarmed to Yzerman over the years — and there have been a slew of them — Yzerman himself doesn't have a lot of his own memorabilia. Although he admits now to wishing his personal collection was more complete, he insists that the remembrances are more than enough to satisfy as reminders of his incredible career. "I really wasn't a big collector," he said in a 2010 interview. "When I look back, I wish I had kept more things, but obviously I have great memories, and that's the best collection."

MONTREAL CANADIENS

There's no denying it. In the long, illustrious history of hockey, no teams is as collected as the Montreal Canadiens. The reasons for this are many, but Erle Schneidman, who penned the book *The Memorabilia of the Montreal Canadiens*, attributes the popularity to two primary factors. "Having such a successful franchise, winning all those Stanley Cups and having the heroes, that makes them all that much more desirable — people like Howie Morenz and Rocket Richard. Jean Beliveau, Guy Lafleur . . . they're just larger than life icons."

The latter point is one of par-

ticular interest. Ask any member of the Habs lineage of alumni and they'll tell you that there is an unparalleled prestige to donning the *bleu, blanc, et rouge*. As a result, the team was home to the lion's share of superstars. While many came to the Habs system naturally — a de facto result of being French Canadian — others came to the team simply for the prestige of wanting to play for the organization.

The decline of the mighty Habs franchise in recent years, however, has meant that the lineage of superstars has tailed off. Yes, names in recent years have been heralded as stars, but these are more so regional favourites than true hockey superstars. "The last icon was Roy, and since then there hasn't been a hero," Schneidman assesses. "We've had moments like Saku Koivu when he came back from cancer, but really no hero to go with."

As a result of this distinct lack of a superstar to hang their hat on, many Habs collectors have instead gone back into the team's history and sought out names from the past. This has partly been made easier thanks to the recent centennial celebration of the franchise, which saw a glut of new memorabilia hit the market, everything from replica throwback jerseys to game pucks to stamps to impressive framed, autographed pieces. Amid this rush of nostalgia came the ultimate question: Who is the greatest Canadien of all time? Is there one that stands head and shoulders above all else, one that crosses all generational gaps? The answer, perhaps not surprisingly, is a resounding no. "I think it depends who you're speaking to and the age of the person. Everyone goes back to their childhood; so if you grew up in the Rocket Richard era, it was Richard, if you grew up in the Jean Beliveau era, it was Beliveau," Schneidman says.

So the established feeling is that even though there is no true superstar today, nor is there one definitive player, the Habs' regionalized identity is large enough to practically sustain an entire memorabilia industry unto itself. No other sport is so closely identified by a cultural group as being "theirs" and, more specifically, is so singularly the focus of their recreation time than hockey for Canada's francophone community. "French Canadians have hockey in their blood. They live and they breathe hockey," Schneidman explains. "They know their hockey and their players — it's just a different mentality."

Aside from or, more appropriately, alongside the team's rich history is the famed Montreal Forum. From its opening in 1924, the Forum played host to a wide array of sporting events, but the feature attraction was always hockey. Originally it hosted the Montreal Maroons, but the Canadiens moved in in 1926, and the two teams shared the Forum until the Maroons folded in 1938. Other Montreal hockey teams have called the Forum home, namely those in the QMJHL and AHL, and it also played host to numerous other hockey events, including one of the Summit Series games and the Memorial Cup on several occasions. Most infamously, it was home of the Richard Riots and the funeral for Howie Morenz.

When the Bell Centre became the new home of the Habs, the Forum was dismantled and parts were sold off in one of hockey's greatest auctions. Bricks and seats were only the start to this — just about anything that wasn't nailed down (and quite a few items that were) were sold off to hungry collectors. Since then, the number of pieces on the market has decreased as more become part of permanent collections. "It's drying up," Schneidman says. "With the auction houses and the Internet, things are drying up, but they're still very desirable."

When the Forum closed, it was more than just the end of a building that was home to so many dynasties — it really did end an era in Montreal hockey. For the vast majority of their existence, the Habs were the top team in the NHL. This led to much debate over which was the better era for the club — the team in the late 1950s that won five straight Cups led by the likes of Plante, Harvey, and Richard, or the late-1970s edition

that featured Dryden, Lapointe, and Lafleur. Both teams certainly have their claims to this coveted title, and much like the aforementioned eternal player debate, it's one that will not get resolved. But those two editions of the franchise, even still, only account for nine Cups, just over a third of their total championships. The first Cup reign predated the formation of the NHL, and the last came in one of the most epic encounters in NHL history — Patrick Roy versus Wayne Gretzky in 1993.

In between, the Habs featured more Hall of Famers and superstars than any team in hockey history. Part of this came from exclusive access — for some time — to Canada's francophone community. Regardless of the politics behind it, the undeniable result is a collector thirst for memorabilia that will never be quenched. From Aurel Joliat to Carey Price, there is always demand for anything featuring a Habs player, and as a result they have the single largest database of any team in hockey history.

Exclusive trade card sets, stickers, commemorative pucks, coins . . . you name it, a Habs superstar (or at least a star) has been

RONALD ENG ▸

featured on it, including some of the most quirky pieces ever issued. Take a 1996 McDonald's offering, for example. That year, the Habs teamed with the famed fast-food chain to issue four commemorative placemats depicting action or famous events from the team's history. Sounds good, right? Well, the images featured illustrations of the infamous "ghosts of the Montreal Forum," which, for example, bent goal posts to help the Habs tally yet another goal or helped Patrick Roy glove a puck. Yep, they're pretty bad. But for every bad piece of memorabilia, there are quite a few really, really good ones, and none

come under as much scrutiny and demand as those that belonged to Habs players themselves. Several players, like Beliveau and Lafleur, or their estates, have donated their items for public auction. The result has been mega profits for auction holders and indispensable memory pieces for hobbyists.

For those collectors looking for more of a challenge, perhaps something a little more mysterious in nature, Schneidman points to a set of pinback buttons issued in 1948. "Not much is known about them — we've never seen a cereal box back or an advertisement; but they're really nice looking," he says.

★ MAURICE RICHARD ★

No player is more emblematic of hockey's dedication to its fans than The Rocket. Always generous with his time and pen, Richard was frequently surrounded in airports by legions of admirers, and like a true professional he signed and signed until every child, old and young, had their coveted moment with the man considered by many to be the best all-around player in NHL history. His signature is so popular, in fact, that had he not been as willing to sign for any and all, chances are his autograph would command a higher dollar than it currently does. When the sports card craze began in the 1990s, Richard was among the first to ink an autograph deal, aligning himself with Score Brands for the 1992–93 season. Even in the waning years of his life, Richard would still take opportunities to meet his fans and greet them wherever possible, becoming part of the "Oldtimers Hockey Challenge" tour among several appearances on the autograph circuit.

Long before he was a legend to fans of the game's history, Richard was its elite hero on the ice. A career-long leader of the Montreal Canadiens, the "Rocket" was a threat to score any time he was on the ice. He was the leader of Canadiens dynasties, the first player to score 50 goals in 50 games and the cause of hockey's most infamous clash between fans and authorities. On March 17, 1955, four days after Richard was suspended for the remainder of the season by the NHL for hitting a referee, then NHL president Clarence Campbell made an appearance at the Forum. This caused fans to react, shall we say, negatively, with fights breaking out in the stands, spilling outside the rink, and causing $100,000 in property damage. Forever known as the Richard Riot, the day lives on famously in the minds of the Habs faithful.

When the Montreal Forum closed its doors, the Canadiens held an elaborate ceremony, where the torchbearers of the team were all present. At centre ice stood Richard, who held the final flame for the Habs, in tribute to his immeasurable influence on the franchise and its years of unparalleled success. The numbers for Richard's career speak for themselves. He was the first player to score 50 goals in 50 NHL games. In an era where scoring was not yet as inflated as it is today and

by Quebec writer Roch Carrier. The book, an instant classic — and sought after by collectors seeking first editions and autographed copies — has since been turned into an animated short and for a long time was also part of Canadian currency, with images and quotes appearing on an iteration of the five-dollar bill.

NEW YORK RANGERS

The long history of the New York Rangers isn't always memorable. After all, the team wasn't exactly an on-ice success — they had an unheard of 54-year run between league championships — but what the Rangers lack in playoff success they more than make up for in prestige. Being in the epicentre of American sports will have that effect, especially when your home base is what many argue is the most famed arena still standing on this continent — Madison Square Garden. The circular stadium has played host to virtually every form of entertainment at the most elite level, and one of the main attractions has been the Broadway Blueshirts.

seasons only ran 70 contests, he still amassed 544 goals and 965 points. He was the major player in eight Stanley Cups and, when he retired, the normal three-year waiting period was waived for his entry into the Hockey Hall of Fame.

To millions of Canadian kids, Richard remains famous as the subject of the book *The Hockey Sweater*

Born in the 1920s, the Rangers were the second New York–based team to enter the NHL, following hot on the heels of the New York Americans. Both teams were owned by Tex Rickard, with the newer squad so nicknamed because there were dubbed "Tex's Rangers" (light years before Chuck Norris would earn a similar moniker). The squad found early success, earning the Stanley Cup in just its second year of existence. The series was particularly memorable for the emergence of 44-year-old Lester Patrick between the pipes as he filled in for an injured Lorne Chabot. The team would again win the Cup in 1932–33 and once more in 1939–40.

For the remainder of the Original Six era, the Rangers were on the outside looking in during the Stanley Cup chase. Superstars like Gump Worsley and Andy Bathgate weren't augmented with the manpower needed to make a serious run to the post-season. There was a stretch where the club would not even make the playoffs for 12 out of 16 years. When the NHL finally expanded, the Rangers were feeling the heat. Essentially a dead entity, they did reach the championship round of the playoffs a few times (most notably in 1971–72), but they didn't have enough strength to bring

home the Cup. By this time, the league was expanding at a steady pace and the Rangers became a championship afterthought.

Instead of the promise of a Cup run to draw fans, the Rangers formed fierce rivalries with the arrival of close-proximity clubs. Thanks to the emergence of the New York Islanders, Buffalo Sabres, and later the New Jersey Devils, the Rangers now had interstate teams to battle with. In particular, Isles games drew massive crowds, as both squads played high-calibre hockey.

Late in the 1970s, the Rangers

Victory on Ice

A panoramic view in Madison Square Garden – photographer Rob Arra

again resembled a championship contender, with a squad that included Boston imports Phil Esposito and Ken Hodge, as well as Winnipeg Jets grabs Ulf Nilsson and Anders Hedberg. The pinnacle of this squad's play came in the 1978–79 season, when they again made the Cup Finals after defeating the soon-to-be dynasty Isles team, only to bow out to the Canadiens. As the 1970s turned into the 1980s, the Rangers remained competitive, making the post-season annually. The problem, however, was that they were battling either the Islanders, Canadiens, Bruins, or Philadelphia Flyers. Even when the team seem poised to take a serious run to the Cup — such as in the 1991–92 season when they

captured the President's Trophy — they would end up on the sidelines thanks to a ferocious rival (in this case, the Pittsburgh Penguins).

Finally, in 1993–94, the stars aligned. After a year of missing the playoffs, Rangers brass imported a slew of talent, including Glenn Anderson and Kevin Lowe, with the sole purpose of bringing the Cup back to Broadway for the first time since 1940. With Mark Messier up front, Brian Leetch on defence, Mike Richter between the wickets, and now Mike Keenan as coach, destiny struck for the Rangers and after two emotional rides through a seven-game series, they finally regained Lord Stanley's famed trophy.

As quick as the rise was, the fall was just as fast. Rangers executives

RUSS COHEN ▲

panicked and, similar to baseball's Yankees, began hunting major name players in an attempt to bolster their struggling roster, including Wayne Gretzky, Eric Lindros, Pavel Bure, and Jaromir Jagr. The success, however, never came.

It took the reformation of the NHL following the lockout year of 2005–06 for the Rangers to get back to the fundamentals of development. A new breed of stars like Henrik Lundqvist and Marc Staal emerged from within, while free agent pickups were more precisely geared toward players whose best years were still in the present, like Rick Nash. That the team is considered a Cup contender has led to debate among fans over the eras of the Rangers' best years. "There's a real separation in your Ranger fanbase," says Russ Cohen, co-author of *100 Ranger Greats*. "You've got your younger fans who weren't born or knew what was going on in 1994, and then you've got people like me. If you go online, you'll see wars with people saying 1994 was in the past and you've got to forget about it, then you've got people saying it was one of their greatest years ever. It doesn't go on in a lot of fanbases."

No matter which side of the

debate you're on, there's no question that the Rangers' 1994 Cup victory is the franchise's defining year through the pre-lockout eras. As such, one of the most popular items in the team's rich memorabilia history is a before-its-time panoramic shot of the celebration of that Cup win, held at the famed Madison Square Garden.

★ MARK MESSIER ★

In the pantheon of hockey's rich history, debates about who is the greatest player of all time are never-ending. Most often, these debates involve names like Gretzky, Howe, and Orr, but the case can certainly be made that Mark Messier is the best all-around player in league history.

A native of Edmonton whose career encompassed five Stanley Cups with the Edmonton Oilers, Messier moved to New York following the 1990–91 season, demanding a trade publicly during the 1991 Canada Cup after citing poor decisions by Oilers brass. Messier quickly gained the captaincy, having already proven to be a true leader with the Oilers. He would instantly give the Rangers the boost they needed, helping the team secure the President's Trophy and gaining the Hart Trophy in his first season in New York.

Come the 1993–94 season, Messier again led the Rangers to the President's Trophy and this time was destined to fulfill the promise of bringing a Cup back to New York for the first time in more than half a century. Most prominently, Messier guaranteed victory in what would have been the Rangers' elimination game in the Eastern Conference Finals against the New Jersey Devils. That contest, Game Six, saw Messier single-handedly stave off a trip to the golf course by overcoming a deficit and winning the game with a natural hat trick. One Game-Seven, double-overtime contest later, the Rangers were on to the Stanley Cup. Another seven-game series was all that stood between Messier and immortality as he became the first, and thus far only, player to captain two franchises to the championship.

While the Rangers tapered off soon after, Messier continued strong play, scoring at better than a point-per-game pace in the following three NHL seasons. In 1997, Messier left New York — just one season after former teammate Wayne Gretzky joined the Rangers — signing with the Vancouver Canucks. The venture lasted three seasons before Messier returned to New York to play four additional seasons. Messier concluded his career with the second highest point total in NHL history, came just a few games shy of beating Gordie Howe's all-time record after playing 25 NHL seasons, and was the last member of the WHA to skate in an elite-level game of North American hockey. His career would be capped off by Hall of Fame induction, and speculation continues that he will be the next guiding force behind the Rangers.

For hobbyists, Messier will

forever be known as one of the toughest signers in hockey, as he would routinely shy away from opportunities and duck crowds. Thus, certified autographs of his still command a hefty premium, and there is none more revered by card collectors than his first — the 1996-97 Be A Player autograph — which appeared a full five years after signed cards started appearing in packs.

TORONTO MAPLE LEAFS

Look back into the early to mid-1900s and you'll see the birth of broadcasting in Canada, and one of the first major attractions on radio was hockey. In Quebec, this meant hearing calls for the Montreal Canadiens, but for the majority of the country, the action described by famous voices were contests featuring the blue-and-white Toronto Maple Leafs.

"Radio came into play in the late 1920s, and in Canada, excluding Quebec because of the language differences, we had play-by-play of the Toronto Maple Leafs. We first had it locally and then Foster Hewitt built a national network from Victoria to St. John's," explains author Kevin Shea. "Most of the major centres carried *Hockey Night in Canada.* Because radio was such a big part of people's lives and a huge source of entertainment, it became 'have your Saturday night bath then gather around the radio together — let's listen to *Hockey Night in Canada.*'"

For much of those days of radio, the Leafs were the subject of all *Hockey Night in Canada* broadcasts. It was natural — English-speaking radio would tailor to English-speaking audiences. This wasn't the U.S., which had baseball teams like the Yankees, Red Sox, Reds, and other teams to choose from. This was Canada, where, by default, the Maple Leafs were the anglophone heroes; and the Maple Leafs lived up to that pressure.

While the Montreal Canadiens were far and away the most powerful team in the NHL, the Maple Leafs, up until league expansion, were also incredibly successful. From their early days until 1967, the Leafs won 13 Stanley Cups, including two dynasty runs of three straight championships.

Interestingly, the city's NHL history does not begin with the Leafs. Instead, the team's roots trace back to the Toronto Arenas, who entered

NHL SCRAPBOOK

TIM HORTON

the NHL in a move that essentially was out of spite against the Toronto Blueshirts. The Blueshirts were members of the National Hockey Association (NHA), a predecessor to the NHL that operated between 1909 and 1917. As the story goes, the NHA was disbanded due to Eddie Livingstone, owner of the Blueshirts. Livingstone previously owned the Toronto Shamrocks but suspended the team after a raid by the Pacific Coast Hockey Association emptied the Blueshirts' roster and he chose to transfer his Shamrock players to his new squad. Livingstone was at constant odds with the other NHA owners, a struggle that heightened when a team representing the Canadian army (but centred in Toronto) was added in 1916–17, infuriating Livingstone. Though this Battalion team pulled out of play after being called overseas, Livingstone had angered the other owners enough that the league suspended operations in 1917 and subsequently formed the NHL, without the Blueshirts.

The new team formed in Toronto, primarily featuring players from the Blueshirts, won the first Stanley Cup of the NHL era. Soon after, however, Blueshirt ownership began filing suit after suit against the Arenas, helping lead the team to declare bankruptcy. The team would be partly owned by the NHL before it would be picked up by a group that once owned the St. Patricks senior amateur club in Toronto. Now known as the St. Pats, the team would again win the Cup in 1922 before yet more financial issues would lead to the team being sold to Conn Smythe (after a Philadelphia-based purchase offer was rejected), who changed the team's name forever to the Maple Leafs.

The new era for the Toronto club, whose nickname purportedly originated from the Maple Leaf Regiment, began where the old finished — at the Arena Gardens — but moved to the new Maple Leaf Gardens in 1931. The Gardens immediately hosted its first Stanley Cup championship squad, as the Leafs, led by the Kid Line (Busher Jackson, Joe Primeau, and Charlie Conacher) won the 1931–32 Stanley Cup. That first Cup win, however, was the only one for a decade. The Leafs made the finals five additional times, but lost each time to a different squad, including the Rangers,

Montreal Maroons, Red Wings, Bruins, and Black Hawks. The Leafs finally rebounded in 1941–42, taking home the first of five Cups during the 1940s, including a three-year run as champs, a first for the NHL.

What followed can be described as a curse on the franchise. In 1951, Bill Barilko scored the Cup-winning goal and soon after disappeared during a fishing trip. The Leafs wouldn't win again until 1962, which wasn't only the year Barilko's body was found but also the first under new ownership. That season, Conn Smythe sold the Leafs to a group that included his son Stafford and, perhaps most famously, Harold Ballard. Ballard is remembered as one of the most animated and involved owners in all of hockey. With new management in place and a new set of heroes that included Johnny Bower, Frank Mahovlich, Red Kelly, and several others, the Leafs would go on another tear that saw them win three more consecutive Stanley Cups. The final Cup, coming in a victory over the forever rival Montreal Canadiens, took place in 1967, the final year before the NHL's true expansion began. The Leafs that year were a powerhouse team featuring Bower and Terry

Sawchuk as a goaltending tandem; Tim Horton, Bobby Baun, and Allan Stanley on defence; and Kelly, George Armstrong, Mahovlich, and a host of other legends upfront.

The end of the Original Six era signalled the end of the Leafs' dominance in the NHL. Over the next seven seasons, as players retired, were traded, or signed elsewhere, the team struggled immensely, missing the playoffs three times during the stretch, and being quickly eliminated any time they did make them. The Leafs finished the 1970s with five straight years of making it past that fateful first round on the strength of a new generation of heroes like Darryl Sittler and Lanny McDonald, but they couldn't make it to the final series.

The 1980s proved to be even more unproductive than the previous decade. Players like Allan Bester and Wendel Clark were popular with the Toronto faithful, but there was a general sense that the team was headed nowhere fast. The Leafs missed the playoffs four times in the 1980s and twice in the 1990s before a turnaround started in the 1992–93 season thanks to the acquisition of Doug Gilmour and Dave Andreychuk and the emergence of goaltender Felix Potvin. For two straight seasons, the Leafs made the Conference Finals.

The momentum stopped suddenly when Wendel Clark, arguably the most popular player of the era, was dealt to Quebec for Mats Sundin. The acquisition was originally chided, although it would ultimately be a great move for Toronto as Sundin would captain the Leafs back to the Conference Finals twice in the next five seasons.

Even with Sundin at the helm, however, the curse of the expansion era still weighed heavily on the Leafs Nation. A rotating cast that included Curtis Joseph, Ed Belfour, Joe Nieuwendyk, Eric Lindros, and other top-rank names, as well as role players like Darcy Tucker and Tomas Kaberle, pushed the Leafs into the playoffs more often than not in the years before the 2004–05 NHL lockout, but never out of their own conference.

Then disaster struck. With John Ferguson Jr. as the new general manager when the NHL resumed play in 2005–06, the Leafs crumbled. Ludicrous contracts that included no-trade clauses were signed, and a battery of other misguided signings (the Jeff Finger contract, in particular,

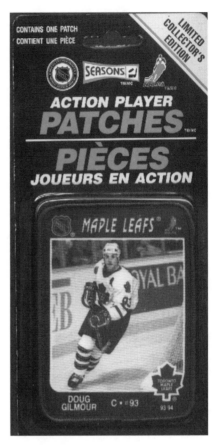

was baffling) handcuffed the Leafs from making deadline acquisitions that may have pushed them to the post-season. Instead, they were the only team in the entire league not to make the playoffs once between the two lockouts, and only after the NHL restarted play following the 2012–13 work stoppage did the team once again make it to the playoffs.

Despite the up-and-down play and decades passing from the last Stanley Cup, the Leafs, more than any other team in hockey, have a

dedicated following that at times seems almost cultlike. As Shea argues, there is a generational aspect to this. And, unlike with other franchises, where the player who scores the most is typically the most popular, in Toronto it's the gifted grinder who might get the most attention. "You have to think that guys like Ted Kennedy were the ultimate Leafs," Shea says. "They worked hard, they were great public relations people, they did all the things that Toronto fans love: that hard-working, dyed-in-the-wool guy who would do anything. So you think of guys like Darcy Tucker and Tie Domi to some degree and Wendel Clark — these are all really good players, but they're all endorsed by the Leafs because they have that same work ethic."

It's possible that this dynamic begets the reason why the most popular Leafs collectibles, of any generation, are those that feature the entire team lineup, rather than items that only feature one particular athlete; and ruling the roost are team-autographed sticks, particularly from the 1960s squads that took home Stanley Cup rings. Now, a team-signed stick from the 1960s may seem like a high-dollar item, and to an extent it is, but not as much as you'd think. Shea recalls a conversation he had with Frozen Pond president Hersh Borenstein about a couple in Shea's collection. "He taught me something," Shea says. "I thought these sticks signed by the 1960s championship teams were really rare, but he said there were two things the Leafs did that decade — they won Stanley Cup championships and they signed a lot of stuff."

★ DOUG GILMOUR ★

"Killer" may have only spent five full seasons in Toronto, but he made a greater mark on the Leafs Nation than he did anywhere else in his 20-year NHL career. Originally a member of the St. Louis Blues, Gilmour was traded to Calgary prior to the 1988–89 season, where he helped the Flames win the Stanley Cup. In 1992, Gilmour was sent to Toronto, as one-time Flames general manager Cliff Fletcher brought him to the Ontario capital in a massive 10-player swap.

Gilmour's playoff experience came into play as he helped the Leafs reach the Western Conference Finals in 1992–93, completing a turnaround from missing the playoffs the year prior. Gilmour also hit the 100-point plateau for the second time in his career and became a leader at both ends of the rink, earning him the Selke Trophy as best defensive forward in the NHL. One year later, Gilmour would again reach triple-digit points, and the Leafs would reach the Western Conference Finals once again. Prior to the lockout-shortened 1994–95 season, Wendel Clark, one of the most popular players in recent Maple Leafs history, was traded, and Gilmour was named the new team captain. Under his watch, the Leafs entered the playoffs twice in three seasons.

Gilmour departed Toronto in the summer of 1998, signing with Chicago as a free agent. He later had short stints in Buffalo and Montreal (of all places) before he was sent back to Toronto at the 2002–03 NHL trade deadline. Gilmour played in only one game with the Leafs, tearing his ACL during the second period against Calgary. The injury led to Gilmour's retirement.

In all, Gilmour played in 1,474 NHL games and tallied 1,414 points (including 450 goals) and was inducted into the Hockey Hall of Fame in 2011; but his greatest accomplishment came as being the face of the Toronto franchise, and as a result he was heavily featured on team souvenirs, including multiple appearances on the team's official calendar that today are unique collectibles for Leafs Nation.

THE EXPANSION SIX

The NHL doubled in size in 1967. The six new squads literally came from across the U.S. From the east, Philadelphia and Pittsburgh joined the fray. On the west coast, Los Angeles and California (Oakland) came on board, and the central United States were represented by Minnesota and St. Louis. Among those six squads, four have been Stanley Cup champions, one other has been a finalist, and the other folded.

It's also worth noting off the top that two of the teams did not remain in their cities, which is why you only see four teams in this chapter. The Minnesota North Stars, of course, moved to Dallas in 1993, while the Seals, after a few failed name changes, became the Cleveland Barons (who, coincidentally, would merge with the North Stars before ownership would essentially split the two, with the new squad becoming the San Jose Sharks). Those teams that did survive have become some of the most successful and famed franchises in the NHL.

LOS ANGELES KINGS

It's hard to say what made the Kings survive so many years, especially when their sister expansion team, the California (later Oakland and later California Golden) Seals, fell from the NHL landscape. Despite being mediocre for many years and their inability to get close to the Cup for all but one year of the majority of their existence — and giving birth to one of the worst jerseys the NHL has ever seen — the Kings have continually been able to attract big names to the franchise, from the early days of Marcel Dionne, to Wayne Gretzky, to Jeff Carter. There's a pretty darn good reason for that too — this is, after all, Tinseltown we're talking about. When the team has been hot, they've attracted Hollywood bigwigs to their games, and even at their low points they've had a certain cachet, primarily thanks to Canada-born actors in attendance.

The problems that the Kings faced for many years were more about obstructions than their own deficiencies. During the 1980s, the club played in one of the toughest divisions in the history of hockey — the Smythe — when the Edmonton Oilers and Calgary Flames were in the Stanley Cup Finals. The only noteworthy post-season game during this era came on April 10, 1982, against the powerful Oilers. The Kings were behind 5-0 going into the third. L.A. pulled off an unheard-of comeback, netting five goals to equalize the game and send it into overtime — where Daryl Evans shot a long tally toward the net, beating Grant Fuhr and pushing the Oilers further than anyone would've imagined. The Kings would end up winning the series.

It was truly the high point for the franchise. Through the 1960s and 1970s, the team was an also-ran. Sure, they enjoyed *some* playoff success, but they were never able to get close to the championship series. Names like Rogie Vachon and Eddie Shack either led or augmented teams with true superstar leaders, but for whatever reason, the clubs could not get deep into the post-season.

After the acquisition of Wayne Gretzky, L.A.'s fortunes began to turn. In 1990–91, with a more

rounded team than ever, the Kings took the Smythe Division for the first time. Two years later, the Kings made it all the way to the Stanley Cup Finals, where one of the greatest marquee matchups in NHL history took place between Gretzky and Patrick Roy. The Kings came out on the losing end and would begin a near 20-year roller coaster ride that would see them get close to greatness one year and the next miss the playoffs completely. Making matters worse for the club was one-time owner Bruce McNall's fall from grace, which left the team

decimated in the years following the 1994–95 lockout-shortened season. In short, the team was in ruins.

As name players came and went through the 1990s and 2000s, fans wondered if the Expansion Six franchise would ever get the opportunity to hoist Lord Stanley's mug. That answer came during the 2011–12 playoffs in one of the most remarkable — and unusual — Cup runs in NHL history. Already with a strong squad that featured young defensive sensation Drew Doughty, superforward Anze Kopitar, and upstart Jonathan Quick between the pipes, the Kings were able to acquire Mike Richards and Jeff Carter — a pair who once led Philadelphia to the Stanley Cup Finals. The acquisitions were the final pieces of the puzzle needed, and the team pulled off a miraculous run to the Cup, in the process becoming the first eighth-seeded team in a conference to knock off the first-, second-, and third-ranked clubs. A second Cup, with much the same nucleus, followed in 2014.

Of course, with a Cup celebration come many great collectibles, but none are more exciting for fans to have than a piece of the game itself. That trick seemed bound to happen thanks to card-maker the Upper Deck Company, who just a couple weeks after the Kings skated away with the Stanley Cup were able to procure one of the two nets used in the final series, including the now-famed Game Six clincher. "Now the question is, what to do with it," wondered Upper Deck's Chris Carlin in a blog posted June 22, 2012. "The obvious thing for us to do would be to cut it up, embed them in trading cards, and insert them into 2012–13 NHL trading card releases for Kings fans to find. Maybe even have some of the Kings players like Jonathan Quick, Anze Kopitar, Dustin Brown,

and others sign those cards. But there's part of us that doesn't want to cut it up. Maybe we can do something else unique with it."

In the end, the net would indeed be cut up and embedded in trading cards and other memorabilia, giving Kings fans the opportunity to share the important piece of history.

★ LUC ROBITAILLE ★

There certainly was an element to Robitaille's career that was "Lucky." After all, not many late-rounders get a fair shake in the NHL. More often than not, these players are veritable token selections by an NHL club, ultimately destined to spend their years in the AHL and maybe get a sniff of the big league. That wasn't the case with Robitaille, who ultimately became one of the greatest left wingers in NHL history.

Robitaille entered the league during the 1986–87 season and made an immediate impact with the Kings, winning the Calder Memorial Trophy and finding a post-season All-Star spot. During this first run in L.A., Robitaille started to show the capabilities of being a leader, gaining the *A*. For a short time, he also held the full captaincy while Gretzky was on the injured list during the 1992–93 season. It was during that season that Robitaille truly had his best experience while wearing the Kings colours as the team advanced all the way to the Stanley Cup Finals before being beaten by Robitaille's hometown Montreal Canadiens.

The Robitaille years concluded — for the first time — prior to the 1994–95 season, when he moved over to Pittsburgh, becoming one of the few players to skate with both Gretzky and Mario Lemieux. His time there, however, was less than memorable, and Luc eventually made his way to the New York Rangers before returning to Los Angeles. Robitaille later signed with the Detroit Red Wings, in time for him to earn his only Stanley Cup ring as a player. When the NHL returned from the 2004–05 lockout, Robitaille once again joined the Kings for his swan song in the NHL. He remained with the club in an executive role, however, and his career came full circle in 2012. On the day that the Kings hoisted their first Stanley Cup, it was Robitaille who got one of the loudest cheers of the night as he stood with the trophy held high above his head.

Robitaille's career included sev-

eral post-season All-Star berths, the Calder Memorial Trophy, the league record for goals by a left winger, and the benchmark of being, arguably, the most beloved player in franchise history and still, long after retirement, at the top of L.A. Kings collector want lists. Among the items highly sought after is a puck that was given to fans on the night of Robitaille's jersey retirement.

PHILADELPHIA FLYERS

Brian Propp, an 11-year veteran of the orange and black, sums up so eloquently the attitude of the Flyers organization. "The way the Flyers played was the way I liked to play hockey. We played as a team, we won as a team, we were tough as a team. We were always there and we

◄ JON WALDMAN

All the play-by-play action, highlights and interviews of the 74-75 championship season and Stanley Cup victory, by Gene Hart. Narrated by Don Earle.

always gave ourselves a chance to win the Stanley Cup."

That style is emblematic not only of the drive and determination of the organization but truly of Philadelphia. In the heart of the northeastern United States lies this city full of American history. It is considered to have one of the most rough-around-the-edges yet most devoted fandoms. The metropolis's nickname is somewhat of a misnomer — when it comes to sports, "The City of Brotherly Love" it isn't; and while a diehard attitude has reigned the day in baseball, football, basketball, and even professional wrestling, it can be argued that nothing epitomizes the raucous behaviour of the Philly faithful more than the Flyers.

Born amid the expansion era of 1967, the Flyers peaked in the 1970s. While Guy Lapointe and "Tiger"

Williams were marquee enforcers on other teams, the Flyers club had a full-team attitude of hit first, ask questions later. Bobby Clarke, Rick MacLeish, and Dave "The Hammer" Schultz were the premier names on a team that was the first non–Original Six squad to capture Lord Stanley's mug; and they did so in consecutive years. Following the first Cup run, a strange occurrence took place. In preparation for the season ahead, miniature Stanley Cup patches were affixed to the team's jerseys. As the story goes, players condemned the boastful logo, and within a day the crests were removed, but not before a series of memorabilia pieces — specifically hockey cards — captured the logo for all time.

As the 1970s gave way to the 1980s, the Flyers continued to be a powerhouse in the league. At this point, a new breed of stars like Dave Poulin and Brian Propp emerged as fan favourites, but the player who would define their decade was Ron Hextall, the first goalie ever to score a goal on the strength of his own shot. The team would again ascend to the Stanley Cup Finals but would run into a steamroller known as the Edmonton Oilers. Into the 1990s, the Flyers continued to be one of the most threatening teams, thanks in large part to Eric Lindros, John LeClair, and Mikael Renberg, affectionately known as the Legion of Doom line. The Flyers once again found their way to the Stanley Cup Finals but would once again fall to the opposition. The same fate would befall the 2000s edition of the club, which featured new heroes Mike Richards and Jeff Carter, as well as longtime defensive veteran and agitator Chris Pronger.

The overall scope of how powerful the Flyers teams of the past were is respected not only by collectors and fans but also by the players, as was demonstrated by Jeremy Roenick. During the 2011 Winter Classic alumni game, which pitted the Flyers against the New York Rangers, Roenick sat on a bench alongside greats like Clarke, Mark Howe, Bernie Parent, Lindros, and LeClair. At one point, Roenick, himself a 500-goal scorer and legend in the game, was shown on the bench with the back of his own sweater covered in signatures. "We're amongst greatness here — some of the greats in the game," Roenick said during an interview with the CBC during the day's

JON WALDMAN ▲

included both full recordings of play-by-plays of Flyer games and themed song compilations and are coveted by Flyer fans, particularly those who remember those championship years.

★ BOBBY CLARKE ★

A native of Flin Flon, Manitoba, Bobby Clarke has done something few in the game have been able to accomplish — have a successful career both on the ice and in the front offices.

First to his on-ice days, where Clarke was a gritty forward and very much looked the part of an NHLer. With an infectious smile that was missing front teeth, the moment of Clarke looking like a young boy in pure joy as he celebrated Philly's Stanley Cup victory has been shown on video screens across the nation over and over again. Clarke had two moments like this, guiding the Flyers to their only two Cup victories — the highlights of a fantastic NHL career that featured three 100-point seasons, three Hart trophies, multiple All-Star Game nods, and a Hockey Hall of Fame ring. Not surprisingly, these moments and others were captured multiple times on film, leading to some amazing photos available on a

broadcast. "It would be a real shame if I left the building and left the city without having a memento of some of the greatest players that I looked up to and had the pleasure to be on the ice with."

That greatness was once captured in a collectible that can best described as . . . well . . . unique. Back in the 1970s, long before MP3s were the musical format of the day, hipsters would spin their tunes on record players, both in large format and smaller 45s. The smaller remain popular with collectors today, especially those who long for the scratchy imperfections that authentic records provided. As the Flyers celebrated their first Stanley Cup win, the team issued a variety of records that commemorated their victory. These variety of collectibles, the most interesting of which may be traditional wire photos that the press would use in newspapers long before the days of digital cameras and network sharing.

As amazing as Clarke's on-ice career was in Philly (one that ended just as the infamous Cooperalls became the legwear of choice for the fashion-unconscious Flyers), his name is etched just as deeply in shinny history for his role in the 1972 Summit Series.

But the second half of Clarke's career is perhaps even more talked about than his playing days. Even before Clarke retired, he took on duties off the rink, becoming an assistant coach while still playing during the 1979–80 season. He became general manager after retiring, guiding the Flyers to two Stanley Cup Finals appearances during his first run with the club. He also led the Minnesota North Stars to a Cup appearance in the midst of a two-year stint with the club before coming back to Philly.

PITTSBURGH PENGUINS

For a team that almost died on more than one occasion, the Pittsburgh Penguins have had more than their fair share of hockey heroes swing through their locker rooms. Think about it — name another team that, just when it seems like it's destined for relocation, comes to life bigger and better than ever.

As the NHL grew from six to 12 teams, the decision was made to bring top-level hockey back to the Steel city (Pittsburgh had hosted the NHL's Pirates during the 1920s). Originally, the team was very distinct, especially considering the territory it called home. While the National Football League's Steelers and Major League Baseball's Pirates took on yellow, black, and white as their colour schemes, the Pens instead adopted baby blue as their primary tone. Yes, the other colours were incorporated, but they were secondary. It wasn't until the 1980s, in fact, that the colour scheme changed. Just a short time prior to the arrival of Mario Lemieux, the team switched to yellow and gold, even going so far as to have a bright yellow jersey at one point. Since then, the colours have evolved into a black-and-gold scheme, while the original baby blue has returned as an alternate jersey.

As a team, the Penguins have enjoyed more success than almost any other non–Original Six squad, despite troubles that have kept the team rumoured to be on the move for the better part of more than two decades. Through this tumultuous time, the team has garnered three Stanley Cups, and in the last 20 years Pens players have earned numerous individual honours. But the jerseys and trophies only tell part of the story of the Penguins, who in their time have drafted extremely well and came up with some Hall of Fame names. Four of those names — Mario Lemieux, Jaromir Jagr, Sidney Crosby, and Evgeni Malkin — are extremely well known and rank as leaders in the memorabilia world; but there is one player who, unfortunately, did not get the opportunity to fully showcase his capabilities to the NHL or its massive fanbase.

Michel Briere entered the NHL in the 1969–70 season and immediately became a force. He placed third on the team in scoring in his rookie season, with 44 points in 76 games, and was a close runner-up for Calder Memorial Trophy honours. In an interview for PittsburghHockey .net, Red Kelly, then Pens coach, said, "He was showing me moves you can't put into a hockey player. He was tough as nails." Briere's

career, however, was cut tragically short. Just weeks after the Penguins' season ended, Briere and two friends were in a car accident that would ultimately cost the young prospect his life. His death would lead to the Penguins retiring his jersey number and naming their rookie-of-the-year trophy after him.

Briere collectibles have rarely been present on the market, and only twice has he had an official trading card — once in 2004–05, produced by In The Game for its Franchises set, and in 2010–11, Panini created a cut signature card of Briere in its Dominion series. Several examples of retro jerseys have also popped up on shopping sites like eBay, as has a playing card that is part of a deck created to tribute Penguins legends.

★ MARIO LEMIEUX ★

Where do you begin with a personality who not once but twice saved a franchise? Perhaps simply with one word: *magnifique*. Born into a hockey-playing family (his brother Alain played for three NHL clubs in his career), Mario Lemieux was reluctant at first to become a Pittsburgh Penguin when the club drafted him in 1984; but he would

Kellogg's

Mario
Lemieux

CORN
FLAKES*

TOASTED FLAKES OF CORN
FLOCONS DE MAÏS
GRILLÉS
COR 246

The original and best
L'original et le meilleur

SUGGESTED SERVING
PRÉSENTATION SUGGÉRÉE

NHL
SPECIAL EDITION
PRINT
See reverse for details.

LNH
PHOTO A
TIRAGE
LIMITÉ
Voir les détails au dos.

soon become the team's leader and spend his entire NHL career with the squad before eventually buying the team.

It's not likely that Pittsburgh's brass knew just how good a player and person they were getting when they selected young Mario way back when. Lemieux became one of the elite centres of his generation, racking up Hart, Art Ross, and Conn Smythe trophies while winning two Stanley Cups and setting multiple NHL records. At the same time, Lemieux made the sort of impact on the squad that can best

▲ JON WALDMAN

be measured by the success of those who played around him. He made Rob Brown a 100-point scorer and Kevin Stevens into a far more elite left winger than anyone would've thought imaginable.

Lemieux's biggest triumph, however, came not on the ice but off it as he battled non-Hodgkin lymphoma during the 1992–93 season. Not only did he beat this form of treatable cancer, but on the day of his final treatment, he flew to Philadelphia for the Penguins game that night and tallied an assist and a goal. Lemieux's career would later include two returns — one after taking off the 1994–95 lockout-shortened season and a second coming three years after initial retirement. He also captained Canada's 2002 Olympic Gold Medal–winning squad.

Of course, Lemieux's role in hockey led to many endorsements and memorabilia pieces, but none is more significant than what he has done for his own charitable organization, the Mario Lemieux Foundation, which raises money for cancer research and patient care. The most important facet of the organization is his own involvement. "Mario is very committed to the foundation and is a big part of our success," says the foundation's executive director, Nancy Angus.

But for all that Lemieux has given to the Pittsburgh, the community has also given back to him in the form of the Mario Mosaic. Assembled from photo submissions from fans, the Mosaic pays tribute to The Magnificent One in a group effort that also saw donations to the foundation. "The Mario Mosaic was a very popular promotion . . . and the photos will be in the Mosaic housed at CONSOL Energy Center for a very, very long time," Angus says.

ST. LOUIS BLUES

The story of the St. Louis Blues is best told not by what they have done in the NHL but rather by what they haven't achieved. In just about every possible scenario, the Blues have faltered. They've had superstar-laden teams, snipers, hot goalies, and the greatest coaches in league history. Heck, they've even challenged for Lord Stanley's mug on multiple occasions. Yet the story of the St. Louis Blues is always summed up by one predominant theme — missed opportunities. Look through their history and I dare you to challenge me on this statement.

The Blues started out as one of the Expansion Six and immediately looked like a squad that would upend the Original Six era. Led by legendary coach Scotty Bowman, the Blues reached the Stanley Cup Finals for three consecutive years (albeit largely due to a format that ensured one expansion club would face off against an Original Six squad in those years, but still . . .). Each time, however, they were dispatched in short order. Then began a 25-year run during which they made the playoffs each and every year. That's right — a quarter-century of playoff appearances. Unheard of no matter how you cut it. The result? Zero Stanley Cups.

Now look up and down the roster of men who have donned the team colors — it's practically like reading through the Hockey Hall of Fame roster. Glenn Hall. Brett Hull. Bernie Federko. Joe Mullen. Scott Stevens. Al MacInnis. Adam Oates. Curtis Joseph. Chris Pronger . . . even Wayne Gretzky suited up for the Blues. And the result? Still zero Stanley Cups.

Need more examples? Look to the 2006 NHL Entry Draft. One year removed from the lockout season, the Blues, who had crumbled in the new NHL, were "rewarded" for their poor play with the first overall pick. Their selection was Erik Johnson, a defenceman who, while dependable, was hardly the star that the Blues thought he would be. And who could the Blues have drafted instead with the ultimate selection opportunity? Jonathan Toews, Jordan Staal, Phil Kessel, Claude Giroux . . . Yep, their drafting hasn't been exactly stellar either . . . at least when they have participated. Yes, you read that right. In 1983, amid financial troubles that almost had the team relocate to Saskatoon, Saskatchewan, the Blues all-out skipped that year's Entry Draft, missing out on super-stars like Pat LaFontaine, Steve Yzerman, Cam Neely, Tom Barrasso, Dominik Hasek, Rick Tocchet, and Slava Fetisov.

Despite these factors and periods of downright incompetence displayed by management, the Blues have one of the most storied histories in all of the NHL. They have a devoted fandom that will follow its beloved team to the ends of the Earth (and probably beyond). They've also been able to foster two different Hart Trophy winners, top goalies and defencemen, and, merchandise-wise, have been among the top teams in NHL history . . .

And there's where the story of what the Blues haven't done gets even more intriguing — specifically, they decided not to move forward with what many call the ugliest jersey in league history. During the 1994–95 lockout-shortened season, the Blues debuted a rather unique sweater that enjoyed some popularity despite some odd diagonals that dominated its look. One year later, however, it seemed those jerseys were going to hang in storage as a new sweater was set to debut . . . at least until head coach "Iron Mike" Keenan put a stop to the madness. You see, this new jersey was highlighted by trumpets, musical notes, and startlingly awful colour blends. It was hideous. Check that, it was beyond hideous. It was fifth-circle-of-hell horrid.

So amid all these bad decisions, has St. Loo made any good ones? As it turns out, yes; and no decision may have been better than giving the fans some power in the franchise. Starting in 1994 and running until 2005, the Blues handed over control of game night programs to their dedicated fans rather than producing them internally. Titled *Game Night Revue*, the programs were, shall we say, rogue in nature. They didn't candycoat opposing teams, nor did they present fluff pieces — they were biting, often humorous looks at the evening's contest while giving statistical analysis that even hockeydb.com would be jealous of. Although today the *Revue* is just a memory, it still tells the story of the odd connection between the loveable losers — the St. Louis Blues — and their fans.

★ BRETT HULL ★

Getting hot any time during your sporting career is always a good thing; but getting hot just when the sports collectibles world is in the midst of its boom era, that's just . . . well . . . golden. Born into the proud tradition of hockey immortality shown by his dad, Bobby, and uncle Dennis, Brett Hull was a standout in junior and college hockey before getting his first crack at the NHL amid the 1986 playoff run of the Calgary Flames, a team that fared well in developing star players. The promise Hull showed in his first full NHL season was enough that the team felt he could be fairly shopped around, and before the 1988 trade deadline, Hull was sent to St. Louis.

Big mistake. In his first season in St. Louis, Hull put together a

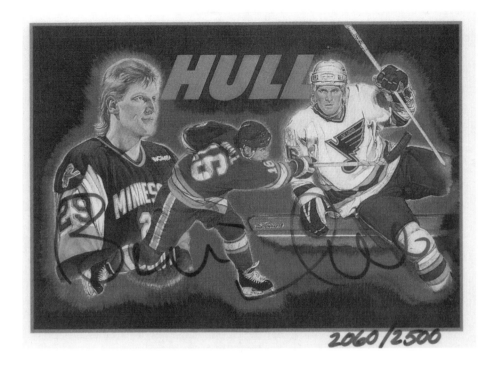

40-goal campaign and a higher than point-per-game pace. One year later, he was a 100-point superstar and tallied an astounding 72 goals.

That was just an appetizer for the main course, which came in 1990–91, right when the hobby boomed. At this point, Hull was already a spokesperson for The Upper Deck Company, and for the 1991-92 season the two made history, issuing one of the first autographed cards to appear in packages. That's right — before Wayne Gretzky signed a single piece of cardboard for Upper Deck, Brett Hull blazed the trail.

Now on to the season itself. Leave aside the 131 points, because

Hull became just the fifth man to hit the 50-goals-in-50-games mark and, even more remarkably, tallied 86 goals. For his efforts, Hull took home the Hart Trophy. One year later, Hull tallied 50-in-50 once again, joining Gretzky in the elite club. He tallied one more 100-point season to make four consecutive seasons at that plateau before his numbers settled down, much like scoring did across the NHL as a defence-first mentality took over. Hull gained the captaincy of the Blues during this time and did what he could to bring the team to playoff glory, but by this time the team was crumbling, thanks in part

◄ STEPHEN LAROCHE

to the departures of Adam Oates and Brendan Shanahan, and so were any thoughts of any sort of championship in St. Louis.

Before the 1998–99 season, Hull signed with the rival Dallas Stars. The move paid immediate dividends for the Stars, who won their first Stanley Cup off of Hull's controversial triple-overtime winner. You see, Hull's skate was in the Buffalo Sabres' crease during that final game, which at the time was practically the eighth deadly sin. Perhaps fittingly, that goal would signal the end of the crease rule for good. A couple years later, Hull moved to the Detroit Red Wings and earned his second Cup ring. Hull's finale on the ice came just after the 2004–05 NHL lockout with the Phoenix Coyotes. During his stint with the franchise, Hull wore No. 9 as the team un-retired his father, Bobby's, sweater. The controversial move may have jinxed Brett, who played in only five games — and tallied no goals — in the desert.

Brett Hull was inducted into the Hockey Hall of Fame in 2009.

BORN IN
THE 1970S
★ ★ ★

More than anything, for professional hockey, the 1970s were about change. Jean Beliveau retired and Guy Lafleur took over. The Maple Leafs were done as a Cup-winning megapower, while the New York Islanders were becoming a dynasty. Plain-faced goalies and crewcutted skaters were slowly eliminated in favour of masks, helmets, moustaches, and long hair. And then there were the new teams.

The 1970s saw the expansion floodgates truly open. While some, like the Kansas City Scouts and Cleveland Barons, did not make it past the end of the decade, others flourished. The 1970s also saw the birth and death of the WHA. Now, only one of its teams remains intact.

So grab your afro pick, turn on your eight-track, and pop in some Aerosmith: it's time to look at the teams born in the 1970s.

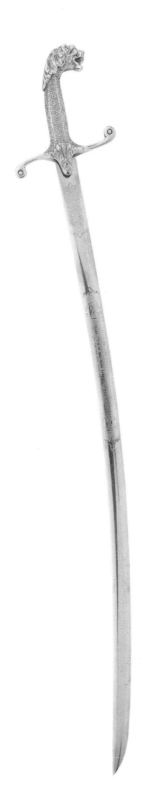

BUFFALO SABRES

Perhaps the best way to describe the Buffalo Sabres is to say they're . . . unique. Buffalo gained its entry into the NHL after hosting the AHL's Bisons for years. Rather than carry the name forward, the Knox family, who owned the franchise, chose to stage the ever-popular "Name the Team" contest, eventually settling on "the Sabres." The Knoxes instantly gave the team front-office credibility by hiring Punch Imlach away from the Toronto Maple Leafs as Sabres general manager and coach.

But the Sabres handle wasn't just another sports cliché moniker. No, the team was also going to create the most dangerous marketing giveaway ever. Afraid an MLB bat night might lead to violence? Try giving out daggers. Yep, that's right. In one of the most violent, yet ultra-cool, bonuses ever offered by a sports team, the Sabres commemorated their inauguration by giving swords to their season ticket holders. Etched with Punch Imlach's replicated signature, the swords featured a two-foot-long blade. That's right; this wasn't a shish kebob stick, this was a real-deal slicer. Over the years, the Sabres sabres

"DES". SMITH

French newspapers took their photographs seriously and for
several years produced collectible, sepia-toned photographs
of the stars of Montreal teams. Maroons standout Des Smith
was among the players featured in the late 1920s. JON WALDMAN

Just as baseball's earliest
treasures were cigarette cards,
hockey had its share of tobacciana.
The origin of this photo dates back
to early 20th-century cigar boxes.
HERITAGE AUCTIONS

FRED. TAYLOR of RENFREW CLUB.

One of the oldest hockey sets,
the C56 series, featured "Cyclone"
Taylor as its lead superstar.
WINSTON HART

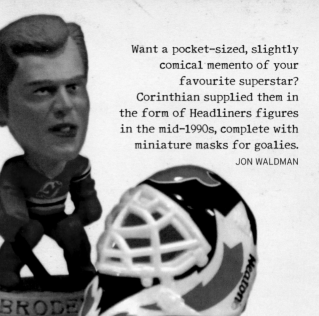

Want a pocket-sized, slightly comical memento of your favourite superstar? Corinthian supplied them in the form of Headliners figures in the mid-1990s, complete with miniature masks for goalies. JON WALDMAN

Breweries created some unique collectibles, but their sponsorships brought them more exposure. Labatt, for example, sponsored the Canada Cup, leading to the creation of unique patches like this crest. These are fairly hard to find in the modern market. JON WALDMAN

Some memorabilia items come from obscure hockey leagues — the Colonial Hockey League, for example. The predecessor to the United Hockey League only ran from 1991 to 1997 but had enough time to produce this patch. JON WALDMAN

STANLEY CUP

TORONTO MAPLE LEAFS

1942

Pin collectors have had a variety of team-produced items to choose from, including this piece produced by the Jets in the 1980s with a sponsor. JON WALDMAN

Commemorative jersey-retirement night items are huge among collectors since so few see the secondary market. This pin was issued the night that Rod Gilbert's number seven was raised to the rafters of MSG. FERNANDO MORENO

Looking for a way to remember championship seasons? Miniature Stanley Cup banners, such as this Toronto Maple Leafs offering, make great additions to a man cave or rear-view mirror.
JON WALDMAN

Miniature zambonis are a cult hit with those who grew up playing with Hot Wheels. Todd McFarlane released this special-edition ice cleaner as a promotion for his comic book antihero, Spawn.

JON WALDMAN

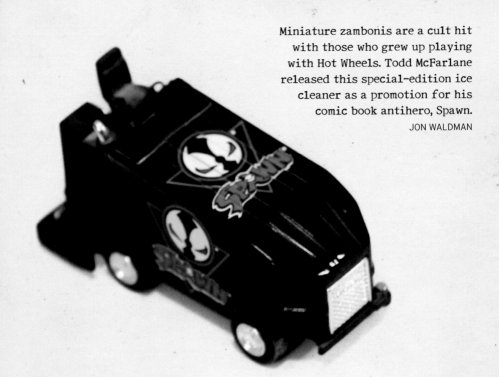

Though not as hotly pursued as other collectibles, table hockey games have long been a part of shinny culture. This model, dubbed "Foster Hewitt Hockey," emerged in the 1940s as one of the first of its kind.

JON WALDMAN

ONLY THE GREAT ONES DELIVER.

Not every collectible is obvious. Advertisements dating back to pre-World War II command high dollars. While this Domino's Pizza flyer won't make anyone rich, it is coveted by hardcore Wayne Gretzky fans. JON WALDMAN

Optimistic printing of tickets for the playoffs has been going on for years, but most ducats that don't come to fruition end up in the garbage. Some, like this Oilers Stanley Cup Finals piece for the non-Finals bound team, make their way into collector hands.

JON WALDMAN

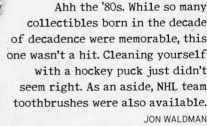

Those who braved horrible
conditions on January 22, 1987, to
see the Devils and Flames square
off were part of "The 334 Club."
Artifacts were later created to
commemorate the lowest-attended
game in NHL history. JEFF MAZZEI

Ahh the '80s. While so many
collectibles born in the decade
of decadence were memorable, this
one wasn't a hit. Cleaning yourself
with a hockey puck just didn't
seem right. As an aside, NHL team
toothbrushes were also available.
JON WALDMAN

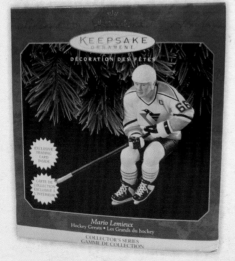

Hockey for the holidays!
Hallmark has produced a variety
of ornaments over the years,
including a couple series of
hangable hockey figurines.
JON WALDMAN

and...
HOWE!

The #1 All-Time Best Seller!

AN AUTHORIZED AUTOBIOGRAPHY
BY GORDIE AND COLLEEN HOWE
WITH TOM DeLISLE

Gordie and Colleen Howe, Mr. & Mrs. Hockey®
Hockey's greatest all around player of all time and the most durable athlete in sports history. Mrs. Hockey™, the most influential woman in hockey history and the publisher and co-author of "and...HOWE!", the best-selling hockey, hardcover autobiography of all time.

Power Play International, Inc.
(248) 960-7500
www.mrhockey.com

Jerseys from all tournaments — including the World Hockey Championships — are highly in demand, especially when the player who wore them is a superstar like Steven Stamkos. JOHN PICHETTE

Books and autographs go together like pucks and sticks. Promotional materials will come from time to time, and it was during the buildup to their book that Gordie and Colleen Howe did the autograph circuit together. JON WALDMAN

proved to be quite coveted by collectors. In 2009, gamewornauctions .net initially listed one for $100 — it wound up selling for $895.

But the swords were hardly unique to the Sabres' arsenal. In Imlach, they had a true character, who showed his bravado in the 1974 NHL Entry Draft. Deciding that his team was done picking up players, Imlach, when called upon to select a player by the NHL brass, invented Taro Tsujimoto, supposedly a star from Japan. The selection was actually made official, and draft history records still list him as a Sabre recruit.

But the intricacies of the Sabres don't end there. In an odd precursor to the current Draft Lottery, the Sabres and fellow expansion team the Vancouver Canucks were both in a position to lay claim to the first overall draft pick in the 1970 NHL Entry Draft, with their fates decided by a spin of the roulette wheel. The Sabres won and claimed the first member of the famed French Connection line, eventual Hall of Famer Gilbert Perreault. One year later, the club picked Rick Martin in the draft and traded for Rene Robert. The formidable line

brought the Sabres to their first Stanley Cup Finals in 1975 — a loss to the steamrolling, rough-and-tumble Philadelphia Flyers. But the series is just as memorable for an incident on the ice as for any other event in the series. Amid Game Three of the series, fog started to form in the Buffalo Memorial Auditorium due to heat and ventilation issues. The game continued on through near-blind conditions, during which time Sabres forward Jim Lorentz spotted — and killed — a bat. Unfortunately, marketing wasn't quite what it is today, and the "Bat Trick" never came to be.

Through the remainder of the

1970s, the Sabres continued to be one of the most dominant teams in the NHL but were unable to make it back to the finals. The true highlight for the team came during the 1979–80 season, when they became the first team to upend the touring Soviet Olympic squad. Into the 1980s, with a new cast of characters that included Dave Andreychuk, Phil Housley, and Tom Barrasso, the club again looked like contenders; but the Sabres were now in the Adams Division, a grinding group of clubs that more often saw the Boston Bruins or Montreal Canadiens advance out of the division-based playoff series.

As the 1980s rolled into the 1990s, a new era dawned. This time was perhaps best known for sharp-minded trading rather than development from within, with the Sabres acquiring Dale Hawerchuk from the Jets, Pat LaFontaine from the Islanders, and, most importantly, Dominik Hasek from the Blackhawks. The turnover also saw a change in uniform as they abandoned the blue and yellow for a red, black, and grey schemata. The new jersey was unique primarily because it did not feature any striping around the lower portion of the sweater.

The updated fashion seemed to bring about a renewed toughness for the Sabres, who now counted players like Maxim Afinogenov and Mike Peca. The squad, led by Hasek, went all the way to the 1999 Stanley Cup Finals, where, in controversial fashion, it was eliminated by the Dallas Stars. The Sabres fell back to reality as they soon were watching the playoffs rather than participating in them, failing to qualify for the post-season in the last three years before the 2004–05 lockout. Once NHL play resumed, however, the Sabres were unquestionably rejuvenated. The arrival of Tomas Vanek up front was spectacular, while goalie Ryan Miller emerged as a top netminder in the NHL. The club reached the conference finals in 2005–06 and 2006–07. Since then, the team has not fared quite as successfully, bouncing between missing the playoffs and being eliminated in the first round.

The team has also undergone a return to their old uniforms, after changing temporarily to a stylized buffalo on their sweaters. Yep, that would be the "Buffaslug," quite possibly the worst logo ever devised (though the rarity of these jerseys does make for temptation for sweater collectors). Thankfully, good taste prevails now, and there's rekindled hope that the Sabres will return to their former playoff glory.

★ GILBERT PERREAULT ★

Spending one's entire tenure in the NHL with one squad is a rare feat, but this was exactly what Gilbert Perreault did as a member of the Sabres.

The first-ever Sabres draft pick, Perreault immediately showed he was a force to be reckoned with as he tallied 72 points in his rookie year, making him the obvious choice as Calder Trophy winner. Perreault quickly became the best player to wear No. 11 in the league, a number that may seem innocuous until you remember that he chose it because it was the winning number in NHL Roulette, the gamble that brought the French Canadian superstar to Buffalo prior to the 1970 draft. Perreault would go on to centre the famed French Connection line alongside Rene Robert and Rick Martin. Perreault amassed ten 30-goal seasons, including three occasions when he hit the 40 mark. He would also surpass the point-per-game rate 11 times, twice exceeding the 100-point milestone. Perreault

was also an international sensation during his career, playing in the 1972 Summit Series and the 1976 and 1981 Canada Cups. When he called it a career midway into the 1986–87 season, Perrault had eclipsed the 500-goal and 1,300-point marks. He was named to the Hockey Hall of Fame in 1990 and today — nearly 30 years removed from the ice — continues to be one of the most in-demand players on the autograph circuit.

EDMONTON OILERS

Edmonton has always had the Oilers, from their days in the WHA; but they weren't always known as the *Edmonton* Oilers. Yes, when they first entered the WHA, they had this name, but when the Calgary Broncos folded, the team became the Alberta Oilers. This lasted for only a year, and soon the Edmonton Oilers were back.

The early days of the Oilers would bring about one player who would become an important cog in their later success — Glen Sather. Following retirement, "Slats" moved behind the bench in Edmonton and be the starting point for what would become one of the greatest rosters ever assembled in hockey. As

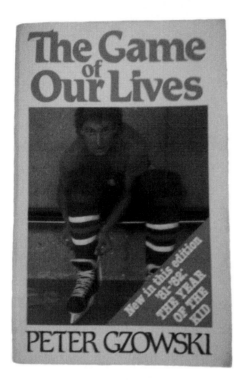

The Game
of
Our Lives

PETER GZOWSKI

far less common in the early 1980s when famed Canadian journalist Peter Gzowski joined the Edmonton Oilers on the road for the 1980–81 season. The result of his work is one of the most iconic books in hockey history, *The Game of Our Lives*. While it has since been reissued several times over, the original hardcover edition, with a spry Gretzky lacing up his skates, is an incredible memento, particularly if you can find a copy autographed by Gzowski.

The Oilers outright dominated the majority of the 1980s. Between the 1982–83 and 1989–90 seasons, the team appeared in six Stanley Cup Finals, hoisting the coveted trophy five times; and each time they did so they beat teams that can hardly be described as slouches. They kicked off their run by ending the Islanders dynasty, then defeated the Philadelphia Flyers and Boston Bruins in back-to-back succession.

their NHL tenure began, the Oilers showed signs of becoming the next big hockey dynasty. Their arrival coincided with the start of the New York Islanders dynasty, and the team quickly assembled a powerhouse group, bringing aboard future Hall of Famers like Mark Messier, Paul Coffey, Jari Kurri, and Grant Fuhr to join Wayne Gretzky in creating a young, phenom-laden squad.

Those early days were captured eloquently, and quite uniquely, on paper. While documentaries featuring behind-the-scenes information are not uncommon today (witness HBO's 24/7 docu-series), it was

After the 1990 victory, the wheels began to fall off the Oilers steam engine. By this time, Gretzky and Coffey had been traded, and they were soon followed by the rest of the dynasty's core — Messier to the Rangers, Fuhr to the Maple Leafs, and Kurri to Italy (before joining Wayne in Los Angeles), all before the end of the 1991–92 season. In 1992–93, the Oilers missed the playoffs for the first time in their NHL tenure.

Unfortunately, succession planning wasn't the Oilers' strongest suit. Young stars like Adam Graves were sent to other teams, and poor draft picks like Jason Bonsignore didn't pan out. To make matters worse, a sharp decline in the value of the Canadian dollar didn't do the Oilers any favours in drawing new talent to their squad (after all, heritage only goes so far). The exception, it seemed, was Curtis Joseph, who played some of the best hockey of his career in Edmonton, and, with a budding leader in Ryan Smyth, the Oilers made a triumphant return to the post-season during the 1996–97 season.

By this time, seemingly irreparable damage had been done to the franchise. They were still a money loser for owner Peter Pocklington, who looked bent on selling the squad to a U.S. investor interested in relocation. The rumour mill had the team moving to Minnesota, replacing the departed North Stars. At one point, Pocklington had a deal on the table that would send the team to Houston under the ownership of Leslie Alexander

(owner of the NBA's Rockets). A consortium, however, rescued the squad from northern extinction. Despite new ownership, there was still instability in Edmonton. With a low Canadian dollar, the Oilers were unable to compete with the American NHL teams. Once the 2004–05 lockout was done and salary caps were in place, things started to turn around, and with a surge in the Canadian dollar, the Oilers became more attractive for players like Chris Pronger, Michael Peca, and Dwayne Roloson. Immediately, these acquisitions paid dividends, and the Oilers made an unexpected run to the Stanley Cup Finals in the first year of renewed play.

The rejuvenation lasted only one season. Just days after losing in the Cup Finals to Carolina, Chris Pronger demanded to be traded amid rumours of an extramarital affair with an Edmonton journalist. Ryan Smyth departed during the 2006–07 season, and the Oilers slumped back down, eventually finishing dead last in the NHL.

Fortunes, it seemed, were ready to turn back in the favour of the Oilers. Starting in 2010, the team went on a three-year run of securing the first overall pick in each season's

NHL Entry Draft. As a result, three future superstars — Taylor Hall, Ryan Nugent-Hopkins, and Nail Yakupov — were brought to Edmonton. Other new heroes like Jordan Eberle and Justin Schultz would also take on leading rolls with the club. Though injuries stinted several of these players in their first seasons, there is now renewed hope in Edmonton that glory days, reminiscent of the 1980s, will return to the Alberta capital.

★ TAYLOR HALL ★

It's hard to pick a single player to represent the new breed of Oilers; there are certainly enough suitable options. Of all the rising stars, Taylor Hall, a three-time gold medallist in international junior tournaments, is the likely marquee name. While the others will fill in the Messier, Kurri, Anderson, and other personality spots, it is most likely that Taylor Hall will be the Gretzky (not that I think he'll hit those scoring levels, but you know what I mean).

Borne from the Windsor Spitfires, Hall had "future star" written all over him even well before the 2010 NHL Entry Draft. There was only one question — whether it would be he or rival Tyler Seguin who would be selected first overall. In the end, the Oilers chose Taylor, and while injuries cut his ice time, he showed enormous potential, hitting the 20-goal plateau each year (lockout aside). Time will ultimately tell the story of Taylor Hall, with expectations that the young superstar will be the Oilers' leader for years to come, filling in the "Gretzky" role in the new edition of Edmonton supremacy.

While Hall's performance on the ice has yet to yield Gretzky-like results — namely playoff supremacy — he has matched The Great One in one department. Oilers collectors of the '80s no doubt recall the Wayne Gretzky doll, and today Hall has his own Bleacher Creature, a stuffed likeness of the phenom.

NEW YORK ISLANDERS

While hockey-mad cities like Toronto and Montreal have gone for decades with only one NHL franchise, New Yorkers have long had the option of which team to cheer for — the mainland Rangers or the team that carried the banner as one of the NHL's greatest dynasties, the New York Islanders.

Hailing from Long Island (as clearly defined in the first EA Sports hockey video game, when EA only having an NHLPA licence meant that teams could not have their nicknames used), the Islanders entered the NHL in the 1972–73 season, thanks in large part to the WHA wanting to establish a team at the Nassau Coliseum. The move meant a team would be hastily put together (along with a franchise in Atlanta), which may have influenced general manager Bill Torrey's desire to let young talent rule the roost rather than acquire wily veterans. Two of these players were Billy Smith and Bobby Nystrom.

The first year for the franchise proved to be what you'd expect from an expansion club — an unmitigated disaster. The team finished dead last in the NHL, "earning" the right to that year's Entry Draft top pick. That selection was Denis Potvin, who immediately paid dividends by capturing the Calder Trophy the following year. Slowly but surely the Isles were putting together a solid franchise, led by the masterful coaching of Al Arbour. As Potvin, Nystrom, and Smith matured, and new draftees Clark Gillies and Bryan Trottier emerged, the club began to have the feel of a true contender. Four consecutive 100-point seasons would do that for a franchise. The

tipping point came in 1977, when the team selected Mike Bossy.

During the 1979–80 season, the first year of the NHL/WHA merger, the Islanders broke through the playoff glass ceiling and earned their first Stanley Cup. It was against one-time dynasty Philadelphia that New York captured the championship, with a heroic overtime goal by Nystrom putting the Cup in their hands. (It's worth noting that, in contrast to Bobby Orr's heroic Cup-clinching goal, there has been very little in the way of souvenirs from this historic marker, save for the jersey Nystrom wore when he scored the goal, which was auctioned by Heritage in the summer of 2013.) The fire created by this crew continued to burn for three more Stanley Cups, the last coming against the team that would succeed them as a dynasty, the Edmonton Oilers. The changing of the NHL's championship guard saw the Islanders' rebuild start almost immediately, as one by one the prime-time players faded into retirement or moved to other NHL squads with little star replacement (save for Pat LaFontaine, Kelly Hrudey, and a handful of others). Soon, the Islanders were bottom dwellers, scraping high draft picks (at times very unsuccessfully), trying to put together a new run of superstars to guide them back to the promised land; and certainly the squad could have done so, if they had been kept together. Just imagine, for a second — Roberto Luongo, Zdeno Chara, Todd Bertuzzi, Olli Jokinen . . .

But such was the legacy of one-time general manager "Mad Mike" Milbury. Milbury was known to make deals that would baffle pundits, often swapping potential talent for immediacy. The result was, pardon the pun, a disenfranchised fanbase that seemed to dissipate year by year, to the point that relocation rumours started to pop up. By the time the 2004–05 NHL lockout was over, not much of a team was left. The days of dynasty were long gone, and the Islanders were in need of new hope, which came in the form of young guns like John Tavares and Michael Grabner.

Oh yeah — they were also in need of as much separation from Captain Highliner as possible. You see, back in the mid-1990s, the Isles, roughly a decade removed from their last dance with the Cup, felt that a fresh look was needed for the team. A new jersey was designed, with the traditional striping at the bottom altered to resemble waves in treacherous waters, topped off with a fisherman bedecked in a blue rain jacket and hat, wielding a hockey stick instead of a harpoon gun as part of the new logo. Yes, it was bad as it sounds; but quickly, good taste saw the fisherman washed away and the new jersey design cast aside. The logo was thankfully not captured on many pieces of memorabilia, primarily appearing on trading cards from those two years; however, he can still be found in all his glory on the Kirk Muller Starting Lineup action figure, issued in 1995.

★ MIKE BOSSY ★

A well-known face in the hobby and the autograph market, Bossy has been called the best pure goal scorer in NHL history and to this day holds the record for the best goals-per-game pace. Born in Montreal, QMJHL graduate Bossy was highly coveted by both WHA and NHL franchises. The knock against him, however, was that he was too much a scorer and too fearful of the checking game, something that was considered a must in the rough-and-tumble days of the 1970s NHL. Bossy would end up being picked by the Isles 17th overall in the 1977 Draft, passed over once by many other teams and twice by the Rangers and Maple Leafs.

Bossy quickly proved that any team that had passed him over had made a terrible mistake, as he tallied 53 goals in his rookie year, establishing a new NHL record for freshmen in the process and starting what would be a string of nine consecutive seasons above the half-century mark. By comparison, Wayne Gretzky, as good as he was, and as many 50-goal seasons as he had (also nine), wasn't able to maintain that level of consistency. Bossy is also one of only five players in NHL history to tally 50 goals in 50 games. Bossy's strong play netted him a Conn Smythe trophy, three Lady Byng trophies, and numerous All-Star nods. Yet for all he did in the NHL, he was unable to win the Hart Trophy, namely because of competition from Gretzky. The two were, however, on the same side during the 1984 Canada Cup, and it was Bossy's goal in the semi-finals against Russia that propelled Canada to the finals and eventual Cup victory.

All of this firepower made Bossy a popular spokesperson for hockey gear. Companies like Titan-Jofa and Scor-Mor would spotlight the

Islanders superstar on their products and in advertisements, and today these items make for some unique collectibles — when they can be found.

Today, Bossy is still involved with the Islanders, having helped found the Islanders Business Club and now serving as the organization's executive director. The organization provides tickets to business owners in the Long Island area, helping them entertain clients and network while enjoying the game of hockey.

VANCOUVER CANUCKS

To get the obvious joke out of the way . . . the most unique collectible associated with the Vancouver Canucks would probably be the handcuffs used during the 2011 riots that broke out after the hometown team folded like a cheap suit at the hands of the Boston Bruins in the Stanley Cup Finals. But in all seriousness, if you wanted to point to one piece that defines the Canucks, it's the rally towel that has been raised above fans' heads three times during the last leg of the journey to Lord Stanley's mug (though none of these ventures has been successful).

The tradition of "towel power" arose from the 1982 Stanley Cup Playoffs when, in signal of mock surrender to poor officiating, Roger Neilson put a towel on a player's stick and waved it in the midst of a playoff game. The trend caught on and ever since has become a sort of call to action for the Canucks faithful, with the team now routinely handing out towels emblazoned with their logo for playoff games.

Unfortunately, that sense of defeat has loomed large in the history of the 'Nucks. Three Cup trips, numerous solid teams, but no Stanley Cup banners hanging in the rafters.

That's not to say that being a Vancouver Canuck is all that bad (well, if you ignore a couple of the ugly uniforms in the early 1980s). Outside the Original Six clubs, the 'Nucks have been the most solid Canadian franchise in the last 30 years, thanks to a strong following that has faithfully trailed its heroes from superstars like Pavel Bure and the Sedins to cult heroes like Harold Snepsts and Alex Burrows. Names like Dale Tallon and Trevor Linden, while having followings outside B.C., are legends on the West Coast.

Vancouver was part of the second stage of NHL expansion in 1970, entering the league alongside the Buffalo Sabres (another bridesmaid team), using the same name as the Pacific Coals/Western Canadian Hockey League club that previously played minor hockey in the area. Twice before, Vancouver had attempted to get an NHL team — once in 1967 as part of the initial expansion and again shortly thereafter as a potential purchaser of the struggling Oakland Seals club.

As was the case with other expansion drafts, the Canucks primarily picked up the dregs of other

▲ RONALD ENG

teams and selected Dale Tallon with their first Entry Draft selection. The early years of the club were nothing short of disastrous, as they failed to earn a playoff berth in their first four seasons, and the rest of the 1970s proved to be just as fruitless. It wasn't until a core of players like Stan Smyl and Richard Brodeur began to come together that the team truly gelled.

The funny thing is, the Canucks started to work well just as they entered into one of hockey's most fashionably disastrous eras — of the infamous "Flying V." Wearing bright yellow jerseys at home, the getup looked horrid, especially with the mix of orange, red, and black also in the design. Eventually, the team came to its senses and exchanged the non-logo for the more recognizable skate (itself looking more postmodern than most authentic NHL symbols). The yellow jerseys stayed with the club until 1989, when the team finally bowed to good taste and instituted a white home sweater. (Incidentally, the NHL would relive the horrid jerseys as retro togs. The ironic commentary of fashion sense gone wrong somehow struck a chord with fans.)

As the 1980s rolled over to the 1990s, the team looked more powerful than ever. Led by Linden, Bure, and Kirk McLean, the club excelled and took over the Smythe (later the Pacific) Division from the once dominant Calgary Flames and

I VOTE
TREVOR LINDEN
FOR NHL
ROOKIE
OF THE YEAR
1989

through on their promise as young prospects, and new faces like Ryan Kesler proved worthy of wearing the club colours (which had reverted back to the blue, green, and white the franchise had originally worn, abandoning a slick black, maroon, silver, and blue look).

Still, despite all the new faces that became popular with fans, the Canucks couldn't seal the deal, which led to the infamous riots in June 2011. Much like in 1994, upon losing the Stanley Cup Finals' seventh and deciding game, the team's faithful (and some disturbers looking for an excuse to create havoc) tore apart the city's downtown, hanging a dark cloud over the franchise. Regardless, the Canucks enjoy one of the most dedicated followings in hockey and in the hobby, becoming one of the NHL's most elite franchises both on and off the ice.

★ TREVOR LINDEN ★

The Canucks weren't quite directionless without Linden, but with Trevor at the helm the 'Nucks were always a threat. Recognized as one of hockey's great leaders in the 1990s, Linden was drafted by the Canucks second overall in 1988

Edmonton Oilers; the only problem was that the teams in the Norris (Central) Division and Eastern Conference were too strong. This was right around the time that the Detroit Red Wings, Colorado Avalanche, and Dallas Stars became the darlings of the NHL. No matter how good the 'Nucks were, there was always a team better than them.

The return of the NHL to active duty following the lockout of 2004–05 brought renewed hope for the franchise, especially with the monumental trade that sent Alex Auld to Florida in exchange for Roberto Luongo. Louie instilled new faith in the club that had previously been led by the tandem of Markus Naslund and Todd Bertuzzi. This was also the time that Daniel and Henrik Sedin finally followed behind Mike Modano. He started his NHL career the next season and instantly became a hit, eventually guiding the club to the 1994 Stanley Cup. Linden would become a perennial NHL All-Star in the process.

Linden's dedication to the team, however, went beyond his time on the ice. He became one of Vancouver's most community-minded personalities, creating the Trevor Linden Foundation in 1995. These efforts later led to a unique tie to the memorabilia world as Linden teamed with Pinnacle Brands to offer collectors a unique autographed card in exchange for a donation to his charity — a first in the collectibles world.

Almost inexplicably, Linden was dealt by the Canucks in 1998 to the New York Islanders, in exchange for Todd Bertuzzi, Bryan McCabe, and a draft pick (Jarkko Ruutu). He would last only a couple seasons on Long Island, much like he would subsequently with the Montreal Canadiens and the Washington Capitals; but during the 2001–02 season, Linden was returned to the Canucks in a Draft Pick–laden deal.

"I think Vancouver was trying to make a move to get me back for a few years," Linden said near the start of the 2002–03 NHL season. "Things weren't really happening in Washington, and they were looking to make a move. It was right time, right place." His new teammates, including one of the men he was initially traded for, were happy he'd returned. "You always thought of Trevor as a Vancouver Canuck," Todd Bertuzzi said in a 2002 interview. "He's back where he wants to be."

Linden was recognized for his charitable efforts and devotion to Vancouver in 1997 with the King Clancy Memorial Trophy.

WASHINGTON CAPITALS

If any single term best describes the Washington Capitals' history, it's *enigmatic*. Every time the Caps have been on the verge of becoming one of the NHL's true elite squads, they've seemed to falter. Scanning their record book you will find a number of standout names, from Hall of Famers Scott Stevens and Mike Gartner to the modern-day heroes Alexander Ovechkin and Mike Green.

That's not to say that the Caps have always had strong teams; in fact, many years the opposite has been

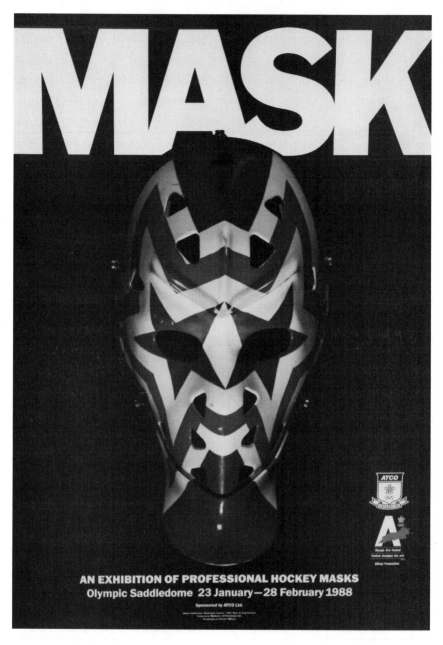

MASK

AN EXHIBITION OF PROFESSIONAL HOCKEY MASKS
Olympic Saddledome 23 January — 28 February 1988

Sponsored by ATCO Ltd.

true. During the 1974–75 season, the team's first in the league, the Caps finished with an 8-67-5 record, the fewest number of wins for any team during the modern era of NHL play.

Granted, the team was formed from the scraps left over from the NHL Expansion Draft (never mind the dilution of the talent pool thanks to WHA recruitment), but the Kansas

City Scouts, the team who formed that same season, had twice the number of points. It ended up taking eight seasons for the Caps to make the playoffs for the first time. By this time, Gartner was already maturing into a leader, Stevens and Bobby Carpenter had joined the team via the NHL Entry Draft, and Pat Riggin was quickly becoming a star goalie. This took place, though, during the New York Islanders' dominance in the Patrick Division (let alone the entire NHL) and sent the Caps packing for three straight seasons. Fortunes reversed, however, for the 1985–86 season, and the Caps swept their rivals in three straight games in the opening round of the playoffs (but were eliminated in the next by the New York Rangers).

By the 1989–90 campaign, the Caps were starting to look like a very competent team and finally broke through the Patrick Division's glass ceiling. They advanced to the Wales Conference Finals for the first time that year, despite having jettisoned leader Mike Gartner and standout defenceman Larry Murphy to Minnesota in exchange for Dino Ciccarelli and Bob Rouse. The Capitals showed an incredible amount of promise, despite losing to Boston, and that they were becoming a force to be reckoned with (or at least a team that would regularly be a playoff club).

This is where the enigmatic history really gets interesting. In the 1996–97 season, almost inexplicably, the Capitals faltered. By this time, the team was more than competent, with a roster that included Peter Bondra, Sergei Gonchar, and Olaf Kolzig, all homegrown talents. Veterans Adam Oates and Phil Housley had also been brought in to help bring the Caps to a new level, and they proved just how dangerous they were one season later, making it all the way to the Stanley Cup Finals, where they were swept by the powerful Detroit Red Wings. Still, they showed enough promise for the future that people started believing in the team once again. But oh, what a difference a year can make. As quickly as they ascended to Cup contention, they just as soon parted from the title picture, failing to make the playoffs in 1998–99. Through the next seasons leading into the NHL lockout, the Caps either missed the playoffs or couldn't make it out of the first round.

What their dismal play did, however, was entitle the team to secure high draft picks, which helped them land Alexander Semin, Alexander Ovechkin, and Niklas Backstrom. These players started a turnaround for the Caps, who, beginning in the 2007–08 season, went on a five-year streak of making the playoffs.

While the Caps have had an up-and-down history, what has remained consistent for the club and its netminders are some of the most beautiful and memorable mask designs in the league. From Ron Low and Mike Palmateer's full-face shields to Don Beaupre and Olaf Kolzig's modern styles, the Caps' colours of red, white, and blue (and even their deep-blue and gold formats used for a few years) have made their goalies' equipment really stand out. Many of these masks, such as Wayne Stephenson's star-emblazoned model, have been exhibited in art galleries and reproduced as sought-after collectibles.

★ ALEXANDER OVECHKIN ★

It's interesting how fickle hockey fans can be. One minute they absolutely despise a player, but the next minute their bitterness turns to admiration. Such was the case with Alexander Ovechkin, but, unlike many players in hockey history, the turn to favour for him is easily explained.

In 2004, Ovechkin was the enemy of North American hockey. As a member of the powerful Russian team that tormented Canada and U.S. squads at the World Junior Hockey Championships, Ovechkin was a lightning rod for spite, partly because he was so good, but partly because he was so cocky. Playing ferociously while wearing a mirrored visor, Ovechkin was nearly impossible to defend against and as a result was the top name on hate lists across the tournament.

Fast-forward to the start of the 2005–06 season, however, and Ovechkin was the subject of much applause. He lit up the league with stellar play as he easily took the Calder Trophy as rookie of the year, defeating rival Sidney Crosby in the process. Part of what made Ovechkin so attractive now was his wizardry. He could score a goal every which way, including, most famously, from his back with his stick above his head, a moment in time that has since become the stuff of early legend and, years and several highlight-reel goals later, is still the most iconic of his career for anyone wanting his autograph.

▲ RONALD ENG

In subsequent years, Ovechkin would further show that he truly was becoming the most dominant Russian ever to enter the NHL. He captured multiple Rocket Richard awards and two consecutive Hart trophies while putting up numbers not seen in the league since the heyday of Pavel Bure. Sixty-goal seasons, even in the post lockout era, were unheard of. Fans were even warm to Ovechkin's push to rejoin Russia's national team for international competition. Repeatedly, Ovechkin threatened the NHL that if the league would not let its players compete at the 2014 Winter Olympics in Sochi, Russia, the proud skater would abandon the league just to be able to play in front of his home country.

Beyond the glitzy play and cockiness, Ovechkin has truly become the NHL's top international star and one of the hottest names for hobbyists on both sides of the Pacific Ocean. What Crosby is to North American hockey, Ovechkin is to the Russian game — a larger-than-life personality who loves the sport and takes every opportunity he can to promote it.

THE 1990s
EXPANSION
★ ★ ★

For the entire decade of the 1980s, the NHL comprised an awkward number of teams — 21. Perhaps league execs expected one of the WHA arrivals to fold, or that the twice-relocated Scouts/Rockies/Devils franchise would finally go belly up — but the league never shrank back to 20 members. Soon, expansion was on everyone's lips.

In 1991, the San Jose Sharks made their debut, and just two years later, they were joined by the Ottawa Senators, Tampa Bay Lightning, Florida Panthers, and Anaheim (Mighty) Ducks, for an even 26 squads. Most of these teams, at one point or another, have been in financial trouble, and yet they have as a group largely excelled in competition while remaining in their initial locales. Two clubs have won the Stanley Cup while two others have reached the Finals.

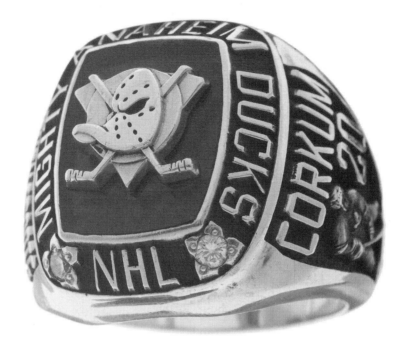

ANAHEIM (MIGHTY) DUCKS

There may be no better example of how a team that starts out as a punchline can become one of a sport's most elite franchises.

In 1993, the NHL was in the midst of an expansion era that would see the league grow to 26 teams in a matter of three seasons. Among those fortunate cities was Anaheim, joining Los Angeles and San Jose as part of a California trio. At the time, Disney was in the midst of a run of sports movies that "inspired" youngsters, including a series of movies about a plucky young group of hockey players coached by Emilio Estevez's

character. *The Mighty Ducks* became one of the best movie series for young fans growing up in the 1990s. The first movie garnered over $50 million at the box office in the U.S., far exceeding its $10 million budget, while the second earned $45 million (the third, however, was a practical bust at nearly $23 million). And so began one of the most unique concepts in all of sport — take a movie-born team and bring it to life.

When the Mighty Ducks of Anaheim skated for the first time in the 1993–94 NHL season, the team did so under much criticism from NHL purists who saw the team moniker as not much more than a publicity stunt to sustain

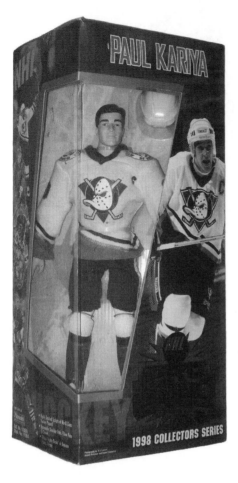

PAUL KARIYA

1998 COLLECTORS SERIES

Mighty Ducks would get to living out a Hollywood-style dream run; but a conversion to the now more familiar Anaheim Ducks moniker in 2006–07 seemed to start them off on the path to the promised land.

Invigorated by young talents like Ryan Getzlaf and Corey Perry, a returning hero in Teemu Selanne, and a dream pairing of Chris Pronger and Scott Niedermayer on defence, the Ducks were dominant in the playoffs as they dispatched the Minnesota Wild, Detroit Red Wings, and Vancouver Canucks in the west before meeting — and beating — the Ottawa Senators.

Throughout their history, the Ducks have gone through identity crisis after identity crisis. Although they are still relatively young by NHL standards, they have played host to some of the best players the NHL has seen. Their position in the NHL is solid, and they are one of few southern U.S. teams that have not been mentioned in the same breath as the term *financial failure*.

But any discussion about the Ducks, inevitably, goes back to their first alternate jersey experiment. While Anaheim has come out with some colourful and unique jerseys in its day, none quite had the horrorful

interest in the movie franchise; but the team barely resembled its pint-sized namesakes. The Ducks were, in fact, anything but mighty, going to the post-season only three times in their first nine years. Fortunes turned around in 2002–03 as they regrouped and put on a show for the ages, coming within one game of hoisting Lord Stanley's grail but ultimately falling to the New Jersey Devils. This was as close as the look of the 1996–97 tog, with team mascot "Wildwing" bursting out of the bottom of the jersey, which was seemingly covered in ice. But even that piece of material is not the worst offender to feature a Ducks logo.

In 1996, Disney took it upon the themselves to make one final cash grab on the Mighty Ducks with kids and produced a cartoon television series centred around Wildwing (voiced by 90210's Ian Ziering) and a group of futuristic fighting ducks, out to save the world from . . . okay, I'm really not sure what they were saving us from. In any case, when Disney goes merch, they go merch in a big way, and so were born the Mighty Ducks action figures, complete with two pieces that are fully equipped in the NHL team's gear. While these toys may not rank high on collector want lists (or at all, more appropriately), they are one of the most vivid reminders of just how bad things got, off the ice, for the Anaheim (Mighty) Ducks.

★ TEEMU SELANNE ★

Teemu Selanne's spectacular career began in Winnipeg, but mere months before the franchise was relocated to Phoenix, Selanne was traded to the Anaheim Ducks for Chad Kilger and Oleg Tverdovsky. The trade shocked the Jets franchise, but it was welcome news for Anaheim's faithful, who embraced the "Finnish Flash" upon his arrival. Selanne would quickly become one of two marquee names in Anaheim, pairing up with Paul Kariya to form one of the deadliest pass-shoot combos in the NHL. The two were virtually unstoppable when on the ice together; and, while Selanne's goal-scoring exploits as a rookie will forever be his calling card, his tally totals in Anaheim were just as incredible. He had three consecutive years of at least 40 goals, two of which were 50-plus seasons, two 100-point seasons, and he picked up the Maurice Richard Trophy once.

Toward the end of the 2000–01 season, however, Selanne was dealt to the San Jose Sharks in a surprising move. During this time, Selanne's numbers faltered, and he failed to hit the 30-goal plateau during the two full seasons he spent with the team. At the end of this stint, he reunited with Kariya in Colorado, but the magic wasn't there — Teemu belonged in Anaheim. After the year-long NHL lockout, Selanne returned to Anaheim with gusto, tallying 40 goals and 90 points and picking up the Bill Masterton Trophy in the process. One year later, with a 48-goal campaign under his belt, Selanne was instrumental in Anaheim winning the Stanley Cup, a first for a California-based hockey franchise.

Following the Ducks' Stanley Cup victory, the question of how much longer Selanne would be in the NHL began to come up. Thus was born an annual tradition in which Selanne would sign one-year contracts as he continually evaluated whether he could hang with the new breed of superstars, and for the next few years the answer was a resounding "yes." Through this time, Selanne remained committed to the NHL's Ducks; and while some European players would skate their swan songs back home, including one-time Anaheim teammate Sergei Fedorov, Selanne always intended on finishing his career in North America. "I think I'd like to retire here. I want to play here as long as I can and then do something else," he said in a 2003 interview.

Perhaps it's for this reason that an otherwise inconspicuous miniature jersey created by Upper Deck is desired by Selanne collectors. Issued for the 2007–08 season, the Selanne comes in both away and home versions (the latter being much rarer), as they did for many other players; but these would be important down the line for Selanne's rabid fans, as they would be the last he would wear.

That's not to say that Selanne neglected his homeland; rather, he holds a very unique record — most points during the Olympics. Selanne also has three medals from the famed competition: a silver and two bronze.

FLORIDA PANTHERS

If it weren't for one season, the Panthers' NHL story would be one of complete disappointment. The Panthers debuted in the 1993–94 season as the South Florida Panthers before dropping their regional name. The team received some early attention, thanks in large part to the unique opportunity they had to pick up the still-hot John Vanbiesbrouck from the New York Rangers in the Expansion Draft (teams could only protect one netminder, and the Broadway Blue Shirts kept Mike Richter).

With Beezer at the helm of a team of gutsy veterans like Scott

▲ CHERYL LAPALME / FLORIDA PANTHERS BOOSTER CLUB

Mellanby and young upstarts such as number-one draft pick Ed Jovanovski, the squad had all the right tools to be an underdog team that made it to the finals of the NHL playoffs. Oh, and having the support of rat-hungry fans certainly helped as well.

For those who don't recall the story, prior to the team's home opener for the 1995–96 season, Scott Mellanby spotted a rat in the Panthers' locker room. After batting the rat across the locker room, killing it, he went on to score two goals in the evening's tilt, scoring the first "rat trick" in NHL history. Once word spread of Mellanby's "heroics," fans began to bring plastic rats to the rink and tossed them onto the ice below whenever the Panthers would score. The result was a veritable plastic rainstorm on the rink, often resulting in defence-less goaltenders cowering in their nets, trapped like . . . well . . . rats.

Cheryl Lapalme of the Florida Panthers Booster Club remembers that the players made extra efforts to show their fans their appreciation: "On the ice, their lunch pail attitude and never-quit mantra was intoxicating and it made us love them more," she explained in a December 2011 interview. "The rats were our way to give back to them. It was our way to say, 'This is our team, this is our time,' and each goal they scored was OUR moment to celebrate."

"This group of guys don't quit, even when they are down a goal or two or three. This team is special and this team has helped bring back the rats with their winning ways. It has absolutely *nothing* to do with the league enforcing any rules. It has to do with the wins. If the team wins, the rats fly; if they don't, we wait until the next game."

While fan groups, including the Booster Club, have painted up rats on occasion and sold them to fans, the team has not fully monetized the rats. Only once — in 2007 — did the team actively sell rodent souvenirs. Perhaps that's because it's only been recently that Panthers fans have had any reason to toss plastic rodents. For years, the Panthers were stuck near the bottom of the league (albeit not low enough to earn a coveted first overall draft pick). Through eras that included superstar goalie Roberto Luongo and ubersniper Pavel Bure, the Panthers rarely contented for a playoff spot — and when they were close, it was unbearably so for fans. With the recent maturation of young stars, however, the Panthers have started to claw their way back into contention, and with it comes renewed hope for the Florida faithful.

Their fans were rabid, and the Panthers advanced all the way to the Stanley Cup Finals before falling to the Colorado Avalanche. After that season, the NHL disallowed the rats being tossed on the ice with the threat of a delay-of-game penalty. In later years, the tradition was renewed, with fans chucking the plastic renditions to the ice following a victory; but those were few and far between until the 2011–12 season.

"It wasn't until . . . Dale Tallon brought in a group of guys that had the same attitude as the '95–96 team that the rat-tossing really began to take hold," Lapalme said.

★ JOHN VANBIESBROUCK ★

On a rather sad-sack team, Beezer was the standout. John Vanbiesbrouck was able to record 21 wins in the Panthers' first season, no small feat as many expansion team goalies can attest.

Vanbiesbrouck's NHL career began with the New York Rangers, where he was an instant hit on Broadway, garnering 31 wins in his second complete season while bringing home the Vezina. Over the next few years he would continue his solid play but never reach the 30-win plateau again. Perhaps that was why the New York club left him unprotected in the Expansion Draft.

Immediately, Beezer became the number-one name in Florida, and thanks to a wicked paint job on his mask, he became one of the most in-demand players for collectors. The lid, while simplistic, was very drawing to the eye and commanded that replicas be produced. Alongside premium mask makers, McDonald's and EA Sports included the lid in product lines.

Once he left Florida, however, Beezer's stock dropped quicker than a share in Enron, as his runs with the New York Islanders, Philadelphia Flyers, and New Jersey Devils were largely forgettable, and controversy surrounding a racial slur during a coaching stint further degraded his profile. Still, he is well regarded for a career that included more than 350 wins, and is best remembered as the first marquee name in Panthers history.

OTTAWA SENATORS

The Ottawa Senators are a perpetual curiosity. They've enjoyed deep playoff runs, going all the way up to the Cup Finals in 2007, but they've have also languished, finishing at the bottom of the NHL.

The Sens joined the NHL officially after the 1991–92 season, adopting the nickname of the legendary franchise that dominated Stanley Cup competition prior to the formation of the NHL and skated in the new league until the 1930s, winning 11 Stanley Cups in its history. Thus, there was no question what moniker the team would use for its new iteration, especially with a "Bring Back the Senators" campaign launched by would-be owners Bruce Firestone, Cyril Leeder, and Randy Sexton.

The only question was whether

the team would be as successful as the original, and in the short term of its first few years, the answer was a resounding "no." The Sens finished last in the NHL in their first season, with a paltry 10 wins in 84 games, amid accusations that they threw their final contests in order to secure the first overall pick in the 1993 NHL Entry Draft, which they used to nab Alexandre Daigle. This led to the Draft Lottery system we're now familiar with today. Whether the Sens did this purposely or not, they didn't fare much better with Daigle in their ranks and one year later had another first overall pick, this time making the quirky selection of Bryan Berard then almost immediately trading him to the New York Islanders for the number-two pick — Wade Redden. One year later, the Sens completed the first-overall hat trick and took Chris Phillips number one.

While Daigle was a bust, the original Senators pick, Alexei Yashin, became a legitimate star and a young Daniel Alfredsson looked extremely promising. The Sens finally earned their first playoff spot in 1996–97. Over the next few seasons, Ottawa continued to find itself in the playoff mix, but Yashin was proving to be more

trouble than he was worth. Twice he had been a contract holdout, and he clearly did not display the work ethic the club expected, especially given his role as team captain. As a result, he was swapped to the Islanders at the 2001 NHL Entry Draft for a group of players that included the behemoth Zdeno Chara, Bill Muckault, and the second overall pick in that draft: Jason Spezza.

The new acquisitions paid off. While off-ice the club was mired in financial woes, on-ice they were better than ever, winning the President's Trophy with the most regular season points and making it to the Conference Finals for the first time in team history. The Sens also soon got a boost from a new collective bargaining agreement instituted before the 2005–06 season, which helped the team achieve a more level playing field against their American counterparts.

But before the new era could begin, the Sens first established a rivalry with the Toronto Maple Leafs. The Battle of Ontario created major hatred between Ottawa and Toronto as fans would regularly deride one another whether it was a playoff game or even exhibition play. Even past the days where the Leafs

were post-season regulars, the rivalry would still be a featured component of broadcasts on Canadian television.

When the new NHL era began, the Sens looked a lot different. Bryan Murray was brought in as the team's new coach, and Dany Heatley joined Alfredsson and Spezza on the team's top line, replacing the at-times-enigmatic Marian Hossa. The changes paid off, as the Sens advanced to the Stanley Cup Finals in 2006–07. The advancement caused a celebration in the streets of Ottawa but was unfortunately too short-lived as the team bowed out in five games to Anaheim.

Following the defeat, the Sens started to unravel. Ray Emery, who had been Ottawa's netminder for the amazing Cup run, was now becoming troublesome off the ice and was released in 2008, while Heatley was dealt after demanding to be traded. As a result of the turmoil and changing cast, the Sens missed the playoffs twice over the five seasons that followed their finals appearance.

Amid their up-and-down fortunes, no time was harder for the franchise than when Roger Neilson passed away June 21, 2003. Roughly a year prior, Neilson, primarily an

assistant coach with the squad, had been given the opportunity to be the bench boss for two games in order to allow him to reach 1,000 head-coaching contests for his career. The following year he remained part of the coaching staff even as his health deteriorated.

Following Neilson's passing, the Senators engineered several tributes, including naming their coaches' office the Roger Neilson Room, and the Ottawa Senators Foundation announced plans to found Roger's

House for pediatric palliative care, which opened in 2006. The Senators also wore commemorative patches for Neilson on their jerseys during the 2003–04 season and playoffs. The sweaters now stand as some of, if not *the* most important in the history of the franchise.

★ DANIEL ALFREDSSON ★

Trade rumours haunted his career almost since day one, and for more than 1,100 games Daniel Alfredsson remained loyal to Ottawa before leaving the team in 2013 for Detroit.

A sixth-round draft pick in 1994, Alfredsson performed right out of the gates, winning the Calder Trophy in the 1995–96 season and earning a rare All-Star Game berth for a first-year player. Following a fantastic sophomore campaign where he hit the 70-point mark, Alfredsson's third season was shortened due to contract disputes and an ankle injury. The trend of incomplete seasons continued for the rest of Alfie's career. In particular, the next three campaigns would see him lose at least 14 games to injury.

Despite this, Alfredsson became the unquestioned leader of the Senators, especially following the departure of Alexei Yashin. Alfie was named captain in 1999 and did not relinquish his leadership role until his departure. It is these jerseys – with the captain's "C" on the front, that are far and away the most desireable Daniel Alfredsson collectible.

Leading by example, Alfredsson has had at least 80 points four times, including a personal-best 103 points in 2005–06, and has twice hit the 40-goal plateau. Alfredsson's leadership was never more vibrant than in the 2007 Stanley Cup Playoffs, where he tallied 14 goals and 22 points in 20 games, leading the Senators all the way to the final series. In doing so, Alfie became the first European–born and bred player to captain a team to the finals.

SAN JOSE SHARKS

No one was sure what to expect when California was awarded a second go at hosting two NHL clubs; but the San Jose Sharks have established themselves in the face of adversity. Right out of the gate, the Sharks were a hit. Their teal jerseys were very different than what fans were used to seeing. The vicious shark logo, chomping through a hockey stick, was a hit, and apparel was snapped up quickly.

At the forefront of the new squad were what could best be described as castaways, with the likes of Jeff Hackett and Doug Wilson as featured players on the new team. Young Pat Falloon, fresh from the 1991 NHL Entry Draft, was anointed the team's first true "in demand player," but this lasted only a short time before he succumbed to pressure and faded into hockey oblivion. As their first decade wore on, the Sharks gradually improved, thanks in large part to smart drafting that yielded the likes of Evgeni Nabokov, Jeff Friesen, and, perhaps the team's most venerable player, Patrick Marleau. By the time the millennium rolled over, the Sharks had become a marquee attraction. Annual guides began to tout that the Sharks were Cup contenders, especially once Joe Thornton was acquired from the Bruins in one of the most shocking trades of the NHL's new era.

And yet, as good as the Sharks have been in the regular season, they've been haunted by a distinct inability to reach that final brass ring and advance to the Stanley Cup Finals. They've come close on several occasions, but whether it's rival Detroit or another hot Western Conference team in their way, the Sharks have not been able to get to the fourth and final round of the Stanley Cup Playoffs. As a result, playoff-friendly collectibles for the Sharks are few and (really) far between. Instead, the most unique piece of memorabilia associated with the Sharks comes from a game that never was.

As fans will recall, the NHL locked out its players in the summer of 1994 for a large part of the

forthcoming season. By the time an agreement between the league and its Players' Association was made, a reduced schedule meant that the planned All-Star Game in San Jose had to be cancelled. The Sharks would get a second opportunity to hold the All-Star Game later on, but the non-game had made its mark with a variety of souvenirs already available in retail outlets. The result was an instantly hot collectible in the form of the commemorative game puck. Theme pucks have long been an easy souvenir sale (samples of All-Star Game commemorative pucks exist from the 1980s), but nothing draws a crowd quite like an item that isn't supposed to exist; and in this case a puck from an event that never happened drew huge demand immediately. Interest in the puck has slowed to the point where a larger lot of 1995 and 1996 All-Star Game pucks sold for just $100 in a Classic Collectibles November 2011 auction.

★ PATRICK MARLEAU ★

Patrick Marleau was, coincidentally, chosen second overall by the San Jose Sharks in 1997 behind future team-mate Joe Thornton, and while he hasn't put up the same point totals,

it's arguable that he has been even more important to the franchise.

Marleau's pro career started right out of junior, and almost immediately he showed the signs of becoming a leader. Originally, he was an understudy to the likes of Owen Nolan and Mike Ricci, but he became Sharks captain before the end of the 2003–04 season. When the NHL resumed following the first lockout, Marleau was one of the emerging NHL superstars. Prior to the work stoppage, Marleau had not had a single 30-goal season. After, he's had six seasons tallying at least 30, including one 44-goal campaign in 2009–10. Marleau's play over the years has made him a popular choice

for Hockey Canada, which has made Patrick a regular on international tournament squads. Patrick owns a gold and silver from the World Championships to go along with a gold medal from the 2010 Olympics. He has also been a prominent figure for autograph seekers and more often than not is happy to oblige.

TAMPA BAY LIGHTNING

Almost every franchise created during the 1990s expansion has been to the Stanley Cup Finals; but of the five clubs, only one has a perfect record in the final series — the Tampa Bay Lightning.

Tampa was announced as an

NHL city prior to the 1991–92 season, but, as was the case with the Ottawa Senators, they took to the ice a year later. Per tradition, the Lightning put their team together via an expansion draft, but then also signed a variety of other NHLers.

Their first official night in the league, October 7, 1992, was quite memorable. The team upended the Chicago Blackhawks 7-3 on the strength of four goals by upstart scorer Chris Kontos. Kontos returned to his standard form (that being inconsistent play) in subsequent games, but the Lightning were looking like a playoff contender thanks to castaways like Daren Puppa and Brian Bradley. By season's end, however, the wheels fell off and Tampa missed postseason play. It was the beginning of a string of unsuccessful seasons that saw them make the playoffs only once in their first decade.

During this run, the Lightning quietly put together a solid team of prospects, thanks in large part to great drafting and trading. In fact, they put together one of the most fearsome frontlines of the era — Vincent Lecavalier, Brad Richards, and Marty St. Louis. By the time the 2002–03 season rolled around, the team's fortunes began to turn, and one year later, led by long-time veteran Dave Andreychuk, the Lightning put together a true Cinderella run to the Stanley Cup. The image of Andreychuk kissing Lord Stanley's mug, something he had been unable to do with powerhouse teams in Toronto and Detroit, is as memorable as anything seen in the last couple decades of NHL hockey.

When the 2004–05 NHL lockout concluded, the Lightning struggled and lost two of their key Cup cogs in Nikolai Khabibulin and Brad Richards. Since then, the team has been inconsistent as it has rebuilt and reshaped its corps, with Steven Stamkos and Viktor Hedman leading the new generation. At times now they look like Cup contenders, and at other times like draft lottery fodder. Nonetheless, the remarkable Cup run will never be forgotten, especially by fans who have since been able to share in the experience thanks to unique collectibles such as one produced by the Danbury Mint, which reproduced the miniature Stanley Cup given to players following the celebration with the authentic Lord Stanley's mug.

★ STEVEN STAMKOS ★

Before Steven Stamkos, the Tampa Bay Lightning had two first overall draft picks (Roman Hamrlik and Vinnie Lecavalier); but neither, nor anyone who will be drafted first overall by Tampa after Steven Stamkos (yes, I am making a very bold prediction), will be able to repeat the success of the blond-haired superstar who made the Lightning faithful forget that the team had even fallen from the glory of its 2004 Stanley Cup championship.

Stamkos came into NHL stardom at the exact right time. The

league was carrying one heck of a hangover after celebrating Sidney Crosby's Stanley Cup victory when the young Stamkos was coming off what many pundits saw as a disappointing rookie season. Rather than challenge for the Calder Trophy, Stamkos spent much of his freshman year on the bench, at times limited to as little as 10 minutes of ice time per game. One year later, Stamkos was showing the maturity and talent of men who had far more experience. That year he counted 51 goals, enough to tie Crosby for the league lead. He would follow that up with 45- and 60-goal seasons.

Stamkos's success brought endorsements, which included the cover of an EA Sports game and deals with both Nike and Tissot. Further evidence of his popularity came in the form of collector pursuit as his autograph grew in demand, and coveted rookie cards hit heights that had not been seen by a player on a southeastern U.S. team since . . . well . . . ever.

THE 30-TEAM
LEAGUE
★ ★ ★

The latest round of NHL expansion came with the introduction of four teams between 1998 and 2000. The spread of these clubs, in comparison to the early 1990s expansion, was a bit more unique. Rather than being primarily based in California and Florida, the new breed of NHL expansion teams were situated in Ohio, Minnesota, Georgia, and Tennessee, a wider variety of markets than the sun states.

Initially there were high hopes for all four markets. One was a no-brainer — the Minnesota Wild — while the Columbus Blue Jackets, the Nashville Predators, and the Atlanta Thashers were a bit more of a crapshoot, one that proved to already have holes by 2011, when the latter moved to Winnipeg. As the NHL grows into the 2010s, expansion talks are less vocal, and the chance for Quebec City, Hamilton, and Kansas City to gain squads seems more likely to come via relocation.

NASHVILLE PREDATORS

Long before the Predators first took to the Nashville ice, there were strong rumours that the New Jersey Devils would be moving to the southern U.S. metropolis.

And then they won the Stanley Cup.

As the story was told on June 8, 1995, in the *New York Times*, the city of Nashville, amid the construction of a 20,000-seat arena, was providing quite the lure for a team interested in switching cities. "Nashville has prepared a sweetheart offer to lure a team, including a $20 million relocation fee," said writer Richard Sandomir. But in the end, the Devils stayed put, and Nashville, already a rumoured NHL expansion destination, was promised a team if it sold 12,000 season tickets in advance of the 1998–99 season. And so the Predators were born.

Like most expansion franchises, the Preds were an on-ice bust. Their first appearance in the playoffs didn't come until the 2003–04 season. Nashville picked up some veterans like Cliff Ronning early in their run, but it was the emergence of homegrown talent like David Legwand and Martin Erat that brought the team maturity quickly.

When the NHL resumed play post-lockout in 2005–06, Nashville looked like a contender, posting a 100-point-plus season. Though unceremoniously dumped by the San Jose Sharks in the first round, the Preds served notice that they had arrived. One year later, with Shea Weber beginning to emerge and Peter Forsberg on board after a blockbuster trade, the Predators again made an early playoff exit to the Sharks. The story played out the same the following campaign — great regular season, terrible playoffs. Aside from a hiccup season where the Preds finished outside of post-season contention, the team continued its early exit trend until 2010–11, when they finally won a playoff series, defeating the Anaheim Ducks.

Throughout their history, the Preds have treated their fans to some of the top players in the modern era. To augment homegrown talents like Weber and Legwand, the team brought in the aforementioned Forsberg, Paul Kariya, and Tomas

Vokoun. The team has become stronger at the box office. Once pursued by Research In Motion co-founder and former co-CEO Jim Balsillie as a franchise to move to Hamilton, the Preds are now seeing sold-out crowds at home, something many never thought possible.

These accomplishments make the Predators' milestones that much more impressive. Whereas teams like the Cleveland Barons and Colorado Rockies made quick exits, the Preds have proven that hockey can sell in the heart of NASCAR country. As a result, the 10th anniversary patch that the Preds put on their jerseys is one of the more meaningful pieces of memorabilia available, either on its own or, better yet, attached to a game-worn sweater.

★ SHEA WEBER ★

When the 2005 World Junior Hockey Championship team for Canada was put together, there was a glut of stars on the roster that many expected to be leaders in the NHL. Players like Sidney Crosby, Ryan Getzlaf, Dion Phaneuf, and Andrew Ladd have already become the captains of their respective teams; but no player has proven to be a better leader than Nashville's captain, Shea Weber. Both in size and stature, the 6-foot-4 defender has one of the biggest physical presences on the ice. A lot of Weber's ability to stand out and be a leader can be attributed to the vast experience he's already had in his young career. Along with the 2005 World Junior squad and their gold medal performance, Weber won the CHL's Memorial Cup with the Kelowna Rockets and was part of the Milwaukee Admirals squad that made their way to the 2006 AHL Calder Cup Finals.

In 2006–07, his sophomore year in the league, Weber firmly established his position in the NHL as one of the bright prospects on defence. He played in the NHL Young Stars Game and finished the year with 40 points. Just a couple years later, Weber was an All-Star Game regular and was earning post-season First-Team All-Star berths regularly as well as Norris Trophy consideration. Weber has also become an international sensation, earning World Men's Hockey Championship and Olympic gold.

He also has one of the more . . . shall we say . . . unique collectibles on the market. While with the Milwaukee Admirals of the AHL (Nashville's farm team), Weber was immortalized on a giveaway night with a bobblehead figure; the catch, though, is that the jersey he's "wearing" is a flannel style, more akin to a Don Cherry suit jacket than a hockey sweater.

COLUMBUS BLUE JACKETS

Defining the history of some teams is straightforward — others, not so much. The Columbus Blue Jackets fall into the latter category. The Jackets have primarily been an afterthought, dismissed by pundits and fans as perennial losers that have yet to truly make an impact. For the most part, this assessment is correct.

Through the 2012–13 NHL season, the Jackets have only made one post-season appearance. The result is that the team has become the NHL's underdogs, a squad that even fans of rival teams hope to see in the playoffs.

The Jackets came to be officially

in 2000 but had actually been granted entry into the NHL in 1997. As the second NHL team to take up residency in Ohio (the first being the long-defunct Cleveland Barons), the Jackets began their first NHL campaign with castaway players picked up in that season's expansion draft. The team was a disaster from the start, despite the efforts of Ron Tugnutt, who tied a league record for the most wins by a goalie with an expansion franchise. In fact, outside of Rick Nash, the Jackets' success (as little as there has been) can almost be fully attributed to their netminders, a roll call that has also included Steve Mason and Sergei Bobrovsky. The lone year that the Jackets advanced in the playoffs, it was almost solely due to the work of Mason, then a freshman in the NHL.

Despite their lack of success, the Jackets have established a franchise that sits on fairly stable ground. While attendance is among the lowest in the league (80 percent of arena capacity in 2011–12, according to ESPN), they have established somewhat of a cult following as they have made efforts to encourage fans to keep coming through the turnstiles. One method the Jackets used in recent years was arena giveaways, a common practice

by many NHL teams. These promotions have included ceramic bobblehead dolls that pay tribute to star and/or favourite players. The Jackets also made a bobble of their mascot, Stinger.

You all remember Stinger, don't you? The fictional insect (resembling a yellow jacket)? For a long period,

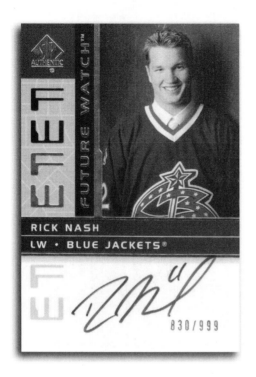

FUTURE WATCH

RICK NASH
LW · BLUE JACKETS®

830/999

Jackets who requested to be moved at the 2012 Trade Deadline (a request that wouldn't be fulfilled until the following summer), he was the revered face of the Columbus franchise.

A junior sensation, Nash made the immediate leap from draft podium to NHL ice. At one point, it had been more commonplace for a top pick to take the time in juniors and/or minors to further develop his skills; more recently though, the first overall selection has been found on his team's opening day roster. In this case, the Jackets were in desperate need of a boost for their struggling on-ice play. Yes, they had only been around for two years, but they were already quickly gaining the reputation of being a sad-sack franchise; plus, they needed that true superstar they could market.

Nash fit the bill. As a rookie, he tallied 39 points across 71 contests after becoming just the eighth first overall pick to score in his first NHL game. Nash was a Calder Trophy finalist that year, setting the stage for an incredible individual effort the following season, when he tied Jarome Iginla and Ilya Kovalchuk for the league lead in goals and a share of the Maurice Richard Trophy, with 41 tallies. Soon after, he became captain

the beloved character was more than just the team's mascot — he was also the subject of cresting on the team's jersey during their early years. Yes, the players looked odd at times with a cartoon insect on their chests, but there was a kitsch factor to the jerseys that appealed to many fans. After all, this wasn't a sweater designed for failure — it was a god's honest effort to have something different that reflected the region's heritage.

★ RICK NASH ★

Before Rick Nash was famously a disgruntled employee of the Blue of the Blue Jackets, and young fans took the opportunity to plaster their rooms with posters, stickers, and one of the more recent advents in bedroom collectibles, player-specific pennants, which actually have a pretty cool niche appeal.

Despite the lockout derailing Nash's momentum somewhat, he had six seasons of 30 goals or more in the next seven campaigns, including a streak of five straight years. Nash also hit the point-per-game clip twice. Unfortunately, Nash's talents couldn't propel the Jackets to the playoffs more than just once. Frustrations boiled over, but not before he wrote his name in the record books as the greatest player in Columbus's history.

MINNESOTA WILD

The state of Minnesota has one of the richest cultures in the history of hockey, and that culture has carried through to today's iteration of pro shinny — the Wild. Born in time for the 2000–01 season, the team filled a void left open by the departure of the North Stars after the 1992–93 season. The team took up residency in the Xcel Energy Centre and were an instant hit with fans who

DECEMBER 29, 2000 - FRI. 7:00 PM

| 217 | 6 | 18 |
| SEC. | ROW | SEAT |

VS. PHOENIX COYOTES
XCEL ENERGY CENTER - ST. PAUL, MN - GAME 20

had been starved for hockey since Norm Green uprooted the beloved franchise and took them to Dallas. The rebirth was nothing short of remarkable as the centre sold out immediately. On the ice, two seasons passed before the Wild had a taste of true playoff success (the 2002–03 season saw them reach the Western Conference Final).

Since those early days, the franchise's success can best be described as "up and down." They've seemed, at times, on the brink of being a true championship contender, then other nights have turned back into a bottom-feeder team of ragtags. In the Wild's entire run, they have been somewhat starved for a true hockey superstar. The biggest name to don the squad colours — red, white, and green, with hints of gold — was Marian Gaborik. Other standouts like Andrew Brunette, Niklas Backstrom, and Brent Burns have plied their trade on St. Paul ice, but none have reached the level of elite play that is more commonly seen on Broadway. Instead, the Wild franchise has been primarily composed of gifted grinders. Some, like Brian Rolston, are journeymen who seemed to not quite fit in with other NHL franchises. The team has also taken to native Minnesotans, the most notable of late being Matt Cullen.

As stated off the top, the Wild are far from the first to lay down roots in Minnesota. Its icy winters has fostered the game's popularity and helped build success at virtually every level of play. This has included the famed Minnesota Golden Gophers of the NCAA. The celebration of hockey's rich history has taken a few different forms with the Wild franchise and was first seen in their inaugural season ticket stubs. Rather than debut a flashy design that celebrated the state's return to hockey, the tickets instead had an old image of Minnesota boys in a team photo, stirring up a feeling not of the newness of the franchise, but rather of the tradition of the sport.

★ MARIAN GABORIK ★

Few draft picks make an immediate impact, but Marian Gaborik was different. Taken third overall by the Wild in their first-ever draft (2000), "Gabby" made his presence felt in his very first NHL game, scoring the first goal in Minnesota Wild history. He became the number-one player in Minny very quickly.

"After he made the team as an 18-year old, and then scored their first ever goal in team history, I was hooked on the kid," says radio host and card collector Curt Johnson.

"[I've been] collecting his cards ever since then."

Curt wasn't the only Gaborik collector by any stretch, and even a 2003-04 contract dispute didn't slow his popularity in the Twin Cities. In the 2005–06 season, Gaborik showed the type of form expected of a high draft pick. In the last four seasons of play in Minnesota, Gaborik played point-per-game hockey through seasons in which he accumulated an unfortunately large number of injuries (at one point he missed 65 games in a single season). Gaborik left the Wild after the 2008–09 campaign, settling in on Broadway with the New York Rangers. He left as the final member of the opening-night roster and the all-time leader in goals, assists, and points on the Wild and, inarguably, the biggest name ever to play for the squad. While with the Rangers, Gaborik maintained a strong scoring touch amid continued injury woes. In 2014, Gaborik moved to the Los Angeles Kings where he claimed his first Stanley Cup ring. He has also continued to be a national icon for Slovakia, donning his country's colours every opportunity he has had.

RELOCATION

★ ★ ★

Moving, for a pro sports franchise, is never the first option. A pro league admitting that a market can't sustain a team is not easy; but when revenues dry up and stands are vacant, at times there is no other option than to relocate to a more suitable city.

Usually these efforts are successes. Rarely does a team move from one city, then move again; more often they find a new permanent residence that is better suited for hosting the game. But failure in a market doesn't mean that a second go-around is impossible. This was the case in Colorado, Winnipeg, and Minnesota, and could very well be the case in Kansas City and Quebec City. (The exception that makes the rule here is the two-time failure of Atlanta.) In these relocations, a team finds a new life, and for the hobbyist, a new world opens up, with hundreds of new collectibles to pursue.

CALGARY FLAMES

Long before Winnipeg laid claim to the ruins of the Atlanta Thrashers, Calgary blazed a trail for northern relocation from Turnerland. Following the 1979–80 season, the Atlanta Flames franchise moved to Cowtown under Nelson Skalbania, better known in hockey circles as the man who brought Wayne Gretzky to Edmonton. The team retained much of the spirit of the old squad, including its moniker and colour scheme, and was an instant hit, unlike the previous pro hockey team in Calgary, the WHA's Cowboys.

On the strength of Kent Nilsson's stick, the Flames immediately made an impact in their new surroundings, progressing all the way to the Campbell Conference Finals and a date with the Minnesota North Stars. This was as close as they came to Lord Stanley's mug for a number of years, thanks to the emergence of their cross-province rivals, the Edmonton Oilers. That's not to say that the Flames played second fiddle in Alberta. The squad was really well stacked, with the likes of Lanny McDonald, Al MacInnis, Joel Otto, and Rejean Lemelin. So impressive were they that in 1986, the Flames were able to advance to the Stanley Cup Finals against Montreal (albeit with the help of an errant Steve Smith pass) before falling at the hands of young prospect Patrick Roy. After that memorable year, the Flames continued to be a threat and added to their depth. Through drafting and trades, the team brought Joe Nieuwendyk, Doug Gilmour, Mike Vernon, and Theo Fleury on board, leading to a memorable return Cup series against the Habs in 1989. This time, the Flames were ready and took home Lord Stanley's mug.

Those were the glory years for the franchise, before the Canadian dollar tanked and the team became a veritable wasteland. Yes, they remained competitive to an extent, primarily through smart trading that brought Jarome Iginla to the squad, but they were a shell of their former selves when games mattered most — in the playoffs. The squad at times seemed directionless, especially when they underwent a facelift, changing their jerseys from the traditional striping to one that featured a diagonal pointing to the big flaming C logo. The team also almost relocated toward the end of the decade.

As the new millennium began, however, a spark ignited. Iginla was developing into one of the NHL's great leaders and with Darryl Sutter behind the bench, the payoff came in 2003–04. The Flames, who had recently added Miikka Kiprusoff in goal, charged to the Stanley Cup Finals. The support was incredible, as thousands of fans poured onto what became known as the Red Mile, decked out in a redesigned, primarily red Flames jersey with a black C as the chest emblem. Unfortunately, the team bowed out to the upstart Tampa Bay Lightning in the finals.

Since the lockout, Calgary has been somewhat enigmatic, at times seeming on the cusp of greatness but having immense trouble getting any forward momentum, especially come playoffs; regardless, the team sits as one of only four active Canadian teams to hold Lord Stanley's mug aloft, and not surprisingly, it is the souvenirs of that 1989 championship that resonate the most with hobbyists. But what really ignited the Flames (pardon the pun) more than any movement was a simple hockey sweater. The club had experimented with third jerseys a couple times prior, including the unique horsehead tog, but it was that Red Mile jersey — the deep-red version of its standard jersey with a black flaming C logo — that really caught on, so much so that when the team went to the 2004 Finals, the Saddledome became a sea of red with fans wearing the famed sweater in every part of the arena.

★ JAROME IGINLA ★

"Iggy" was originally a first-round pick of the Dallas Stars, highly touted for play that resulted in his Kamloops Blazers winning back-to-back Memorial Cups; but the need to move Joe Nieuwendyk brought Iginla to Calgary, something one wouldn't expect to work for an Edmontonian. Iginla made his debut in the 1995–96 playoffs, tallying two points — including a goal — in two contests. One year later, he was a full-time Flame, putting up 50 points in his rookie campaign.

Quickly, Iginla soared to the top of collector want lists, even amid a dismal sophomore campaign. Following that forgettable year, Iginla went on a 13-season tear (through 2011–12), scoring at least 20 goals a year. The stretch, one of the longest in the NHL, is highlighted by two

50-goal seasons and two Maurice Richard Trophy wins. His consistency led him to become one of a select few players whose prime was in the Dead Puck Era to join the 500-goal club. He would also win the Art Ross Trophy and the Lester B. Pearson Award in 2002, the King Clancy Trophy and the NHL Foundation Player Award in 2004, and the Mark Messier Leadership Award in 2009.

Iginla was named the captain of the Flames in 2003–04, and even though he was traded during the 2012–13 season (and later signed with the Boston Bruins), Iginla has staked his claim as one of the best Flames of all time, one validated when he became the team's all-time points leader in 2009. Sherwood later produced a commemorative puck in honour of the accomplishment.

Carolina Hurricanes 2008-09 Season Schedule

CAROLINA HURRICANES

At the end of the 1996–97 season, the Hartford Whalers joined their WHA brethren — the Quebec Nordiques and the Winnipeg Jets — in hockey's history books. The team moved to become the newest southern U.S. franchise.

And so were born the Carolina Hurricanes. Decked out in a pretty snazzy jersey and boasting a fairly good lineup, the Canes were a hit in the NHL — well, except on home ice. The team arrived to a not-so-subtle sentiment of indifference. The region, after all, is collegiate country. Any desire to see professional sport was tided over by the NBA and NFL, and fans were slow to warm up to a sport that was played on ice.

Eventually, the Canes did win over those fans. Yes, it took more time than it probably should have for the citizens to adapt to their new team, and heavily critical NHL fans cried for the Canes to be dealt the same fate as other failed U.S. experiments like Cleveland and Oakland; but the Canes now sit as the NHL's most unique franchise to ever lay claim to Lord Stanley's mug. Following the return of the NHL after the 2004–05 lockout, the Hurricanes found themselves in a very enviable spot with a solid lineup. Captain Rod Brind'Amour was recognized in league circles as one of hockey's premier leaders, and the Canes also had the fantastic young phenom Eric Staal and well-travelled veteran Mark Recchi in their midst. Oh yeah, and they also had one heck of a young upstart goaltender — Cam Ward. Ward, at first glance, was not expected to be the most successful rookie in the 2005–06 season, which featured a double cohort of fresh faces thanks to the previous year's lockout; yet it was not Sidney Crosby, Alex Ovechkin, Mike Richards, or Dion Phaneuf who outlasted all others. It was Ward who not only took part in the victory but was also the recipient of the Conn Smythe Trophy as playoff MVP.

Since that victory, the Canes have suffered through some lean years, but they are still a threat on any given night while fans reminisce about that amazing run in 2006. Several commemorative products were created following the victory, including a 24-karat gold coin issued by the Highland Mint, one of the leading North American companies when it comes to valued, high-quality memorabilia pieces.

★ RON FRANCIS ★

Ronnie Francis's best days were already behind him when the Canes (re-)acquired the former leader of the Whalers, but his return to

the organization that made him a household name was greatly anticipated. Francis was an extraordinary talent who by all accounts has never received the acclaim he rightfully deserves. He was the lifeblood of Hartford hockey, and when he was dealt to the Pittsburgh Penguins in 1991, it was the first nail in the team's coffin. Francis helped the Pens win two Stanley Cups and cement his own legacy by winning the Selke Trophy and Lady Byng Trophy (twice) during this period.

Flash-forward to his return to the Whalers/Hurricanes franchise. Whereas he was once the plucky, budding superstar, Francis was now in a senior role with the club, mentoring a team that was young and full of energy. In 2002, he was the key cog in a run to the Stanley Cup Finals, an improbable trek by every account. That same year, Francis received both the Lady Byng and the King Clancy Trophy.

When it was all said and done, Francis ranked as one of the NHL's most elite players. Just as Mike Gartner had with his goal totals, Ronnie Franchise quietly put together a remarkable point total that, as of the summer of 2013, ranked him fourth on the NHL's all-time list. He was also third in games played and a member in both the 500-goal club and the NHL's Hockey Hall of Fame.

As one would expect, Francis's number was retired by the Hurricanes soon after his retirement from the game before the start of the 2005–06 season. On January 28, 2006, his famed No. 10 was raised to the rafters, with fans in attendance getting a keepsake replica of the banner for their own collections.

COLORADO AVALANCHE

When historians look back at the history of the Avalanche, they'll usually say that Joe Sakic was the franchise's most valuable player; and with good reason, since he was the foundation of their multiple Stanley Cup victories and the team has been a shell of its former self since his retirement. But the real most valuable player may be a guy who never even wore the team's jersey — Eric Lindros. You may remember "The Big E." Drafted in 1991 by the Quebec Nordiques, Lindros refused to suit up, going so far as to refuse to don their jersey at the Draft. Eventually, Lindros was dealt, and the players the Nords received in return became the building blocks for the franchise's Stanley Cup run. Let's play Six Degrees of the Stanley Cup, the 1995–96 edition.

In exchange for Lindros, the team received:

- Peter Forsberg, Mike Ricci, and Chris Simon, who would be part of that winning team

- Ron Hextall, whose trade path ended up with the draft selection of Adam Deadmarsh

- Kerry Huffman, who ended up being a dead-end as a waiver claim

- Steve Duchesne, who later

would be a part of the trade that brought Wendel Clark (and Cup team D-man Sylvain Lefebvre) to Quebec (Clark would later be dealt for Claude Lemieux)

- 1993 First Round Draft Pick Jocelyn Thibault, who ended up traded for Patrick Roy

- 1994 First Round Draft Pick (later sent to the Washington Capitals who used it to select Nolan Baumgartner)

- $15 million in cash

So as you can see, Lindros, in a detached sense, did more to bring a Cup to the recently imported franchise than anyone; but in the grander scheme of things, the Avs have been among if not *the* outright best traders in recent NHL history. Yes, they have a lot of homegrown talent in their history, but the Avs/Nordiques franchise also procured a strong number of all-time great players for their various Stanley Cup runs. Along with the players listed above were immeasurably large names like Ray Bourque and Rob Blake.

Throughout their NHL tenure, the Avalanche has continued to be one of the league's most robust teams. The Avs have become a darling of the NHL through smart executive decisions and strong player development. Names like Milan Hejduk, Alex Tanguay, Matt Duchene, Paul Stastny, and a host of others started their careers — or played their entire tenure — in Colorado.

As a team, the Avs have been fun to collect, in large part because of the players they have had. Even diehard hockey centres like Montreal and Boston who've had trouble accepting collectibles of their players in any other team colours will take interest in Patrick Roy and Ray Bourque in their Avalanche unis. Add to this another factor — the very look of the Avalanche jersey, especially the pre-lockout version, has struck a chord with collectors. The unique combination of maroon, blue, silver, and white really jumps out among the NHL jerseys.

The Avs have also done a remarkable job in recognition of the fans' desire to be as close to the action as possible, and there's no better example of this than that 1996 Stanley Cup win. Following the finals, the Avalanche offered its faithful a unique prize, a "Slice of the Ice." Encased in a commemorative puck holder is a clear plastic puck containing melted ice from the McNichols Sports Arena, which was skated on during the Stanley Cup Finals. This, by the way, preceded game-used jerseys being cut up for use in cards, where you more commonly find materials of this nature Though this unique piece has somewhat faded from collector consciousness, it stands as one of the most intriguing collectibles ever offered.

★ JOE SAKIC ★

Known as "Burnaby Joe," Joe Sakic was the heart and soul of the Quebec/Colorado franchise and continues to be its marquee name to this day. Plucked from his junior club, the WHL's Swift Current Broncos, Sakic arrived in the NHL during the 1989–90 season and immediately showed he belonged in the big leagues. In his first year he tallied more than 70 points, and he followed this with two consecutive 100-plus point seasons. In those early years, Sakic was somewhat overshadowed, particularly amid all the talk of Eric Lindros and the other two first-overall picks on his team (Owen Nolan and Mats Sundin). Sakic responded admirably and with pure class in those early years as he developed into a leader in Quebec. His patience paid off in spades, and he went on become one of the NHL's premier players and, in Colorado, one of its most dominant leaders.

Often compared with Steve Yzerman, Sakic was at the helm of the Avs' Cup runs in 1996 and 2001. It was in the latter victory that Sakic showed his true colours when, instead of hoisting the Cup himself for the first time among his teammates, he passed it straight to Ray Bourque.

Sakic's career total of 1,641 points ranked him ninth on the all-time list (as of the end of the 2013–14 season). He is also a member of the 600-goal and 1,000-assist clubs, holds virtually every Avalanche/Nordiques record, has won the Conn Smythe, Hart, Lady Byng, and Lester B. Pearson awards, and is undoubtedly the greatest player to ever suit up for the franchise. Thus it's not a surprise that his retirement was closely followed by his famous

▲ JON WALDMAN

jersey number (19) being raised to the rafters. Fans in attendance that night got to take home replica banners as a souvenir of the event.

DALLAS STARS

One of the most controversial teams in NHL history, the Dallas Stars were born as franchise owner Norm Green transferred the beloved Minnesota North Stars from the Midwestern U.S. and brought them deep into the heart

DALLAS STARS

**INAUGURAL YEAR
1993-94**

of the Lonestar State — ripping out the hearts of thousands of rabid hockey fans in the process. In the Texas capital, the Stars found a surprisingly hot fanbase who quickly re-embraced pro hockey (the Houston Aeros, now an AHL team, had once been a WHA squad), finding their niche in the middle of a population obsessed with football.

The summit for the Stars came in 1999, when the superstar-laden team put together an unforgettable run to the championship. Remember — this was right smack in the middle of a period when Western Conference rivals the Colorado Avalanche and Detroit Red Wings were also peaking and had already won Cups themselves. Expectations for Dallas, thanks in part to recent acquisitions Ed Belfour and Brett Hull, were huge to say the least. In the final series of that magical year, Dallas squared off against the Buffalo Sabres. It was the showdown of two former Chicago Blackhawk netminders — Belfour versus Dominik Hasek.

The series went six games and

ended — with controversy — in overtime. Right at the peak of the "in the crease" rule era, when a skater was for all intents and purposes forbidden from entering the opposing netminder's blue-painted zone, Hull potted the Stanley Cup–winning goal with his foot clearly in Hasek's space. Buffalo erupted in anger and pleaded its case, but it was too late — the Stanley Cup celebration was on. Dallas, one of the most unlikely cities to even have an NHL team, was going to host a Stanley Cup parade.

One year later, Dallas found itself back in the Cup Finals against the New Jersey Devils. Good fortune was not on their side this time, however, as the Jersey boys took the championship handily. Dallas remained a Cup contender for the next couple years but failed to pass the resurging Avs and Red Wings, who were the champions of the West (and indeed the Cup winners). The time for Dallas to rank as an elite NHL club was drawing to a close. By the time the NHL resumed play in 2005–06 following a year-long lockout, the Stars were a shell of their former selves. Dallas quickly became a team who challenged for a playoff spot rather than a championship. The team went on a four-year streak of not making the playoffs in and around the departures of Mike Modano, Marty Turco, and other longtime heroes, as they struggled to find new leaders to take their places.

In these more recent tumultuous times, the Stars have gone through bankruptcy protection and ownership changes, much like other teams in the southern U.S. expansion/transfer. Despite this, the Stars continue to be one of the most talked-about teams night in and night out on NHL broadcasts. And after all these years, the Stars' original departure from the Land of 10,000 Lakes is still, perhaps, the most talked-about part of their legacy. The team is still heckled when they come to the Xcel Energy Center for road games, and likely will be for the remainder of their days. As such, inaugural-season collectibles from the Stars have both their fans and detractors. Among those first-year items was a simple, somewhat innocuous item — a lapel pin that still attracts attention when it goes up for sale online (though it's safe to assume this purchase is not made by Minnesota fans, unless there's an effigy being planned).

★ MIKE MODANO ★

Even before they became true Cup contenders, the Stars were able to hang their hats on American hero Mike Modano. The first overall pick in the 1988 NHL Entry Draft was the face of the Dallas franchise. A former standout with the WHL's Prince Albert Raiders, Modano tallied 75 points in 80 games in his rookie year with the North Stars. Similar debut success happened for Modano in his first year in Dallas as he hit the 50-goal mark for the first and only time in his career. He continued to be a strong scorer, adding six seasons of more than 30 goals and six seasons of more than 80 points following that first Dallas season. Off the ice, Modano was a true rockstar personality, even before he married singer and TV personality Willa Ford (they announced their divorced in 2012). He is a strong advocate for abused children, starting a foundation bearing his name to help various charities across the area.

Modano's peak came in the 1999 Stanley Cup pursuit. He was in a state of unbridled determination, and raising Lord Stanley's mug high above his head was the moment of vindication that silenced critics who thought that the closest he would ever come to the championship was in 1991 as a member of the Minnesota North Stars. The moment was reproduced later by McFarlane Toys, who created a limited figurine of Modano holding the Stanley Cup and sold it exclusively to attendees of the NHL All-Star Game Fanfest hosted by Dallas in 2007.

Amazingly, it took Modano until 2003 to wear the C for the Stars, but the time he spent as official on-ice leader was less than memorable. Shortly after the C was transferred to Brendan Morrow, Modano reached a major career summit, tallying the 500th goal of his career and soon after surpassing Joe Mullen to become the all-time leading scorer among American-born players. Modano spent a couple more years in Dallas before ultimately ending his career with rival Detroit. With his departure imminent, Modano skated for the last time on Dallas ice as a member of the Stars on April 10, 2010. The game, fittingly, was against the Minnesota Wild, and in this last game, Modano was named the first star, taking his victory lap adorned in North Stars gear.

NEW JERSEY DEVILS

Who knew Mickey Mouse was so powerful?

During the 1983–84 season, Wayne Gretzky and his dominant Edmonton Oilers took the floundering Devils behind the woodshed in a 13–4 drubbing. Following the game, The Great One famously derided the inferior organization: "Well, it's time they got their act together, folks. They're ruining the whole league. They had better stop running a Mickey Mouse organization and put somebody on ice," Gretzky said. It was a sobering assessment and, unfortunately, true. Up until that point (and even for a couple years afterward), the New Jersey Devils franchise had been horrible, the team at times seemingly playing without motivation; but as you'll soon see, things turned around big-time for the franchise in the 1990s.

The Devils' history began in the 1970s in Kansas City. Playing out of the Kemper Arena, the Scouts survived two years before relocating to Colorado to become the Rockies. Neither team was able to truly put together a decent run as playoff hockey eluded the franchise for the

most part. In the works for a couple of seasons, the move to New Jersey finally took place in 1982, but the team kept up the losing tradition it had established. It wasn't until the 1987–88 season, in fact, that the club made the playoffs. By that time, it had built up a solid core, with names like Pat Verbeek and John MacLean leading the way. This season also saw the debut of Brendan Shanahan, who indirectly led the increasingly powerful team to the promised land. Following the 1990–91 season,

Shanahan, a restricted free agent, signed on with the St. Louis Blues. Already owing draft picks to other teams, the Blues were unable to meet the requirements set out by the NHL in acquiring a player with RFA status from another club. As a result, the team had to send one of its active players to the Devils — and so they acquired Scott Stevens.

The acquisition was one part of what had been a long-term build by the club. In a slow progression, the Devils quietly amassed a team that became a legitimate Cup contender, primarily through smart drafting. In consecutive years, Jersey took Martin Brodeur and Scott Niedermayer in the first round of the NHL Entry Draft (1990 and 1991 respectively), while long-time veteran leadership was being established by home-grown players like Ken Daneyko. Stevens became the linchpin for the franchise, and with a solid defensive corps that included Niedermayer, Daneyko, and Brodeur between the pipes, the Devils advanced to the finals in 1994–95, defeating the powerful Detroit Red Wings for the Stanley Cup. It was the only time that the two clubs met in the finals during the 10-year period that the two teams dominated the Cup scene (only twice during that span did two teams other than the Devils and Wings battle for the championship).

The Devils' first Cup victory was dismissed by much of the league's fanbase, who saw their defensive play, which included the infamous "neutral zone trap," as boring; but you can't deny their success, which also garnered Cup victories in 2000 and 2002. Amid those latter years, the team added more of a scoring touch, bringing on firepower in the form of Patrik Elias, among others.

After the NHL lockout, the Devils bounced into a "pretender" role, never seeming to be able to put themselves together enough to make a serious run; but they remain one of those teams that always seems to pop up in championship conversations, and rightfully so. Quietly, and unsuspectingly, the Devils showed that, despite having a new cast of characters like Zach Parise and Adam Henrique, they were still one of the top teams to contend with, and in 2011–12 they battled through three series as underdogs and made yet another Stanley Cup Finals appearance, this time against the Los Angeles Kings. Coming up short in this series meant nothing long-term — the Devils once again solidified their position in today's shinny world.

Not surprisingly, with three Cup wins under their belts and two other finals appearances, the Devils have plenty of Stanley Cup gear to go around, the most important of which, naturally, are Cup rings that have popped up on the secondary market a few times through auction houses.

★ MARTIN BRODEUR ★

For most players, having a trading card that served as a painful reminder of the awkward years of bad teen-aged moustaches would be something they'd rather forget; but that's not the case for Brodeur. "It's somewhat of a dream come true — when you're young and hope to see your first hockey card," Brodeur says.

That first card for Brodeur was in the 1990–91 Score series. Unlike many players in that first year of the card industry's "boom" era, it is the only rookie Brodeur has. Since then, Brodeur has been featured on just about every type of memorabilia available. Pucks, posters, growth charts — you name it. The enjoyment that Brodeur has of seeing his cards or other collectibles is matched by his offspring. "I have four kids and they enjoy seeing me as a figurine," Brodeur said with a laugh in 2003.

That time in Brodeur's career was an interesting one to say the least. He had not yet earned a Vezina Trophy but was well on his way to making the case for being labelled the greatest goalie in NHL history. Some even said he was better than his idol, Patrick Roy. Three Stanley Cup wins and a pace to overtake Terry Sawchuk for the seemingly untouchable shutout record would do that.

At this point in 2003, Brodeur was still spry, with only a decade of full-time NHL hockey under his belt. Amid an NHL conference call with media, he was asked by Pierre LeBrun (then of the Canadian Press) about the possibility of pulling off an even rarer feat than holding an NHL record — staying with one team for his entire career. "It's something really hard to do these days with all the young guys coming in and free agency. Being a Devil all my career is something I would like to happen." Fast-forward to 2013, and it looks as though Brodeur's wish will be granted. He has cemented a legacy that includes four Vezinas, the Calder Memorial Trophy, Olympic and World Cup championships, three Stanley Cups and 16 NHL records, including both the titles of "most wins" and "most shutouts."

PHOENIX COYOTES

Informally, the Coyotes are known as the Desert Dogs, but at times it

since 1996–97, the Coyotes were a franchise that seemed one or two pieces away from having a serious Stanley Cup contender. Names like Jeremy Roenick, Keith Tkachuk, Mike Gartner, and Shane Doan helped bring the Coyotes success on the ice in the regular season. They also housed some exciting prospects in those early years, including emerging goalie sensation Nikolai Khabibulin and dangerous forward Danny Briere. Through their first six seasons, the Coyotes made the playoffs five times; but the 2002–03 season saw the team fall apart and commence a six-year run of the Yotes not making the post-season, which only served to further fan apathy. By the time the run was done, the Coyotes were under league control.

The playoff-starved years for the Coyotes were seasons that did not have much in terms of star power on the ice. The organization's most prominent name was their one-time team owner, Wayne Gretzky, who also served as the team's head coach for a period following the NHL lockout; but, like superstars before him, Gretz was unable to make a successful transition behind the bench and later left the Coyotes while being owed millions of dollars.

feels more like the team should be known as the "Deserted Dogs." The Coyotes, in recent years, have been one of if not *the* financially weakest NHL clubs. They were owned by the NHL while a long, drawn-out, and dramatic search for new backing took place. Ticket sales for the club were slow, save for when snowbirding Canadians ventured to Glendale.

That's not to say that the Coyotes have had a poor product on the ice. For many of their seasons

Ultimately it was Dave Tippett who guided the Coyotes back to the post-season. In each of his first three years behind the bench, the Coyotes made it into the playoffs, and for the first time in the desert, they won a playoff series in 2011–12 and later advanced to the Conference Finals, a first for the entire 30-plus years of the Winnipeg/Phoenix franchise in the NHL.

The Coyotes' popularity in the hobby, as a collective, has been just as mixed as their on-ice performance. Aforementioned superstars aside, the perilous club has had trouble finding its niche in the collector market. Part of that discomfort can be attributed to their first jersey, which had a very non-traditional look for hockey, incorporating logos that seemed at times more likely to be seen in a Picasso art exhibit than in an NHL arena. Today, those jerseys do have a certain cachet and have gained a measure of popularity in aftermarket auction houses.

In addition to those jerseys, Coyote fans have also been treated to some unique collectibles as incentives to drive people into the often-empty arena seats. Around the time that Brett Hull signed with the Coyotes, father Bobby was part of a giveaway of mini McFarlane figurines (wearing the uniform of the Winnipeg Jets, naturally). Free T-shirt promos were also a regular at the games. But the pièce de résistance came during the 2011–12 season, when the Coyotes, in a somewhat puzzling move, chose to partner up with Alice Cooper for a bobblehead promotion. The figures proved to be a hit on eBay in the weeks following the giveaway as rock 'n' roll hit the ice in a big way.

★ SHANE DOAN ★

The last remaining tie to the Winnipeg Jets franchise is Shane Doan, who was mentored by two of hockey's great power forwards — Keith Tkachuk and Jeremy Roenick — something many young leaders go without as they progress in their careers (or, more accurately, don't progress). Doan's career was highlighted by nine consecutive seasons with at least 20 goals, levels that were akin to another Coyotes alumn, Mike Gartner. Doan has amassed six seasons of at least 60 points, participated in two NHL All-Star Games, and won the King Clancy Memorial Trophy in 2010. All this has come during a tenure when his leadership of the Coyotes was never in doubt, and his dedication to the franchise — even amidst its ownership turmoil — never waivered.

Doan's career has also prominently featured time with Canada's international program as he's been both an Olympian and a five-time medallist with the World Senior Men's team (three silvers, two golds). It was unfortunately during this time that Doan caused a bit of a national uproar, thanks to an alleged racial slur against a francophone referee during an NHL game. Many in politics felt that because of the incident, Doan wasn't a proper representative to be part of the team, let alone be in a leadership role as he was in some World tourneys.

Ultimately, Doan is the face of the Coyotes franchise and as its longest-serving athlete has endeared himself to the Phoenix faithful. It's not surprising, thus, that he is extremely in demand by autograph seekers, and thankfully they have a number of options of photos to get signed by Doan, including highlight moments from his time with the Coyotes (such as a cool locker-room picture of him holding three pucks from a hat trick) and raising the World Cup of Hockey trophy in celebration.

WINNIPEG JETS

For 15 years, the good people of Winnipeg waited. Year in and year out, the city whose beloved Jets left for Phoenix in 1996 was taunted by rumours of the big league returning to the Manitoba capital. They bided their time by showing phenomenal support for the IHL/AHL's Manitoba Moose and playing favourable host to the 1999 World Junior Hockey Championships and the 2007 Women's World Hockey Championships. Truly, Winnipeg was branding itself as a hockey haven and certainly made itself an attractive option for those teams that were rumoured to want to make the move, including, at various junctures, the Florida Panthers, the Pittsburgh Penguins, and the Nashville Predators.

But the strongest relocation rumours came, ironically, from Phoenix. The Coyotes were deep in financial trouble for years, eventually filing for bankruptcy under the ownership of Jerry Moyes. The team was owned by the NHL when, during the 2010–11 season, a number of groups — including Winnipeg's True North Sports and Entertainment — made their voices

◄ MICHAEL COODIN

of interest heard. The original Jets came painfully close to coming home before the NHL brass decided to hold the Coyotes in Phoenix for one more season while they found a new ownership group — one that would keep the team in the desert.

"We literally came within 10 minutes of acquiring [the Coyotes] in May 2010 when the City of Glendale met a 5 p.m. Eastern Standard Time deadline to wire the funds necessary to pay for the league's losses for the [2010–11] season," Mark Chipman told the Winnipeg Chamber of Commerce in June 2011. "We left somewhat disappointed but uplifted by the fact that the league had taken us so seriously and, as a consequence, had indicated it would just be a matter of time before we would actually acquire a team."

That "matter of time" assessment proved to be truer than anyone would anticipate. Prior to the Coyotes sale talk starting, there had been rumour that the Atlanta Thrashers could be on the move as well, and that Winnipeg could be a likely destination. Soon after the

Coyotes were confirmed to stay in Phoenix for another year, reporter Stephen Brunt announced in the *Globe and Mail* that True North had purchased the Atlanta franchise and was relocating the team to Winnipeg.

The rather informal announcement touched off an instant celebration on May 19, 2011 — one that was only superseded on May 31, when official word came: the NHL was coming back to Winnipeg.

There was only one problem — no one knew what the team would be called. Several names, ranging

from the Ice to the Falcons, were bandied about, but there was no official moniker attached to the franchise during the May 31 press conference. "The name has not been chosen," Chipman said during the presser. "[NHL commissioner] Gary [Bettman] was quite accurate when he said we worked right until the very early hours of this morning to conclude this transaction. We have been singularly focused on that effort for many weeks now."

Chipman himself had his own favourite. During a July 2011 interview, he revealed that he liked the name "Bears" for the new franchise, pointing to the polar bear as a symbol of prosperity for the province of Manitoba. And yet it seemed inevitable that only one name would be suitable, and that speculation was made official at the 2011 NHL Entry Draft, suitably hosted in St. Paul, Minnesota, close enough for Winnipeggers to make the cross-border drive.

"It's now my pleasure," Chipman said to the crowd at the Xcel Energy Center and to the thousands of Winnipeggers watching at the MTS Centre and in homes across the city, "to introduce our executive vice president and general manager,

Mr. Kevin Cheveldayoff, who will make our first pick, on behalf of the Winnipeg Jets."

Excitement grew in Winnipeg, and in the summer of 2011 the franchise also revealed the new logo as well as jerseys, hats, and T-shirts, all of which sold out in mere minutes at the team's official store at the MTS Centre. But if you really wanted to see memorabilia fly, then you had to be in attendance at the opening game. Ticket holders received commemorative versions of the valuable paper they held in their hands, and serial-numbered programs were available throughout the arena. The memorabilia craze continued through the season. Replicas of the first game tickets in bronze or silver were available, as were panoramic shots of the first puck drop. While the Jets failed to make the playoffs in their return campaign, it didn't seem like anyone cared. The MTS Centre was a madhouse as fans cheered the Jets and thoroughly booed their enemies. Creativity peaked in a battle against Washington, when Alex Ovechkin was taunted with a chant of "Crosby's better!"

Despite all of the memorabilia and memorable moments, nothing was quite as unique as a specially made beer. Dubbed "Fan Brew" by Budweiser, the unique concoction featured the usual ingredients that go into the tasty adult treat but also included water from a number of locations across the city, including the MTS Centre and the famed tourist location "The Forks."

★ ANDREW LADD ★

Two-time Stanley Cup champ Andrew Ladd was barely settled in as Thrashers captain when the announcement came that the team was relocating to Winnipeg. Still young in the NHL, Ladd, who previously had been with the Carolina Hurricanes and Chicago Blackhawks, was only six years into his career when he was all of a sudden thrust into the spotlight of a hockey-mad city. In a summer 2011 interview, he looked back on what had been a crazy ride. "It really happened quickly. There had been a little bit of talk throughout the year, but mostly it was about Phoenix and Winnipeg and didn't have anything to do with Atlanta," Ladd said, "but in a two-week span, it became 'Maybe it is Atlanta' and then all the sudden it was 'Okay, you guys are moving.' For us, it was really quick and it was kind of a shock for everyone in the organization."

But Ladd, who retained the C in Winnipeg and signed a five-year contract with the new Jets, was ready for the new challenge that lay ahead for him. In the first season in Winnipeg, Ladd tallied 28 goals and 50 points while being a spokesman for the team. He also knew the responsibilities that came with being not only an NHL captain but a player in general. "As hockey players, for us as a culture, I think we're one of the best sports in terms of how open we are with our fans, but it's a big thing for us to be part of the community and help out with charities," he said.

One of the charitable efforts Ladd has been involved in came on the Jets' opening night. While the festivities ruled on ice, Ladd and other Jets raised money for the families of KHL Lokomotiv plane crash victims by signing inaugural season pucks and selling them at the game.

HOT PLAYERS
IN THE HOBBY
★ ★ ★

Picking a single player to represent each NHL team meant that a lot of skilled athletes were kept off the list, including several notable Hall of Famers and up-and-coming prospects. Still, it's important to give these heroes their due. Here now are 50 of hockey's hottest players (past and present), starting with the man who may be not only the greatest goalie of all time but also one of the hobby's greatest ambassadors.

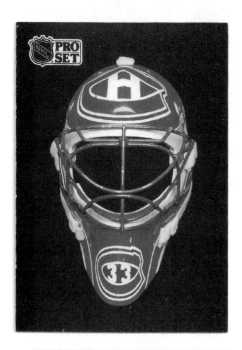

PATRICK ROY

Goaltenders are an interesting group of players. Today, they are among the players most hotly pursued by hobbyists, but for decades they were practically taken for granted. If you look back to the 1970s, for example, the players who you'd see get endorsements or appear on the side of table hockey games were forwards like Guy Lafleur or uberdefencemen like Bobby Orr. Sure, the Tony Espositos, Ken Drydens, and Billy Smiths of the world had their legions of fans, but they didn't have the marquee status that skaters had — well, at least not until Patrick Roy made waves in the hobby in the early 1990s.

Roy, of course, had already proven to be the new patron saint of Montreal. Hitting the NHL during the 1985–86 season, he not only debuted in the famed *bleu, blanc, et rouge* but guided the squad to Lord Stanley's Cup. Through the early part of his career, Roy practically owned the Jennings Trophy (best save percentage), sharing it with backups like Brian Hayward, and he was a multi-time Vezina Trophy winner.

But Roy's best times were inarguably in the playoffs, and just seven years after he won his first Cup and a few years removed from a stinging championship loss to the Calgary Flames, Roy was pitted against Wayne Gretzky in the post-season. Not since the days of Richard versus Sawchuk or Howe versus Plante had the marquee offence and defence squared off in such a legendary battle. To say that Roy was dominant would be an understatement, as he led the Habs to another Cup and his second Conn Smythe Trophy as playoff MVP. The win gave birth to Roy's superstardom. Almost overnight, Roy became a marquee name for the league and established his position as one that kids wanted to play. No longer were you the sacrificial lamb

— now you *wanted* to go between the pipes.

Who knew, however, that Roy's time in Montreal would soon draw to a close. A general decline in the team culminated on December 2, 1995, when they were thumped 11-1 by the Detroit Red Wings. Roy was kept in net for nine of the goals, an unheard-of number for any netminder. As soon as he was yanked, Roy scooted across the Habs bench and told team president Ronald Corey, "It's my last game in Montreal." Soon after, Roy was sent to Colorado, where he won two more Stanley Cups, including one in that same season.

In all, Roy's career saw him set numerous standards for the NHL. Upon retirement, he was the leader in career wins and games played by a goaltender. Though those marks would fall to Martin Brodeur, as of the 2011–12 season Roy still had the most career wins in the post-season and second-most playoff games of any player in any position. His three Conn Smythe trophies as playoff MVP are still the standard-bearer, rendering any argument for any other player to be considered the best playoff performer moot.

But Roy was more than just a great player — he is a collector too. Roy famously has a trading card stash of a mix of his own cardboard and those of his heroes. He also happily lent his name and signature to just about any company who wanted to do business with him or reproduce one of his two famous masks — the simple logo mask of the Habs or the beautiful mountain range visage of the Avs. He remained connected to the game following his career, first as an owner and coach in the CHL and later joining the Avalanche (alongside Joe Sakic) as head coach and vice-president of hockey operations.

BILL BARILKO

Bill Barilko's fame centres around one goal — one life-changing goal. It was the Cup winner in 1951, an overtime beauty past Montreal's Gerry McNeil. It would be the last of his career as Barilko went missing during a fishing trip and was pronounced dead when he could not be found. Eleven years later, Barilko's body was discovered and, coincidentally, that year was the first time the Leafs captured the Stanley Cup since his disappearance. The story became the stuff of legend,

especially thanks to The Tragically Hip, who wrote the hit song "Fifty Mission Cap" based on a 1991–92 Pro Set hockey card that commemorated Barilko and his famed goal.

BRIAN LEETCH

Hardly the bottom feeder that the sound of his name implies, Leetch was a marvel on the ice who captured the Norris Trophy twice and the Calder once, and took home the Conn Smythe as playoff MVP when the Rangers won their 1994 championship. He tallied four seasons of point-per-game shinny, something virtually unheard of for a modern-era defenceman. Leetch spent most of his career on Broadway, also suiting up in Toronto and Boston. Leetch was a popular defenceman for collectors in the early to mid-

'90s, and today one of the more distinguishable pieces is a Russian nesting doll in his likeness.

DALE HAWERCHUK

"Ducky" was the heart and soul of the Winnipeg Jets during the 1980s. A Calder Trophy winner, Hawerchuk carried the Jets to the biggest single-season turnaround in NHL history. Hawerchuk was so revered in Winnipeg that he was made president of the Junior Jets Fan Club, and as a result some unique collectibles exist. Hawerchuk eclipsed the 100-point plateau six times with the Jets before being traded to Buffalo in a blockbuster deal. Hawerchuk continued to be an offensive leader in Buffalo, scoring at above a point-per-game pace before finishing his career with St. Louis and Philadelphia.

led the Czech Republic to the gold medal. That same year, Hasek won his second-straight Hart Trophy as NHL MVP (to go along with his third and fourth Vezinas). By the time he was done in the NHL, Hasek also had two Stanley Cup rings. In the Starting Lineup craze of the '90s, Hasek was among the most desirable, partly due to the company being able to easily replicate his unique "helmet-and-cage" mask.

DREW DOUGHTY

A standout for Canada in underage international play, Drew Doughty was picked up by the Los Angeles Kings second overall in the 2008 NHL Entry Draft. Doughty was a (pleasant) surprise selection to the 2010 Winter Olympic team and was an integral part of his NHL team's run to the Stanley Cup in 2012 and 2014. The future looks very bright for this budding superstar, who is breaking through the collector barrier that usually shuns defencemen. For modern collectors, there are new sorts of memorabilia to pursue, such as a Fathead replaceable large sticker, like one of Doughty and the Stanley Cup.

DOMINIK HASEK

Drafted in 1983 by Chicago, Dominik Hasek didn't play in the NHL until 1990–91. He was somewhat vilified in North America in part due to the 1998 Winter Olympics, where he

EDDIE SHORE

Purchased by Art Ross after the collapse of the Western Hockey League, Eddie Shore immediately paid dividends for a still wet-behind-the-ears Bruins squad, tallying 18 points in just 40 games. Two years later, he was one of the centrepieces of the team that won the Stanley Cup. What makes him attractive to collectors, however, is less his offensive output and more so his toughness. Shore's career was highlighted by four Hart Trophies, the most of any player not named Gretzky or Howe. Wise fans back in the day would pursue Shore for his autograph, and today signed pucks by the Bruins legend can be found in online auction houses.

ERIC STAAL

At one point in the 2011–12 NHL season, Winnipeg Jets fans chanted, "Jordan's better!" at Eric Staal (Jordan being the second of the Staal brothers to reach the NHL). Rather than let the taunts throw him from his game, Staal feasted on them, tallying two goals that night and leading his team to victory. It was

just one example of Staal's prowess, which has seen him become an elite scorer in his young career, decorated with international gold and a Stanley Cup ring. Though it's more of a European pursuit, collectible pins have been created of NHLers, including Staal, whose Hurricanes jersey has been replicated.

EVGENI MALKIN

As of 2012, Malkin had two Art Ross, a Conn Smythe, and a Hart Trophy to his name, in addition to a Stanley Cup ring and World Championship gold medal. In 2012, Malkin was named the winner of the Kharlamov Trophy as the best Russian hockey player, and he remains a national hero who continues to make his name stronger each year in the NHL. Malkin is part of a new wave of young superstars who have taken

JON WALDMAN

the hobby by storm, and he has become a favourite for premium products like this McDonald's mini helmet.

GERRY CHEEVERS

It's hard to imagine what Gerry Cheevers would look like today if he had not worn a mask during his pro hockey career, but we get a good idea based on his legendary mask. Cheevers painted up the mask each time it took a ding from a puck. The result is one of if not *the* most iconic designs in hockey history (and most sought after as a replica or still print), fitting for one of the greatest goalies to play in both the NHL and WHA. Cheevers' career is highlighted by two Stanley Cup victories with the Bruins.

GRANT FUHR

The eighth overall pick in the 1981 NHL Entry Draft, Grant Fuhr started his career teaming up in

goal with Andy Moog. The tandem helped guide the Oilers to three Stanley Cups before Moog was dealt to Boston. Fuhr shone on his own, and in his first season as the unquestioned starting netminder, Fuhr played 75 of Edmonton's 80 games, winning 40 contests and tying nine others, a performance worthy of the Vezina Trophy. When it was all said and done, Fuhr had four Cup rings and more than 400 wins to his credit. Unquestionably, the most desirable Fuhr piece is a Starting Lineup figurine (goalies were and still are the most desirable pieces), which unfortunately didn't colour well.

GUY LAFLEUR

Guy Lafleur was an integral part of the Habs' 1970s dynasty. "The Flower" was famed for his end-to-end rushes, which showed his long blond hair flowing behind him as he dashed on his steel blades to pot yet another goal behind an opposing netminder. Lafleur won the Art Ross trophy three times, the Hart and Lester B. Pearson once apiece, and multiple Stanley Cups before first retiring in 1985. He would later return to the NHL before finally calling it quits with the Nordiques in 1991. Given that Lafleur's popularity came during the disco era, it's not surprising that his most unique collectible is a vinyl record.

HENRIK LUNDQVIST

"King Henrik" arrived in the NHL with the Rangers to much anticipation after originally being drafted in 2000 and spending five years honing his craft in the Swedish Elite League. The time playing against men proved valuable for Henrik Lundqvist's development, as he went on to have seven consecutive seasons of 30-plus wins to start his NHL career, a league record. Considered the sharpest dresser of all the NHL superstars, Lundqvist was named to *People Magazine*'s list of the world's 100 Most Beautiful People in 2006, and was the subject of a Duracell hockey mask keychain.

HOWIE MORENZ

Howie Morenz's status as one of the first superstars the NHL has resulted in sustained collector interest decades after he played his last game. Morenz was a three-time Cup champ and three-time Hart Trophy winner with the Habs and tallied 472 points in 550 NHL games, unheard-of stats for the era. His funeral at the Montreal Forum is still regarded as one of the saddest days in the city's sports history. Morenz is also the patriarch (in-law) of four generations of hockey players (his son-in-law is Bernie "Boom Boom" Geoffrion, who fathered Dan Geoffrion and was the grandfather of Blake Geoffrion). Morenz's fateful passing was later commemorated by the NHL in one of the first All-Star Games, with game-used pieces like jerseys popping up from time to time at auction.

ILYA KOVALCHUK

Ilya Kovalchuk was drafted first overall by the Thrashers in 2001 and immediately made the NHL sit up and take notice, collecting 29 goals in 65 games. He followed that performance with two 40-plus and two 50-plus-goal seasons in Atlanta before moving to New Jersey amid the 2009–10 season. There he gave the Devils new firepower, helping them reach the 2012 Stanley Cup Finals. Kovalchuk's dedication to his homeland of Russia was best seen after the Lokomotiv plane crash in 2011, when he was a leader in raising money for the players' families, giving out autographed photos in

exchange for a donation. Kovalchuk left the NHL in 2013 to return to Russia to finish his playing career.

JACQUES PLANTE

Jacques Plante is best remembered for bringing the mask into regular play in the NHL, but it was not his only innovation. As a junior, he was known for carrying the puck beyond his goal crease, essentially becoming a third defenceman. Plante's NHL career saw him backstop six Stanley Cups and earn six Vezinas and the Hart Trophy (one of only six goalies to do so). His play was primarily for the Habs, but he also suited up in Toronto, Boston, St. Louis, and Edmonton in the WHA. While Plante's mask is one of the most famed in hockey, aesthetically it doesn't measure up to others, which is possibly why

pictures of the netminder's face, like this glass, are in demand still.

JARI KURRI

One of the greatest players to cross the Atlantic, Finland's Jari Kurri was among the first European superstars. Playing alongside Wayne Gretzky and Mark Messier for most of his career, he was the benefactor of their generosity with the puck and as a result amassed point totals worthy

of his Hall of Fame induction. A five-time Stanley Cup champ, Kurri finished his NHL career as the highest-scoring European, eclipsing the 600-goal mark and finishing just shy of 1,400 points. Kurri's popularity and power on the ice made him a perennial NHL All-Star, and stickers like this O-Pee-Chee sample were heavily papered on lockers and albums.

JAROMIR JAGR

Drafted fifth overall by the Penguins in 1990, Jagr hit the ice hard in the 1990–91 season, making an early contribution to two consecutive Cup-winning squads. His stellar play made him an instant hit in the league, but it was the years following the 1994–95

NHL lockout when Jagr truly showed his dominance. Jagr won the Hart and Art Ross trophies in Pittsburgh and become the marquee name wherever he went, including the Kontinental Hockey League (KHL), where he moved for several years after the 2004–05 lockout. During his career in Pittsburgh, Jagr became a spokesperson for several companies and even earned his own brand of peanut butter.

JEAN BELIVEAU

"Le Gros Bill" (the nickname references a French folk hero) was already a legend in French Canada before he joined the NHL, choosing to start in the Quebec Senior Hockey League as a member, and leader, of the Quebec Aces before turning pro. Once in the NHL, Jean Beliveau showed remarkable maturity. He captained the Habs from 1961 to 1971, and won the Art Ross Trophy once and the Hart Trophy twice. His biggest accomplishment, by far, is his unheard-of 17 Stanley Cup rings as a player and executive with the fabled Montreal Canadiens. Beliveau's popularity meant that several magazines that featured him on the cover, such as *Sports Illustrated*, were saved and preserved.

JEREMY ROENICK

JR was an ambassador for American hockey unlike any other player in history. Jeremy Roenick was incredibly outspoken when it came to the game's speed, penalties, and rough play. He began his career in Chicago but had his most productive (and playoff-successful) seasons in the NHL and went on to raise his profile in Phoenix, where he was paired with fellow American Keith Tkachuk. Roenick also played in Philadelphia, L.A., and San Jose and joined the 500-goal club before hanging up his skates. Roenick's personality made him attractive to companies like 2k Sports, who made him the coverboy of one of their video games. Today, it's a niche collectible for JR fans.

JOHN TAVARES

Tavares was well acquainted with hobby folk long before he was drafted into the NHL. He broke single-season and career-goal scoring records in the Ontario Hockey League (OHL) and starred in international tournaments, including the Junior Summit Series and the World Junior Hockey Championships. The first overall pick in 2009 became the face of a struggling Islanders franchise battling an aging building and relocation rumours. Tavares tallied a goal and an assist in his first game and now regularly ranks among NHL scoring leaders. That first tally (or more specifically the celebration) was captured brilliantly, and today signed and framed pieces are highly pursued by collectors.

JOHNNY BOWER

The "China Wall" is the true face of durability in hockey. Johnny Bower soldiered through eight years in the American Hockey League before he got his first sniff of NHL action with the New York Rangers. After one season, however, he returned to the AHL before eventually coming back to the big league with the Maple Leafs. He paid dividends immediately with three straight 30-plus-win seasons and backstopped the Buds to four Stanley Cups. Remarkably, Bower, 89 at press time, is still taking time to meet fans and sign autographs and is one of the most popular figures in Toronto.

JONATHAN TOEWS

Born in Winnipeg, Manitoba, Jonathan Toews grew up with a backyard rink that he and his brother, David, spent endless hours on. "We always provided our boys with opportunities, whether it was for hockey or whatever," said father Bryan Toews. Jonathan was a star in the World Junior Championships and would go on to captain the Hawks to the Stanley Cup in 2010 (as well as 2013), earning the Conn Smythe in the process. He also won the Olympic gold medal the same year — an insanely rare feat. If there is any collectible of Toews that is the antithesis of his "Captain Serious" moniker, it's a bobblehead that was produced as an arena giveaway in Chicago.

KEN DRYDEN

Outside of the statue that stands in the Hockey Hall of Fame, there has never been a replication of Dryden's famed pose, leaning on his stick, primarily due to Dryden's overall reluctance toward the memorabilia world. The Habs goalie won four Vezinas, one Conn Smythe, and the Calder Trophy during his eight-season NHL career, along with six Stanley Cups. Post-hockey, Dryden became a noted author, executive, and broadcaster in hockey. Dryden has been a notoriously stingy signer, and as a result the few

certified autographs available, such as a Future Trends trading card, are highly coveted.

LANNY MCDONALD

Originally a member of the Toronto Maple Leafs, McDonald came to the Flames via the Colorado Rockies in a trade for Don Lever and Bob MacMillan. McDonald was much more than a moustache — he was a talented scorer who once scored 66

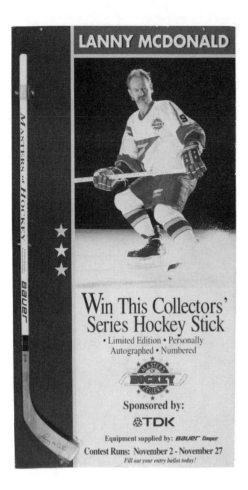

LANNY MCDONALD

Win This Collectors' Series Hockey Stick
• Limited Edition • Personally Autographed • Numbered

MASTERS OF HOCKEY • ZELLERS

Sponsored by:

⊕TDK

Equipment supplied by: *Bauer Cooper*

Contest Runs: November 2 - November 27
Fill out your entry ballot today!

times in a single season. As injuries mounted, however, the call of the Flames centred on getting Lanny the coveted Stanley Cup, a feat that he reached in his final NHL game in 1989. Following his career, Lanny remained closely tied to the NHL and the Flames as an ambassador and team official. Lanny's prowess and unmistakable persona led him to be included in several products, including the Zellers Masters of Hockey line of autographed memorabilia.

MARCEL DIONNE

Before Wayne Gretzky, Marcel Dionne was arguably the greatest player to ever don the colours of the Los Angeles Kings. Dionne began his career in Detroit but came over to the Kings in a trade. Playing alongside Charlie Simmer and Dave Taylor on the famed Triple Crown Line, Dionne won the Art Ross Trophy once, two Lady Byng trophies, and two Lester B. Pearson awards. Post-career, Dionne stayed involved in the game, working with fellow retired players through events and promotion. Dionne's Hall of Fame career has been tributed several times, most notably with a McFarlane Toys figurine which came as a result of his own working with the company on a group Legends deal.

MARTIN ST. LOUIS

Once an afterthought, Martin St. Louis now seems destined for the Hockey Hall of Fame. Undrafted, St. Louis signed his first pro contract with the Calgary Flames but starred with the Tampa Bay Lightning, where he won the Stanley Cup and several individual honours, including the Hart Trophy. He's also a collector to boot. "I remember a few years ago I was so excited seeing my first cards," St. Louis said. "I like to collect my stuff. I like to get one of each I see." He's not the only one who picks up Martin St. Louis cards, by the way.

MATS SUNDIN

The Nordiques selected Mats Sundin first overall in the 1989 NHL Entry Draft; but before long, he became highly coveted by the Maple Leafs, who made him the centrepiece in a large trade that sent Wendel Clark to Quebec. In short order, Sundin became a leader in Toronto. He picked up the captaincy from Doug Gilmour and proudly wore the C on his sweater until his departure in 2007–08, a letter he also carried in the 2006 Winter Olympics for gold medal–winning Sweden. Sundin became the face of the Leafs franchise and appeared on team promotional materials such as pocket schedules.

NICKLAS LIDSTROM

When Nicklas Lidstrom left the NHL following the 2011–12 season, he did so with as good a claim as any defenceman had to being the greatest in the history of the league. Mentored by Paul Coffey and Slava Fetisov, Lidstrom developed a signature style of truly being a two-way defenceman, which resulted in 1,142 points in his 1,500-plus-game career. Lidstrom also became the first European to captain a team to the Stanley Cup and spent his entire career in Detroit, a rare feat in today's NHL. Because of the ownership tie between the Red Wings and Little Caesars, the pizza chain has issued quite a few Red Wings collectibles, including a mini figurine of Lidstrom.

PATRICK KANE

The subject of an incidental cameo on a Pinnacle hockey card of Sylvain Turgeon when he was a youngster, Kane is one of the driving forces behind the revitalized Chicago Blackhawks. A Calder Trophy winner, Kane's career-defining moment came in the 2010 Stanley Cup Finals as he rifled a shot that not only tucked in underneath the Flyers' crossbar but stuck there. Amid confusion, for a brief few seconds, Kane was able to celebrate his moment — the Cup-winning goal — by himself. Kane also received the Conn Smythe Trophy (as playoff MVP) during the Blackhawks' 2013 Stanley Cup Championship run. The Turgeon card, by the way, is the most popular in that set, by far.

PAVEL BURE

Players like Bure come along once in a generation. Like Mike Bossy, the Russian Rocket was a pure goal scorer and perennial All-Star. It can be argued that Bure, a stud young gun in Vancouver, was more influential during his time with the Panthers, where he gave the young team its first true superstar. He twice led the league in goals during this period. Bure was inducted into the Hockey Hall of Fame in 2012. When his number was retired by the Canucks, several mementos were issued to fans, including a commemorative pin.

PETER FORSBERG

When he was drafted fifth overall in 1991, Forsberg was considered one of the top Swedes playing shinny,

and by 1994, he was considered the best player, period, not just in the NHL. While his antics on NHL ice — which included two Stanley Cups, a Hart Trophy, an Art Ross Trophy, and one of the top point-per-game averages in NHL history — were Hall of Fame worthy, his greatest accomplishment was the 1994 Olympic gold medal–winning shootout tally, commemorated later by Sweden's postal system with a beautiful stamp.

PETER STASTNY

Canadians may have the Sutters, but the province of Quebec has the Stastnys. Brothers Marian, Anton, and Peter all played at the same time for the Nordiques, with Peter standing head and shoulders above the others. A Czechoslovakia native who defected to Canada, Stosh was one of the most prolific scorers of his era, hitting the 100-point mark seven times. The Hall of Famer unfortunately never got a taste of playoff success, either in Quebec, New Jersey, or St. Louis. Since his retirement, a number of Stastny's game-used jerseys have gone up on the auction block.

PHIL ESPOSITO

Phil Esposito was one of the greatest pure goal scorers of all time. Drafted in 1964, Espo was on the path to being the next great Black Hawk before he was inexplicably traded to Boston. He was one of the key cogs in the Bruins 1970 and 1972 Stanley Cups and in four consecutive seasons (1970–71 through 1973–74) won the Art Ross Trophy. He captured the Hart Trophy in 1971 and 1974 and was a leader during the 1972 Summit Series. Like many Boston legends, Esposito would end his career outside Beantown with the New York Rangers. His habit of making headlines led to his being captured for a variety of wire photos, once used by newspapers and now highly collectible.

ROBERTO LUONGO

What endears Bobbie Lou to the collecting public? He was one of us growing up. "I was a big card collector when I was a kid; I was especially trying to get goalie cards," he said in 2004. During his time with the Florida Panthers, Roberto Luongo amassed more minutes of ice time and faced more rubber than any other goalie in the league. In Vancouver, Luongo essentially replaced the one-time tandem of Dan Cloutier and Alex Auld in one fell swoop. He has also starred on the international stage, including attaining Olympic gold in 2010.

DANIEL AND HENRIK SEDIN

Born into a hockey-playing family (their father, Tommy, played for the famed MoDo club in the Swedish

Elite League), the Sedins are the only brother combination to win consecutive scoring titles in the history of the NHL (Henrik in 2009–10, Daniel in 2010–11). The two were integral parts of the 2006 Olympic champion Swedish team and the Canucks team that went to the NHL Stanley Cup Finals in 2011 and also played in multiple NHL All-Star Games. Naturally, the most in-demand collectible pieces feature both brothers, such as a dual-signed photo.

STAN MIKITA

Living in St. Catherines, Mikita played for the local Teepees squad in the Ontario Hockey Association, which was essentially a feeder for the Chicago Black Hawks. With the parent club, Mikita formed one of hockey's most dangerous combinations with Bobby Hull. Their innovative banana-curve sticks helped Mikita become a master at centre ice and helped the Black Hawks win the Stanley Cup in 1961. Mikita's production led him to win the Art Ross Trophy four times and the Hart and Lady Byng twice, along with numerous team awards. These coveted trophies since have entered the marketplace via auctions.

TED LINDSAY

One of the founding fathers of the NHLPA, Ted Lindsay was largely responsible for the players getting their fair share in NHL revenue and even more for their post-career comfort. "It's a great satisfaction, for me, to see how well everything has gone for the players," Lindsay said at the 2004 Lester B. Pearson Award presentation, a trophy that later bore his name. Lindsay's on-ice career was highlighted by four Stanley Cups and an Art Ross Trophy. Lindsay was part of a limited run of commemorative stamps issued by Canada Post in the early '00s.

TERRY SAWCHUK

Nicknamed "Mr. Zero," Terry Sawchuk is considered one of the greatest goalies in the history of hockey. Sawchuk won four Stanley

JON WALDMAN

Cups and four Vezinas on tours through four of the Original Six cities (along with a run through Los Angeles). He is perhaps best known for his 14 seasons (over two runs) in Detroit. Sawchuk's mask — a complex mesh — is considered one of the true classics and today can be found in full-scale versions or miniature replicas.

TONY ESPOSITO

Tony O still holds the record for shutouts in a season. Originally part of the Canadiens, Esposito spent the vast majority of his career wearing the colours of the Chicago Black Hawks, where he reeled off seven consecutive 30-win campaigns. Esposito's cage-over-face-shield mask was one of the most unique in hockey. He was also one of two goalies for Canada during the famed 1972 Summit Series and was featured, rather obscurely, on a jigsaw puzzle in the early 1980s.

THE NEXT ONES

While today's stars draw fans to rinks and yesteryear's heroes bring auto-graph seekers to collector shows, there is a third group that gets attention — the next ones. Spurred by media who provide regular coverage of hot draft prospects and memorabilia companies rolling out products dedicated to rookies, the chase to grab collectibles of "the next big thing" in hockey is never-ending. Every time a Taylor Hall makes an impact in the NHL or a Nathan MacKinnon grabs headlines in the CHL, the hockey world is put on notice that yesterday's can't-miss prospect is already old news.

Prospect collecting hearkens back ages. In their junior careers, players like Bobby Orr and Wayne Gretzky were under intense media scrutiny and pre-hobby pundits were collecting autographs of the next men to lead the hockey world; but the hobby boom in the early 1990s, which coincided with the rise of Eric Lindros, saw the first true superstar born before he even was drafted.

Later on, other prospects would be hotly pursued through memorabilia, including the likes of Joe Thornton, Ilya Kovalchuk. Sidney Crosby, and Alexander Ovechkin.

Prospecting in the hobby can be extremely fun, but it brings out a certain core of collectors — investors. This group will hang on the words of NHL insiders and try to get a leg up on hobbyists by snagging autographs, rookie cards, and other memorabilia of players very early in their careers with the hope of being able to get excellent return on their investment; but for every "can't miss" prospect who blossoms into a bona fide NHL superstar, there are countless more who don't make it. Every Alexander Ovechkin has an Alexandre Daigle, after all; and yet, even the player who doesn't make that immediate impact still has investors and collectors clamouring for their keepsakes. Why? Because you never know who will end up being a superstar once they reach their prime.

Witness Markus Naslund. In 1991, Naslund was a first-round draft pick of the Philadelphia Flyers. When he didn't produce, he was traded to Pittsburgh for Alex Stojanov. Wise collectors kept his rookie cards and had their supply of autographs ready for resale by the time he emerged as an All-Star in Vancouver. Naslund offered his own analysis as to why it took him longer to live up to his high draft position. "It takes longer for some guys than for others. Not only are you expected, from others, to step right in and play good right away," he said, "but coming over from Sweden and having success throughout my career, I thought it would be an easy adjustment; but it was tougher than I [expected]. It was a big adjustment and I think patience, for young players, is key."

So as we can see, the risk can definitely result in a handsome reward; but that same risk has snake-bitten so many collectors that one might assume the madness would cease at one point or another. That's far from the case, however. Speculation still fuels the hobby and drives a lot of expectation on the shoulders of teenagers not yet in their maturity. No one understood this pressure more than Sidney Crosby. Ages before he was a Hart Trophy winner, Crosby was a headliner across Canada, and his name was bandied about in hobby shops. Autograph seekers hounded young Sidney severely, while memorabilia companies were working with him early into his CHL career. Being the subject of such demand was something Crosby took in stride. At the 2005 World Junior Hockey Championship selection camp, Crosby talked about how he dealt with the pressure, choosing to focus only on that which he put on his own shoulders, not what anyone else did.

"I think the only pressure you have is the pressure you put on yourself," the very young Crosby said in December 2004. "I don't put that pressure on myself. I just do what I'm capable of doing. I don't put any expectations on. I just try to do that and see what happens."

Still, one cannot ignore the attention one gets as a stud rookie in wait, and Crosby, even at that young age, was constantly in demand for his coveted signature. Already showing maturity well beyond his years, Crosby knew that this was an integral part of the career path he was choosing for himself. "Everyone loves hockey. They want autographs and I'm fine with that — hockey's the biggest sport in Canada and it's to be expected," Crosby said in the same 2004 interview. "I'm fine with that and I accept it; it's part of being a hockey player."

★ ERIC LINDROS ★

There may be no player in NHL history who was as heavily hyped as a junior as Eric Lindros. Before he was even drafted, The Big E had an autobiography, a dedicated trading card series, and an autograph hound following unlike anything the league had seen up until then.

Some of the hype around "The Next One" was self-propelled, as Lindros famously declared that he would never suit up for the Quebec Nordiques, prior to the 1991 NHL Entry Draft. He didn't even wear the jersey on Draft Day. Soon after, Lindros suited up for the Canada Cup tournament. As part of the host squad, young Eric skated alongside the likes of Wayne Gretzky and Mark Messier as his NHL future held a giant question mark. It was a year before the fate of the unhappy Nordiques prospect would be decided. Around Draft Day 1992, two trades were engineered, one that had Lindros going to the New York Rangers, the other to the Philadelphia Flyers. It took arbitration to make the final decision about Lindros's destination, and in the end the Flyers came out the victors.

Lindros's NHL debut largely lived up to the hype, though he fell short in his bid for the Calder behind Teemu Selanne and Joe Juneau. Undeterred, however, Lindros performed incredibly well in Philly, leading his squad to the Stanley Cup Finals and also picking up the Hart Trophy as league MVP in 1994–95. This season, however, proved to be the best he would deliver on the ice, as concussions soon took their toll, limiting his prowess. Arguments with Flyers General Manager Bobby Clarke led to his departure from Philly. Lindros rounded out his career with a variety of teams, including the Rangers, Dallas Stars, and Toronto Maple Leafs, before hanging up his skates permanently.

Because Lindros came into the NHL at the peak of the hockey card boom, it's not surprising that he is perhaps best known in the memorabilia world for the variety of cardboard that has been dedicated to him, especially from Score, who took full advantage of its exclusive contract and created a cornucopia of products, including a set of three cards available only via the purchase of the aforementioned autobiography and a holiday card. Trumping the Score cards is a product that was never supposed to see the light of day. During the 1991–92 NHL season, Pro Set teamed with memorabilia company Ace to produce a dual-packaged card and pin, which included Lindros on the checklist. Because of the exclusive deal Lindros had with Score, the combination never made it to retail, but several pins have popped up online in recent years.

★ ALEXANDRE DAIGLE ★

Despite the potential that players like Paul Kariya and Chris Pronger had, Alexandre Daigle was seen as the unquestioned first overall pick in 1993's draft, especially in his own mind (he once said, "I'm glad I got drafted first, because no one remembers number two"). Daigle was taken first overall by the Ottawa Senators, a sad-sack squad at the time, who were even rumoured to have thrown the last few games of the 1992–93 season in order to draft Daigle (whether true or not, it was speculated that to prevent such a move by a team, the NHL moved to the lottery system to determine the draft order). By Draft Day, card company Score had signed an exclusive agreement with the prospect and produced early cards of Daigle. First, it issued a special card at the Draft, which lit on fire in the secondary market and is still a tough card to find today. Later Score issued a redemption for his first fully licensed NHL trading card. In promoting the chance to get the first card of Daigle in his NHL duds, Score created the single worst advertisement in the history of hockey-related product. Rather than putting Daigle in hockey skates and a jersey, Score dressed him up in a variety of other uniforms. Among them were a Mountie uniform (which created controversy because he was saluting with the wrong hand) and a nurse's WWII–style uniform.

Daigle was barely in consideration for the Calder Memorial Trophy in his first season and soon ended up on the outs with Senators fans. He was shipped around the NHL a couple times before leaving hockey to pursue an acting career but later attempted a comeback. He seemed

to have regained his promise when he landed with the Pittsburgh Penguins and later moved to the fledgling Minnesota Wild. Daigle even led the team in scoring during the 2003–04 season (with 51 points, mind you) but didn't stick well for the 2005–06 season and was eventually moved to the AHL. One year later, Daigle moved to the Swiss league and found a permanent home there. Now far removed from the NHL, Daigle is regarded as one of the worst number-one selections in Entry Draft history. He totalled 327 points in 616 league games, including a paltry 129 goals. To say he did not meet expectations would be an understatement.

▲ JON WALDMAN

★ SIDNEY CROSBY ★

When the NHL announced its return from the 2004–05 lockout, numerous questions needed to be answered; but the one that was on the minds of most every NHL fan was the fate of phenom Sidney Crosby. Like other junior stars before him, Crosby had set hockey prospect pundits ablaze with his fantastic play on both the CHL and global stages. Even before licensed companies got on the Crosby bandwagon, his junior team, the Rimouski Oceanic, issued a special credit card–sized DVD of an amazing lacrosse-style goal Cros scored. This is what separated El

Sid from the pack, however: his uncanny desire to be the best in the world. Crosby knew what looked to be his destiny and took advantage of his marketability. Like Lindros and Daigle before him, Crosby was already an autograph hound's dream, and he took advantage of the opportunity presented to him, teaming with Frameworth on autographed collectibles.

During the 2004–05 NHL lockout, one of the biggest questions surrounded Crosby and which team would be lucky enough to gain the number-one pick in the following NHL Entry Draft. With no season to base rankings on, it was decided that the year's Draft Lottery would encompass all 30 member teams. Crosby was quite literally thrust into the national spotlight. If you thought the LeBron James free-agency-decision special on ESPN was a media circus, you should have seen the lengths the NHL and TSN went to with the lottery, as teams were eliminated one by one from Crosby contention until only the Pittsburgh Penguins and Anaheim Mighty Ducks were left standing. In the end, the Penguins won out, and No. 87 was headed to Steeltown.

Crosby made an immediate

impact with the Penguins, and while he finished second to Alexander Ovechkin in Calder Trophy voting, "Sid the Kid" showed that he was the head of the class of his rookie year. He set a torrid pace, garnering a Hart Trophy win one year later and became the youngest player to captain a Stanley Cup–winning team. Crosby's career was further accentuated in 2010 as he scored what Chris Cuthbert dubbed "The Golden Goal" at the 2010 Winter Olympics in Vancouver, but soon after that moment of glory, Crosby's career would start to be derailed by concussion and neck issues. And yet, whenever it seemed his promising future was in jeopardy, he showed that he hadn't lost his step, continuing a torrid scoring pace and each time re-establishing that he was the true heart and soul of the Penguins.

THE DEFUNCT FRANCHISES

Teams never die — they just leave their home cities once in a while. It might sound somewhat cliché to say this, but it's true — long after a franchise departs from the NHL, you'll still see the indelible mark it made on a market and its fans. Years after a departure, the evidence is still there in the jerseys that fans wear to games or the photos they prefer to gather in their collections.

Though early clubs like the Philadelphia Quakers or Hamilton Tigers are all but forgotten franchises, the post-expansion era has seen a multitude of teams come and go. Among these are two of the Expansion Six clubs (the Minnesota North Stars and Oakland Seals), a few from the 1970s (the Atlanta Flames, Kansas City Scouts, Cleveland Barons, and Colorado Rockies), three WHA imports (the Winnipeg Jets, Hartford Whalers, and Quebec Nordiques), and even a more modern squad (the Atlanta Thrashers), and this is just in the National Hockey League — I could be sitting for days listing off expired WHA, AHL, and CHL franchises from years gone by.

These historic teams, the vast majority of whose players and fans have passed on — taking with them the connections to those former clubs — are well remembered. Witness fans' tie to the Montreal Maroons, Quebec Bulldogs, or original Ottawa Senators for evidence. Thus, it's important to remember these teams — and the multitude of memorabilia generated for former franchises — including five standout organizations that, though long departed, are still very much remembered by the NHL's faithful.

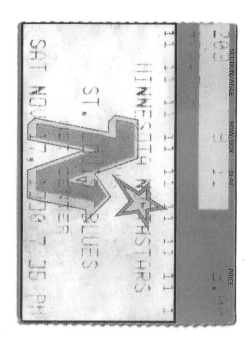

JON WALDMAN

MINNESOTA NORTH STARS

One of the Expansion Six, the North Stars filled a pretty obvious void on the NHL's map — the heartland of U.S. hockey. Over the course of 26 years in the NHL, the North Stars volleyed between being Cup contenders and one of the poorest-performing teams in the league. They came within one game of going to the Stanley Cup Finals in their first year but struggled to regain that magic in subsequent years.

Through the 1970s, the North Stars were without a true superstar; they were a lunchbox-style squad, with names like JP Parise, Danny Grant, and Jude Drouin being part of the club. Once the squad merged with the Cleveland Barons and drafted Bobby Smith in 1978, the team started to make a turnaround. Subsequent drafts brought the likes of Dino Ciccarelli and Neal Broten on board, helping solidify a roster that made it to the championship round in 1981 against the New York Islanders (the less said about that series, the better).

Undeterred, the North Stars continued to put together a solid lineup, adding Brian Bellows and trading for Keith Acton and Mark Napier; but the wheels began to fall off slowly, to the point that the club ended the 1987–88 season the worst in the NHL. The blessing in disguise here was the selection of Mike Modano, arguably the most beloved player in North Stars history. With Modano at the helm of the club and Jon Casey in net, the team became a Cinderella story in 1991, reaching the Stanley Cup Finals. The clock struck midnight a little too early, however, and they fell to the Pittsburgh Penguins.

Soon after that series in 1991 ended, the fate of the Minnesota team changed forever. That summer, the North Stars were essentially split in two. The Gund family, who had previously owned the Barons, separated from the franchise and took with them a number of players to their new team — the San Jose Sharks — via a Dispersal Draft. One year prior, arrangements had been made for a group to buy the North Stars franchise, and the ultimate controlling owner turned out to be Norm Green. Green, just a couple short years later, sealed the North Stars' fate, relocating the team to Dallas.

With Modano having retired in 2010–11, the North Stars lost their final active alumn. Now all that remains for the small-market franchise is commemorative memorabilia, including an excellent book entitled *Minnesota North Stars: History and Memories with Lou Nanne*, produced by the hard work of author Bob Flowers and, of course, the former player–coach–general manager (and yes, for a time Nanne held all three positions at once).

QUEBEC NORDIQUES

One can argue that throughout the 1980s there was no greater feud in hockey than the Battle of Quebec. While the Calgary Flames and Edmonton Oilers had highly spirited standoffs on the western front, the pure and unadulterated hatred that Montreal Canadiens and Quebec Nordiques fans had for each other was a whole other level of competitiveness, most vividly seen in the famed "Good Friday Massacre." During the April 20, 1984, playoff contest, competition between the two clubs got vicious. After earlier fights, the two teams cleared their benches, twice, for all-out brawls on the frozen floor of the Montreal Forum (amid the action, Jean Hamel was knocked out cold). A total of 10 ejections took place during that game, which

JON WALDMAN

eventually saw the Habs win the contest and playoff series.

The fight was emblematic of the Nords' NHL tenure. They were certainly talented enough to make noise in the league, featuring the likes of Hall of Famers Michel Goulet and Peter Stastny; but there was something that never quite clicked with the club. Granted, they were playing in an era dominated by the New York Islanders and western Canadian teams, but they just could not get the puck to go their way. As one of the four refugee WHA teams picked up and stripped by the NHL, the Nords brought with them a fierce competitiveness to the league, and up until the late 1980s the team fared well on the ice. But the wheels began to fall off toward the end of the decade. For three straight years, the club drafted first overall in the NHL Entry Draft thanks to their poor play. The result was Mats Sundin and Owen Nolan suiting up for the franchise, and one of the most famous trades in hockey history as the 1991 selection, Eric Lindros, was shipped to Philadelphia for Peter Forsberg, Ron Hextall, and a vast number of other players and picks.

That trade, of course, ended up being very instrumental in the success of the franchise's 1996 Stanley

Cup run, but by that time the Nords had left for Colorado. Amid the 1994–95 lockout-shortened season, the Nords were in deep financial trouble due to the ever-dangerous elixir of being a small-market franchise in a league with escalating salaries. Mix in the descent of the Canadian dollar and the refusal by government for bailout money, and the death knell rang for the franchise.

Currently, there is a renewed optimism about bringing the NHL back to the French Canadian capital. Talk of a new arena, supported heavily by the provincial government, rules the day, while former Nords' faithful make an annual sojourn to New York to see the Islanders play. It is believed by some that the franchise will end up moving to Quebec when the new facility is ready. Until then, hockey fans have been blessed with a number of souvenirs of Les

Nordiques, with retro products, like figurines of Joe Sakic, abounding.

HARTFORD WHALERS

As much as the Whalers were known during their WHA and NHL tenures as a team that had great resiliency and a drive to succeed, their civic government proved even tougher after the team relocated. You see, as the memorabilia craze picked up in the early 2000s and retro team pieces, primarily jerseys, became the most in-demand souvenirs, Whalers items were nowhere to be found. If you wanted a puck emblazoned with the famed W-and-fishtail logo to be signed by Gordie Howe or Ron Francis, you had to scour for an original. The reason for this? For years, the state of Connecticut owned the rights to the logo and seemingly wouldn't release it. It took the expiry of the ownership rights to the insignia for a rush of memorabilia to surface, most notably those jerseys.

Tribute artifacts were scarce for the Whalers up until very recent years, but the memory of the franchise never died. Originally a WHA franchise located in Boston (though known as the New England Whalers throughout their time in the rebel league), the team is historically best known for being the first team to win the Avco Cup and to house Gord, Mark, and Marty Howe. The only non-Canadian team to join the NHL, the Whalers did so as a definite cause célèbre, with two of the league's all-time greats — Howe and Dave Keon — on their roster. Bobby Hull joined the team later on in that season.

After that first season, the Whalers still had tremendous fanfare with the likes of Ron Francis, Kevin Dineen, and Mike Liut cycling through the team but struggled against Adams Division rivals the Montreal Canadiens and Boston Bruins; and when they weren't suffering from their own bad play, they were suffering from bad trades, such as the infamous 1991 blockbuster swap that saw Francis, Ulf Samuelsson, and Grant Jennings

leave for Pittsburgh in exchange for John Cullen, Zarley Zalapski, and Jeff Parker. The result? Two Cups for Francis and Co., none for Hartford.

Even with emerging stars like Geoff Sanderson, Chris Pronger, and Bobby Holik, the Whalers saw their last playoff series in 1992. Other stars and future phenoms spent time in Hartford, but none were able to get the Whalers to the promised land. As season ticket purchases dwindled, talk of relocation began, and in 1997, Peter Karmanos moved the team to Carolina. Though the new Hurricane franchise also struggled at the box office to start, they were ultimately successful on the ice, winning the Stanley Cup in 2006.

WINNIPEG JETS

"It was great to start my career where hockey was such a big deal."

This quote came from NHL legend Teemu Selanne back in 2003; but it could very well have come from any number of NHLers who got their first taste of hockey action skating at the Winnipeg Arena. Look up and down the roster of the original squad, and you'll see a number of notable names who first plied their trade professionally in

1972-1996 WINNIPEG JETS CHERISHED MEMORIES

JON WALDMAN

North America. Dale Hawerchuk, Keith Tkachuk, Nikolai Khabibulin, Kris Draper, and several others are among these men.

The Jets franchise was more than just a breeding ground for future superstars with other franchises. While the team did not enjoy the kind of success it had in the WHA, where it won three Avco championships, it was a team that had flashes of brilliance. Had it not been for powerhouse franchises in Edmonton and Calgary, the Jets' golden years in the mid-1980s may have led to Stanley Cup success.

Ultimately, the Jets faced similar problems to its WHA cousin, the Quebec Nordiques. Financial woes of playing in a small Canadian market and an aging building were ultimately the downfall of the team, whose fans rallied multiple times to save their beloved Jets. Most famously, during the 1994–95 season, everyone from business execs to school children pooled whatever money they could to save their franchise. The result of this devotion, even after a tribute "funeral" where Thomas Steen's jersey number was retired, was a stay of execution, allowing one final season of NHL hockey in Winnipeg.

That final year was a memorable

Born in an era when the NHL was in its infancy, the Americans were a unique group, almost akin to baseball's Brooklyn Dodgers. The team struggled at the gate, especially in comparison to the rival New York Rangers, who battled with their cousins for the right to play in the famed Madison Square Garden. Originally, the Americans (or Amerks, as they were commonly referred to) were the second U.S.–based NHL team, pulled together from refugee Hamilton Tigers talent and outside pick-ups. The original and mainstay owner was Bill Dwyer, a famed bootlegger during the Prohibition era; but with the end of the dry years came misfortune for Dwyer, and after an attempted merger with the equally downtrodden Ottawa Senators, the league ended up wresting control away from the former booze baron.

The Amerks were the definition of sad sack for most of their time in the NHL, only making the playoffs once during the first decade of their existence. In the subsequent 13 years, including their final as the Brooklyn Americans, the team only made the post-season four times. By the end of 1941–42, with many of

one indeed. Dubbed "A Season to Remember" — a slogan that appeared on patches on the team jerseys — the Jets played their hearts out and made one last trip to the Stanley Cup playoffs before being dispatched by the Detroit Red Wings and becoming the Phoenix Coyotes.

NEW YORK AMERICANS

What, you were expecting to see another story from the NHL's modern era? Sure, I could've thrown in an entry about the Colorado Rockies or either of Atlanta's two failed hockey teams, but when you compare these or other franchises to the uniqueness of the Americans, there is little doubt as to which team is more fondly remembered.

the team's players having registered for World War II duty, the team suspended operations, and the league denied them re-entry after the war was complete.

So what is it then about the Americans that makes them so regarded? Well, it's two parts — first, they had decent players at various times during their tenure, including Hall of Famers like Roy Worters, Charlie Conacher, and Nels Stewart; but more importantly, the jersey they wore is so uniquely colourful and their licence plate–like logo look so unmistakably amazing that one can't help but want to pick up a replica sweater or hockey puck that bears the insignia of the long-gone franchise.

Cy Wentworth   Jimmy Ward

Tom Forman

Russ Blinco

Bob Gracie

Earl Robinson

Walter Cowan

Wes Mutch

Mr. Croghan

Bill O'Brien

Bill Beveridge

"Baldy" Northcott

Tommy Cook

Alan Shields

"Charlie" Smith

Bill Burdge

Paul Runge

Herb Cain

Gus Marker

Chuny Johnson

"Pep" Kelly

Buzz Drillon

"Ink" Smith

Babe Davidson

Ronnie Carr

Dave Schriner

Art Chapman

Eddie Wiseman

Joe Lamb

Tommy Anderson

Tim Cole

Syl Apps

Buster Jackson

Chas Conacher

Buzz Boll

Nick Metz

Reg Hamilton

Jack Shill

Johnny Gallagher

"Happy" Day

Al Murray

Tommy Bell

Nelson Stewart

Joe Serva

Earl Robinson

"Red" Hamer

"Jimmie" Fowler

Bingo Kampman

Murph Chamberlain

Bill Thoms

3

★ ★ ★

LEAGUES
AND
NATIONS

★ ★ ★

While the National Hockey League is dominant in virtually every respect, it is far from the only game of shinny in town. Canada and the United States are dotted with junior, minor-pro, and senior leagues with followings — while more localized — that verge on cult status. Take, for example, the ongoing interest in the Canadian Hockey League and the menagerie of team-issued souvenirs as well as commemorative pucks and programs from highlighted tournaments like the Canada/Russia Challenge and the Memorial Cup.

It's also important to bear in mind that North America is not the only hotbed of hockey. The Kontinental Hockey League, Swedish Elite League, Finnish Elite League, and similar bodies are sprawled throughout Eurasia. These, as well, have their own lines of memorabilia and unique souvenirs.

THE REBELS
★ ★ ★

There was no year more influential to the development of North American hockey than 1972. Two key events changed the landscape of the game forever. One was the Canada–Russia Summit Series — the other was the first puck dropping in the World Hockey Association.

The NHL finally had a challenger to its throne in the early 1970s. The new league quickly made its mark with the signing of Bobby Hull to the Winnipeg Jets. Other NHL marquee names like Gerry Cheevers, Frank Mahovlich, and the great Gordie Howe were lured to the WHA, while imported players like Anders Hedberg gave the league an outlet rarely explored by NHL teams at the time, and top prospects like Andre Lacroix, who may have been picked up by NHL clubs, were recruited and chose to suit up in the WHA, which encouraged underagers to join the pro ranks earlier than they could in the NHL.

The very first WHA game took place on October 11, 1972, pitting the Alberta

MARC LYNCH ▸

(later Edmonton) Oilers against the Ottawa Nationals. The Oilers took the game 7-4, kicking off a . . . how shall I say, unique first year. If there was any clear indicator of the trouble that lay ahead for the WHA, it was that the first championship celebration took place without a championship trophy. Instead, the victorious New England (later Hartford) Whalers paraded around the ice with their divisional award. This was just the cap of a forgettable inaugural season, where two teams — the Dayton Arrows and San Francisco Sharks — relocated and another pair — the Calgary Broncos and Miami Screaming Eagles — folded.

Despite the slippery ice the WHA was skating on, it was able to do something few may have expected — it was able to merchandise its product. Tabletop hockey game

company Munro was one buyer. Just as it had done a scant few years earlier, the company produced a game bearing Bobby Hull's name in 1973, only this game was dedicated solely to the new league. In addition to Munro, the WHA was able to ink a pact with O-Pee-Chee, the signature brand of trading cards for Canadian boys and girls. Originally included in the 1972–73 NHL product line as the final series, the cards featured several of the league's recognizable (read: former NHL) stars, including Hull and Cheevers. One year later, the WHAers were included in a fold-up poster series in that year's NHL release before finally breaking out on their own for the 1974–75 season.

This success wasn't felt across the hockey landscape — the NHL's brass weren't quite as willing to work with the new league. Stories of hardships for teams like the Toronto Toros, who clashed with the Maple Leafs over arena issues, emerged. Even before the WHA played its first game, the NHL's hatred of its competition shone through as WHA stars were not allowed to play in the 1972 Summit Series, even though Hull and others were initially invited to become part of the team. Bitter rivalries between the two leagues were able to be put aside at times, however. For four years, the clubs battled in exhibition contests, with the WHA taking more wins than losses. In particular, the Winnipeg Jets, Quebec Nordiques, and New England Whalers were dominant, while the Edmonton Oilers were the only other club to have a winning record against NHL cubs. While the monetization of those contests in the form of souvenirs was rare, game tickets and souvenir programs do pop up from time to time.

Throughout this time, the WHA continued to have franchise issues, with teams folding or relocating. Almost with every passing season, the makeup of the league changed, at times drastically. By the time the WHA folded, clubs had moved multiple times. For example, the Ottawa Nationals would become the Toronto Toros and then the Birmingham Bulls in the space of the seven-year history of the league. If the hobby community had been alive during this time, one can only imagine the success of the eBay sales of any mementos of these teams.

Despite all this, the WHA fostered and bred the development of future NHL superstars and Hall of Famers. Among them: Michel Goulet, Mark Messier, Mike Gartner, and, of course, Wayne Gretzky. Because of the NHL's policies on draft eligibility, Gretzky was able to be signed first by a WHA club, and in 1978, Nelson Skalbania picked up the young phenom and brought him to the Indianapolis Racers. Gretzky lasted eight games with the club before his rights were sold to Peter Pocklington and the Edmonton Oilers. As the story goes, Skalbania, who had signed Gretzky to a personal services contract rather than a player agreement, knew the WHA was set to be absorbed by the NHL, and the Racers were not to be one of the lucky teams to survive; indeed, they folded that December.

Soon after Gretzky's rookie season ended and the Winnipeg Jets

captured the Avco Cup Trophy for the third and final time, the leagues officially amalgamated. Despite objections from several NHL team owners, the Jets, Hartford Whalers, Quebec Nordiques, and Edmonton Oilers all joined the NHL — even if they were shells of their former selves. Each team entering the league was permitted to keep only four players (two skaters and two goalies). They were then expected to restock themselves in an expansion draft. The unprotected players were picked up by various NHL clubs.

Since its death, the WHA has maintained a standing in hockey's history with a subculture of fans that look back fondly on the league. "I wouldn't use the word *cult*, but certainly a smaller group of people are quite interested in the WHA," says Joe Daley, who was between the pipes for the Winnipeg Jets during their days in the rebel league. "I think, over the years, it's solidified itself as a bona fide league because so many players who got their start there turned out to be Hall of Fame players, which gave it credibility."

In recent years, the WHA has become the subject of various film documentaries and a number of books. Retro commemorative jerseys, trading cards, and other souvenirs have also become popular for a collecting world anxiously looking for something "different" than the standard product. It perhaps comes as no surprise that the biggest symbol of its unique approach to hockey remains its most in-demand collectible — the blue puck. The non-logic behind using the colourful disk that first season was that it would appear better on TV (the same bit of "fixing something that wasn't broken" nonsense behind the FoxTrax puck). The experiment lasted only a few months before the league went back to the traditional black slug. Naturally, the blue puck has become a major pursuit of puck collectors, especially those who chase the seemingly rare variants that have a WHA logo on the reverse. Creating confusion around these game pucks, however, was a series produced in 1975 that looked exactly like the originals but were never used in competition. Online hockey museum officialgamepuck .com later got in on the mini memorabilia rush, reproducing the black and original blue slugs with the new WHA logo on the reverse and the series name "Reflections." (It should be noted, however, that due to licensing issues, some of these pucks, like the Jets version, had slightly altered logos, while others, like the Edmonton Oilers', were never produced.)

In 2004, as the NHL headed into full-out shutdown mode for the infamous 2004–05 lockout, the Rebel League appeared to be on the comeback trail. With Bobby Hull as one of the key figures, the WHA seemed indeed to be coming back, so much so that Pacific Trading Cards not only signed on as the new league's official trading card partner but also produced two promotional autographed cards, featuring Lacroix and Hull in the foreground of the new league's logo. Commemorative pucks and other assorted memorabilia were also produced. All the hype died very quickly, and before a single puck could be dropped, the new WHA became merely a developmental league.

THE SUMMIT
SERIES
★ ★ ★

Had Canada lost to the Russians in 1972, the memorabilia landscape would be vastly different. The team-autographed jerseys, the bobbleheads, the DVDs . . . it simply would never have been conceived.

The story of the 1972 Summit Series has been told repeatedly — how Canada's NHL elite took on the powerful Russian national squad in a battle of epic proportions to decide who was the greatest power in hockey. We've relived the disappointment of being downed twice on our home ice by the Russians and having come *this* close to losing the series on their turf.

Devised to be a truly national tournament for the entire country to take part in, the Summit was staged in four cities across Canada, including Montreal, Toronto, Winnipeg, and Vancouver. Once it moved to the then U.S.S.R., all four games took place in Moscow, in an unfriendly environment where chain-link

JON WALDMAN

fencing separated spectators from the action. Truly, the combatants seemed more like they were in a steel-cage death match than a simple hockey game, especially with the Soviets already holding a 2-1-1 series lead (the tie resulted in a true champion being decided). The games had Canadians glued to their televisions like nothing else in history. Stories are still told of school assemblies being organized so that youngsters could watch the action unfold thousands of kilometres away in the Soviet Union, especially after an impassioned Phil Esposito expressed his discontent with the Canadian attitude after Game Four.

The series was not without controversy. WHA players, namely Bobby Hull, were disallowed from competing, while other Canadian heroes like Bobby Orr were unable to play for medical reasons. Had Canada lost the Series, the blame clearly would have been placed on the lack of a true representation of the nation's elite, especially in comparison with the Russians, who fielded their powerful national team that was already wreaking havoc on international tournaments largely ignored by the Canadian faithful.

But with that win came a new jubilation, and in the years following, the Summit Series has been a boon for memorabilia fanatics. Programs, tickets, and newspapers from the time obviously command high dollars, but interest has spawned many more items, including dedicated trading card series, replica jerseys, stamps, and medallions. More importantly, the Summit can also be credited with growing North American interest in international competition. First, it spawned the 1974 Summit, pitting the Russians against the WHA's top Canadian stars, and later the U.S.S.R. barnstorming tours: the Canada Cup and the World Cup of Hockey. Most recently, a "Junior Summit" between Canada and Russia's top underage stars was held to commemorate the 35th anniversary of the original Series.

The other result was that, for the first time, Russian stars were acknowledged by western media. While names like Valeri Kharlamov and Vladislav Tretiak were known in every home in the U.S.S.R., it took the Summit Series for them to have any sort of identity in Canada (as villainous as they were portrayed to be). Both have since been recognized by the Hockey Hall of Fame as Honoured Members. In years since, Tretiak in particular has become an in-demand superstar and

is for hobbyists, without a doubt, the most popular name that never played in the NHL.

THE SUMMIT STAR – PAUL HENDERSON

While Phil Esposito, Frank Mahovlich, and Ken Dryden were already household names before the Summit, Canada's win made a folk hero out of a less-heralded star: Paul Henderson. At the time, Henderson was a standout with the Toronto Maple Leafs, but he was nowhere near as highly touted as some of the others on the Canadian squad. His dominant performances in Russia (game-winning goals in each of the final three games) changed the course of hockey history, and his heroic goal in the eighth and final contest, with time running short, sealed the victory for Canada. As a result, Henderson has become the single most in-demand personality from the Summit. More than 40 years later, he remains one of the most popular men on the autograph circuit, a "job" he relishes.

"I'm very fortunate, I can't think of anyone more fortunate than myself," Henderson said in 2011 during a barnstorming tour. "It's all a part of giving back. I try to be as cordial as I can. I've always been a positive person and always will be."

Just as famous as Henderson himself is the jersey he wore during that final game. It has been passed through numerous collections in its time, most recently selling in a Classic Collectibles auction for $1.2 million, far exceeding any other sweater. The winning bid was placed by Mitchell Goldhar. "It's one of the purest pieces of modern Canadiana that I think there is," Goldhar told the CBC in 2010 following the auction. "I honestly couldn't believe that it was coming up for auction. I never even hesitated."

Originally, Henderson had given the sweater to trainer Joe Sgro, but through the years it had moved around, eventually ending up in the hands of an American collector. "I was amazed, I really was. I didn't even know where it had gone," Henderson said. "I'd heard through the grapevine that Joe had sold it, but I had no clue it had been in the States whatsoever."

The American collector, who at the time of the auction remained anonymous, announced he would be donating part of the proceeds from the sale to charity, much the

▲ JON WALDMAN

same way Henderson had done with all the other equipment that he had acquired during the Series. "All of my stuff went to charity auctions years ago," Henderson said in 2011, noting that, at the time, the pieces went for "next to nothing" compared with what they would command in today's market.

THE CANADA CUP AND OTHER INTERNATIONAL TOURNAMENTS

As discussed earlier, the Summit Series opened the door for larger-scale tournaments that would feature the best from the pro ranks in each country. In 1974, the Summit was relived as the best of the WHA's Canadian players squared off with the Russians, falling handily with an unquestionably weaker squad. Two years later, the notion of elite players playing for their country blew up in the form of the Canada Cup. This time, Canada was at 100 percent full strength, with Bobby Orr and Bobby Hull leading the way. The tournament was also held in 1981, 1984, 1987, and 1991 before giving way to the World Cup of Hockey.

Among these tournaments, the best and most celebrated, without question, was the 1987 edition. Here, another Henderson-like heroic performance came to be, albeit this time it wasn't a previously lesser-known star who delivered the heroics. Instead, it was Mario Lemieux and Wayne Gretzky — playing together competitively for a rare time in their careers — who combined to give Canada the overtime winner in the final contest against (who else?) the Soviets. The moment has rarely been captured in memorabilia, surprising given the stature both men have.

After that 1987 tournament, every international contest seemed to take on more importance. The World Junior Hockey Championship, which at one time was primarily of interest to NHL scouts, took on a life of its own, especially when it became the first time that a national audience got the chance to see Eric Lindros on the ice. The Women's World Hockey Championships also benefited from the newfound attention that the international game was receiving, as its big names, such as Angela James and Cammi Granato, became sensations in Canada and the United States, giving fans new names to cheer for and memorabilia to collect.

THE OLYMPICS
★ ★ ★

"I'm always excited to play any game in Canada. It's always exciting, always sold out . . . it's just one of those feelings and it's always exciting to be part of it," says Mike Richards, a 2010 Canadian Olympian.

Though the NHL is the most dominant organization in all of hockey, international tournaments unite fans unlike any other event. A fierce rivalry like the Flames versus the Oilers will dissolve if Jarome Iginla and Taylor Hall are both wearing the maple leaf on their chest. Similarly, Evgeni Malkin and Alexander Ovechkin may be bitter rivals during the season, but when it comes time for the Olympics they'll join forces to upend Sidney Crosby or Niklas Backstrom.

This is the nature of hockey, the only one of the big four sports that has branded itself so well around the world.

Hockey's first truly international stage was the 1924 Winter Olympics.

Rather than being the superstar-laden squads we see today, teams were primarily amateur clubs or collegiate players. Even the famed Miracle on Ice team comprised players who weren't quite "NHL ready," and Canadian squads were largely players like Chris Kontos or Dave Archibald, who wouldn't crack NHL lineups on a regular basis.

But as the profile of the Olympics grew in North America (and the marketing opportunities and merchandise dollars grew in turn), pressure came down on the NHL to join the NBA in allowing its players to compete in the Games. As far back as the 1988 Games in Calgary, the International Olympic Committee (IOC) had allowed athletes of all competition levels — including professional — to take part in the tournament, but the NHL had been reluctant to let their players take part, lest it affect the regular season (and playoffs). Finally, the decision was made that NHL clubs would stop play amid the 1997–98 season — putting play on hold for two weeks — to allow selected players to go to the pre-eminent international tournament.

And as soon as the announcement was made, you could practically smell the money being printed. While the IOC had been open to an extent with licences (it still trumpets its longstanding relationships with the coin and stamp collecting industries), the 1998 games were the big floodgate-opener for souvenirs and memorabilia. While more than 30 companies were given licensing rights for the 1994 Olympics in Lillehammer, more than 100 licences were approved in 1998. The result was a glut of collectibles the likes of which had not been seen since the hobby's boom in the early 1990s. Longtime Olympic partners like McDonald's and Coca-Cola planned and executed on Olympic-themed memorabilia such as medallions and miniature jerseys, while newer companies like McFarlane Toys went

through the (expensive) process of gaining the coveted Olympic licence. By the 2010 Vancouver-hosted games, expectations were that each Olympic journey would be outfitted with a bevy of promotions, and, to their credit, memorabilia companies delivered each year with both high-end and easily afforded swag for anxious Canadians.

But the collectibles market probably would have died very quickly had it not been for two important moments in modern Canadian Olympic history — the Lucky Loonie and the Golden Goal.

The tradition is now alive and well for Canadians to place a gold-coloured one-dollar coin in the ice during international competition following the 2002 Winter Olympics in Salt Lake City. For the final games for both the men's and women's teams, a loonie was embedded in the ice by the Canadian who was charged with surfacing the rink. The currency piece sparked fervour unlike anything seen in history. Replica and commemorative coins were issued by the Royal Canadian Mint, while the original was housed in the Hockey Hall of Fame. Originally open to public touching (again for good luck), the coin later was completely sealed away from human hands because its surface was fading away from the rubs it received.

Eight years later, the Olympics returned to North America, this time in Vancouver — and there was no way that Canada was going to lose in front of its home crowd. While the other sports produced Canada's highest ever medal count (and its first gold medals on home soil by the bushel), the expectations for Canadian teams were higher than ever. While the women did their part handily (creating a controversial moment of their own by smoking cigars and drinking beer on the ice following their victory — a moment of missed marketing opportunity for Molson Canadian), the men had to battle past the last second of regulation to secure their gold medal.

And it couldn't have come off the stick of a better player — Sidney Crosby. Sid the Kid was already a household name before the 2010 Vancouver Olympics, in part from his play with the Pittsburgh Penguins but also from his experience playing for Hockey Canada in the World Junior Hockey Championships. But his overtime goal past Ryan Miller put the young phenom into a whole other echelon. Soon, magazine covers, signed jerseys, and photographs of every size were produced, commemorating the so-named "Golden Goal," which became a new generation's Paul Henderson marker.

THE MIRACLE

But international success isn't limited to Canada. In the United States, the "Miracle on Ice" produced some of the greatest hockey memories for American children. The story of a group of ragtag amateur players, guided by Herb Brooks to battle against the mighty and rarely defeated Russians, has become the stuff of legend, gaining attention not before seen for U.S. hockey, and it still ranks among the most memorable moments for American Olympic competition. The game, as Pat LaFontaine explains, inspired another surprise U.S. victory on the ice — the 1996 World Cup of Hockey. The Hall of Famer remarks that the group of players who were together on that squad were motivated by that legendary run to the gold medal.

"At the World Cup, we were down one game in Philly and we had to come back and win two in Montreal," LaFontaine recalls. "All

of us were a product of the 1980 team. We were young boys, looking at Mike Eruzione score this miracle goal that really inspired us who were there. We were a generation that watched that game. So for us to maybe make history again, inspiring more boys and girls, was really special. I'm just proud to be part of a generation that inspired more boys and girls to want to pursue and set their sights high, maybe want to play professionally or represent their country."

While the World Cup team has not quite become as heralded, the Miracle on Ice continues to be one of the most heavily chased themes. Players like Eruzione and Jim Craig, whose NHL careers didn't gain much attention from hobbyists, are highly in demand for their autographs, while the team-signed jerseys and large group photos are some of the most demanded collectibles in the market.

American hockey has also jumped on the memorabilia bandwagon, albeit not quite as prominently as its Canadian counterpart. Licensing for the U.S. squads has come more under the banner of the full Olympic program than that of the single sport, such as when the Miracle team was commemorated early on in a U.S. Olympic Hall of Fame trading card series produced in the early 1990s and, more recently, by Topps. One of the exceptions to this is a series of bobblehead figures produced in 2002 by Alexander Global Promotions. Initially available only in Salt Lake City — the site of those Winter Games — the figurines are harder to unearth than those created for Team Canada.

EUROPE

Similar to North American markets, Olympic memorabilia across the pond is a big industry but with one difference: European markets look for more traditional souvenirs such as pucks and jerseys. Even Russia, whose teams were so incredibly dominant, have had few commemorations for their powerful squads, save for game programs and unlicensed pieces that have surfaced in recent years.

The real exception to this, however, has been in crossover markets like pins and stamps, and none are more prominent than one that commemorates the 1994 Games in Lillehammer, Norway.

In the final Olympics before the NHL became part of the largely amateur competition series, there was a marked excitement surrounding the tournament, particularly in Sweden, where Peter Forsberg was already considered the top player outside the NHL. Forsberg had been drafted by the Philadelphia Flyers and traded to the Quebec Nordiques, but he still had not shifted to North American ice. It's a good thing he hadn't, otherwise he might not have been on the ice in the gold medal game, and certainly would not have scored the overtime goal that handed *Tre Kronor* the gold medal during that year's Winter Olympics. Forsberg's goal was captured several times over, most notably in a stamp that is still considered one of the top international pieces for any collector.

THE WOMEN'S GAME

The sport of hockey has evolved a great deal since its early days. The number of players on the ice has changed; the equipment has changed; heck, the very look of the ice, now bedecked in advertisements, is immensely different from what it was just a couple short decades ago.

But the single biggest change in hockey in the last two decades has been the growth of the women's game. What was once an offshoot of the men's game has now grown to become an entity unto its own.

COMPETITION

In the women's game, the ultimate rivalry is between not two league teams but two nations: Canada and the United States of America. The women's game really broke through in 1990 when the International Ice Hockey Federation (IIHF) staged the first Women's World Hockey Championships; and each and every final series since has been played between Canada and the United States.

In part because of the heated

play, women's hockey has grown by leaps and bounds, with participation in North America on a sharp incline, particularly thanks to the inclusion of the sport in the Winter Games, starting in 1998.

"We've seen how much the game has changed in the last 15 years. It's been dramatic," says three-time Olympian Jennifer Botterill. "We've just seen how many girls are starting to sign up for hockey. It's so drastically different from where it was years ago, and I think the Olympics are a huge part of that."

With men's teams having been so dominant for years, not every market — no matter how hockey mad — will take up interest in the women's game.

"I think there's a really fine line between drawing people to the women's game and competing with male professional sports. There are certain cities and places where women's hockey is off-the-charts popular, and then there are cities where you'd think it's popular and it simply doesn't take off," says Delaney Collins, who played defence for Team Canada and in the Western Women's Hockey League (WWHL). "I found in Calgary, women's hockey never truly thrived, even with Hockey Canada there. The Oval Extreme, even with a handful of Olympians, never really drew a lot of fans; but if women's hockey goes to Winnipeg, the city turns upside down and you can't get a ticket.

"I'm coaching in Erie, PA, at Mercyhurst, where the women's game is thriving, and I think that adds to my job satisfaction."

Where women have differentiated themselves is in their efforts to reach out to fans. While hockey players in general are known as some of the most fan-friendly athletes in all of sport, women's players have gone that extra mile, readily handing priceless mementos to their young fans. "I ended up giving my [Olympic] jacket to a girl I knew who was sick," Botterill recalls. "When you can give someone else in your life value, it's pretty special. You keep some stuff, but if you can have an impact for other people too, you like to share some of that."

That impact can also be seen in the variety of charitable work performed by women's hockey players. Whether it's organized efforts at the team or national levels or on a personal level, women's hockey players have generously given back to the communities that have supported

Though several women's players have become hobby darlings simply in their own competition, others made headlines by moving over to the men's game.

Most famous of these women is Manon Rheaume. In 1992, Rheaume broke the gender barrier by suiting up with the Tampa Bay Lighnting during the 1992–93 NHL pre-season. The move had its skeptics, who figured the new club was attempting a publicity stunt, but the intent of bringing Rheaume to the tryouts was genuine, as she had the skills and had also previously played against males in the QMJHL and Junior-A leagues. Though Rheaume didn't make the Lightning roster, she was able to find a spot in the International Hockey League, first with the Atlanta Knights and later with a variety of other clubs, while also backstopping the Canadian Women's team in the Women's World Hockey Championships.

them or need their help. Collins attributes this to the nature of the sport. "Women's hockey has more of a personal tie to fundraising because the women aren't making comparable salaries to professional male athletes. They know what it's like to raise money, and I think women see more value in raising money. It becomes a personal reflection of themselves," she says, adding that a lot of the effort comes as a result of national initiatives and the effect that follows.

"In particular, the Canadian women's team does a lot of fundraising, and now that's trickling down to the women's leagues. At Mercyhurst, we do different fundraising, and one of the evenings we do is for breast cancer. It's pretty neat. Generally, there are ties to these players and raising these funds."

A few years later, the NHL again came calling to the women's game as Hayley Wickenheiser was invited to the Philadelphia Flyers' rookie camp in 1998 and 1999. Wickenheiser was already a very familiar name to hockey fans, having started in the national women's program at age 15, winning gold in her first year. Up until this time, most women who had crossed over to the men's game were goaltenders, but Wickenheiser showed that she could more than hang with the boys, and she would go on to play in Europe and become the first woman to score a goal in a men's pro league.

While Rheaume and Wickenheiser received more hobby attention — both from manufacturers and collectors — as a result of their play, their popularity is hardly isolated.

THE HALLOWED HALL
★ ★ ★

When you want to get serious about the top hockey collections, all conversation begins and ends in Toronto with the Hockey Hall of Fame and Museum.

It was originally a temporary exhibit, set up in the 1950s at the Canada Sports Hall of Fame. The first efforts to find it a permanent home looked to have the building established in Kingston, Ontario, but the funding couldn't be secured.

A few years later, the decision was made to establish the Hall at the Canadian National Exhibition, where it would remain for nearly 40 years before a new permanent home was established in a former Bank of Montreal (BMO) building in BCE Place (now Brookfield Place) near Union Station (and coincidentally a stone's throw from the later home of the Air Canada Centre).

The main reason for this move? Space. The Hall of Fame, despite being

solely able to acquire artifacts via donation, has amassed an insanely large collection, which has allowed the building to rotate its displays year-round for visitors. Few displays are truly "permanent." Sticks, jerseys, pucks, rink remnants . . . just about everything you can imagine can be found in the Hall; and whatever isn't original has been recreated, such as a full-scale version of the locker room at the Montreal Forum, complete with gear. But there are two sections that stand out above and well beyond everything else in the Hall.

The first lies in the old BMO bank vault. Here, fans can check out the original Dominion Challenge Cup, donated by Lord Stanley of Preston. Also in the vault are the rings from previous versions of the Cup, including those that were on the tower version mostly seen in the 1950s and 1960s, as well as "retired" rings from the current incarnation that needed to be removed to make space for new team names.

The second is even more impressive and sits upstairs in the Great Hall. Lying beneath a stained-glass, domed ceiling are the variety of post-season awards like the Hart and Vezina trophies as well as the etched-glass photo displays of honoured members of the Hall of Fame. The Hall brass are insistent that the honoured members are not inducted as part of a particular team (unlike in baseball, where they "wear a cap" when they enter that sport's Hall), but if you look closely there are hints in the etchings as to what team each player is being associated with.

Take Wayne Gretzky, for example. His etching has a distinctly younger look, with his hockey hair (or mullet, if you prefer) sticking out on either side of his neck. That style was most closely associated with his time in Edmonton, particularly the first half of the Oilers' dynasty days. Luc Robitaille's image, on the other hand, is sans mullet but has piping off the shoulders of the jersey. From that, one can deduce that the originating photo was from his final run with the Los Angeles Kings (rather

than the first era, where his black hair flowed like Jaromir Jagr's locks).

Surprisingly, the etched-glass images have never truly been reproduced in any form for a memorabilia series. While baseball's Hall of Fame plaques have been replicated on postcards and other souvenirs, hockey's version of immortal imagery has stayed put in the Hall.

That's not to say that the Hall hasn't taken advantage of the opportunity to market itself around its honoured players. On the contrary — the Hall, particularly through its souvenir store, has a number of items for anxious fans who want a memento of its honoured members.

Most prominent among these items was a series of postcards issued in the 1980s. Primarily sold as individual pieces (though also available as a full set), the cards, featuring artistic renditions of a player's headshot and an action image, were issued over a number of years. Naturally, the Hall has also created pucks and other such items with its logo emblazoned, including for the move to the new building. More often than not, these pucks are autograph fodder for the fan who never knows when they might encounter an honoured member. More recently, auxiliary companies have gotten into the honoured member game, issuing souvenirs such as medallions either individually or as a set for a given class.

But the bread and butter of Hall of Fame souvenirs are those that belonged to the inductees themselves. With several honoured members participating in "legends" games on Induction Weekend, jerseys worn during these contests have from time to time ended up on the auction block. While they're not as in demand as their NHL game-used counterparts, the jerseys do have a following.

More important than those, however, by far, are two artifacts that a player is given upon their induction — their Hockey Hall of Fame ring and jacket. In both cases, for a living player to give up the cherished memento is exceedingly rare; but when a player passes on, it's not uncommon for these items to go on the auction block. A Hall ring can command just as much attention as a Stanley Cup ring and is considered to be one of the ultimate pieces of hockey memorabilia.

CREDITS

Creating a book on hockey memorabilia would not have been possible without the interviews I've been fortunate to do over the years. I'd like to give credit where credit is due. Many of the interviews and quotes that appear in this book were either previously published in articles I prepared for the following media or were clips left on the cutting room floor:

- *The Toronto Sun*
- *The Hockey News*
- *Canadian Sports Collector*
- *Winnipeg Men Magazine / Studio Media Group*
- *Sportsology.net*
- *Beckett Hockey Monthly*

I would like to extend a thank you to the NHL, the NHLPA, the Winnipeg Jets, the AHL (particularly the Manitoba Moose), and Hockey Canada, who have all granted me media access to the players over the years via in-person interviews or media conference calls.